Rome Against Carthage

T. A. DOREY *and* D. R. DUDLEY

Secker & Warburg · London

First published in England 1971 by
Martin Secker & Warburg Limited
14 Carlisle Street, London W1V 6NN

SBN: 436 13130 7

Printed in Great Britain by
C. Tinling & Co. Ltd., London and Prescot

Contents

List of Illustrations

List of Maps

———

Preface and Acknowledgments

THE SECOND PUNIC WAR, the climax of the long struggle between Rome and Carthage, seemed to the Roman poet Lucretius the most appalling episode of the Roman past. It was a struggle for world-empire: 'men looked on to see to which of the two peoples should fall mastery of all human affairs by land and sea.' Such, in retrospect, it might have seemed, for the Hellenistic powers with whom Rome had yet to contend were to prove unexpectedly lightweight opponents. To contemporaries, however, the struggle was for control of the Western Mediterranean. Here it could perhaps be compared to the wars in the 18th and 19th centuries between the great powers of Europe for the possession of colonies. But the campaigns fought on the home territories of the belligerents recall the more lethal wars of the 20th century. And there is a unique conclusion, in that one of the two rivals was completely destroyed. Even our own dreadful age has yet to witness a 'Carthaginian peace'.

This book attempts to give the whole story of the wars, as it now appears in the light of modern scholarship. It has been written as a work of co-operation, and each writer has made himself primarily responsible for different sections, but has reviewed and revised the work of his colleague. In this way it is hoped to avoid unevenness; no doubt a perceptive reader can still remark some individualities of style.

For the photographs used to illustrate this book, and for permission to reproduce them, thanks are due to the British Museum, the Spanish Tourist office, the Department of Tourism of Tunisia, the Bardo Museum of Tunis, Professor H. H. Scullard, and (especially) Fototeca Unione, Rome. The Faculty of Arts of Birmingham University helped with generous financial assistance and with study leave. The maps are due to the cartographic skill of Miss J. L. Wilson. Finally, the authors wish to thank all who helped in the preparation of the typescript and in the correction of proofs, in particular Mrs Penelope Waller, Mrs Patricia Blampied, Mrs Jean Le Conte, and Mrs Heather DuQuesnay.

Introduction

THE THREE WARS between Rome and Carthage were decisive in shaping the course of the civilization of the ancient Mediterranean world. They may be seen as a later counterpart to the struggles of the Greeks and Persians in the 5th century B.C.: in both cases victory went to 'the West'. But the formula is too simplistic. Rome's victory over Carthage ensured that the dominant culture for a millennium was compounded from Roman-Hellenistic-Oriental elements: a victory for Carthage would have been the triumph of another blend on a different formula—Punic-Semitic-Oriental-Hellenistic. The Oriental challenge to the West was not to be renewed on so massive a scale until Islam confronted Christianity.

Of the three Punic Wars, the first and second were hard-fought contests in which the issue was for some time in doubt. The first gave the Romans a foothold in Sicily, the second a foothold in Africa, through their ally Masinissa. The third Punic War was not a struggle but a massacre. In spite of the gross blunders of the Romans and the desperate courage of the Carthaginians, Rome could command such an overwhelming weight of resources that the destruction of Carthage was inevitable. This left Rome with no serious rival in the Mediterranean that could challenge her monopoly of power.

It was as a result of the growth of Roman power during the years 219–167 B.C. that, as Polybius says (Histories, I, 1, 5), almost the whole of the inhabited world came under the supremacy of Rome. This claim has been criticized as an exaggeration (e.g. A. Toynbee, *Hannibal's Legacy*, I, pp. 3–6) and it cannot be regarded as literally true. But we must remember that Polybius makes this statement in his Preface, when he was urging upon his readers the importance of the type of history that he was about to write, and was speaking in a spirit of rhetorical exhortation and not in the sober tones of scientific fact. Moreover, it was in fact true that in 167 B.C. Rome was in direct occupation of Spain, Sicily, and Sardinia, exercised indirect control, through her allies, over parts of southern Gaul, Numidia, and much of Greece, had an effective though un-official protectorate over Egypt, and had decisively defeated the three great military powers of the Mediterranean, Carthage, Macedon and Syria, which at that time included much of the old Persian Empire. Finally, Polybius uses the term 'the inhabited world' (ἡ οὐκουμένη) in a sense commonly employed at that time, to denote those countries that surround the Mediterranean and had political contact with each other. It was, in effect, the world where Greek was spoken and understood, and countries beyond the easternmost boundaries of the former Persian Empire would not have been included in it.

This power accrued to Rome as a direct result of her successes in the first two wars with Carthage. The First Punic War gave to Rome a naval superiority that she never lost, but sometimes unwisely allowed to lapse. The Romans from the start treated sea-fighting merely as an extension of land-fighting; they regarded ships not as sailing vehicles but as fighting-platforms, and they concentrated on courage and skill at arms rather than seamanship or nautical technique. This approach gave them superiority over opponents who were better seamen but did not realize that conditions in ancient naval warfare gave the upper hand to the side that was determined to fight it out at close quarters. Only the introduction of effective missiles would have restored the advantage to seamanship.

Similarly the Second Punic War provided a stimulus for the Roman land forces. The change in the tactical formation, from that of a phalanx to that of a legion (cf. Toynbee, op. cit., pp. 505–518), was accelerated and completed, and the example of Hannibal produced in Scipio Africanus a commander to match him and improve on him. After the war the Roman generals showed a new sophistication that enabled them to make proper use of the superior man-power that Rome and Italy could put at their disposal.

Up to the 3rd century the relations between the two cities had been friendly. In spite of their inherent national differences, there had been nothing to cause any dispute. Rome, founded as a civic entity from a collection of shepherds' huts some time in the 8th century, had produced a stock of citizens with the typical virtues of an agricultural community. In war they made excellent soldiers, intelligent and disciplined, capable of great endurance and fortitude, of a similar pattern to the English yeoman and the early American settlers. Freeing herself just before 500 B.C. from a period of Etruscan domination, Rome had gradually extended her control over the rest of Italy, reaching the southern extremities of the peninsula in the first quarter of the 3rd century.

It was the war with Pyrrhus (280–275) that brought home to the Romans the importance of Sicily to their security. Pyrrhus came to Italy to assist the Greek city of Tarentum in a dispute with Rome. He defeated the Romans in two battles, at Heraclea and Ausculum, but since he could see no prospect of winning a decisive victory over the Romans' greatly superior resources he accepted an invitation from Syracuse to put himself at the head of the Sicilian Greeks in an effort to drive the Carthaginians out of the island. Here again he was unable to win a decisive success. Although he captured all their other towns, the Carthaginians held out in their impregnable base at Lilybaeum, on the western tip of Sicily, and it soon became clear that as soon as Pyrrhus withdrew they would re-assert their control over much of the island. So Pyrrhus turned his attention once more to Italy, where a coalition against Rome had been formed by the Samnites, Lucanians and Bruttians, and was asking for his help. But after an indecisive battle at Beneventum he lost heart and returned to Greece. The coalition was crushed and Tarentum compelled to surrender, but it was now obvious to the Romans that, if ever a hostile power controlled Sicily, it would be used as a base for fomenting revolt, and their mastery of southern Italy would always be precarious and insecure. The same considerations that later induced Caesar and Claudius to attempt the conquest of Britain, Suetonius Paulinus to invade Anglesey, and Agricola to dream of the subjugation of Ireland must have been present in the minds of many Romans after the struggle with Pyrrhus.

There was another lesson to be learnt from this war, as Pyrrhus found to his cost: that in Rome any antagonist would be challenging not a city-state but a nation-state. The power of Rome spread throughout Italy. Apart from Rome itself, there were the Roman garrison towns (*coloniae*) sited at various points of vantage, especially along the coast, as well as individual Roman settlements. There were, too, many communities enjoying some form of modified citizenship, either with Latin rights or with full citizenship apart from the vote. Then there were the Italian subject-allies, generally left with a large measure of self-government but compelled to surrender the conduct of their foreign policy to Rome and supply her with troops from their citizen-militia. Apart from a deep-seated resentment that lingered on among the Samnites, and, to a lesser degree, in Lucania and Bruttium, the rule of Rome was generally found acceptable. For this there were two main reasons, the willingness of the Romans to extend their citizenship to other peoples, and the fact that from the start they avoided imposing the burden that always gave particular offence in the ancient world—the payment of a monetary tribute.

Carthage had been founded from Tyre just before 800 (the traditional date is 814 B.C.) as a means of exercising efficient control over the important trade routes between Phoenicia and the south and west coasts of Spain. Here the Phoenicians derived great profits from the exploitation of the mineral wealth of the kingdom of Tartessus. (Among the mines they worked was the celebrated Rio Tinto Mine, which even now is important as a source of pyrites.) As her parent city became weakened and then absorbed by the extension of the Asiatic empires, Carthage herself grew in strength and prosperity. During the 6th century her main policy was the consolidation of the Phoenician trading monopoly in the western Mediterranean and the checking of the expansion of Greek influence in that area, particularly that of Phocaea. In about 535 Carthage joined with the Etruscans, a people with whom archaeological evidence shows that she had some cultural connections, in defeating the Massiliote fleet at the battle of Alalia, off Corsica. In 509, the year after the expulsion of the Etruscan dynasty from Rome, Carthage took care to secure friendly relations with this newly emergent state by a treaty of friendship (cf. Toynbee, op. cit., pp. 519–555 for the most recent discussion of the dates of this and subsequent treaties). The main purpose of this treaty was to restrict the rights of Romans to trade in north-west Africa in return for an undertaking on the part of the Carthaginians not to raid Latium. During the 5th century the Carthaginians made two attempts to block any possible Greek expansion into the western Mediterranean by gaining control of Sicily, where they had settlements in the west of the island at Motya, Sololis and Panormus (Palermo). But the first attempt, coinciding with the Persian invasion of Greece, was crushed by Gelon and Hieron at Himera. A second attempt made at the end of the century, after Syracuse had been weakened by her war with Athens, had some initial success, but the Sicilians consistently rallied and Carthage was never able to consolidate her gains. An intermittent struggle went on for more than a hundred years. However, after Pyrrhus had failed to drive the Carthaginians out of the island and had crossed back to Italy, the political weakness of the Sicilian cities gave Carthage considerable hopes of winning complete success.

During the 4th century Carthage had extended her power in other directions. The majority of the Phoenician cities in north Africa had accepted her leadership, while she had imposed her control on the Berber peoples in the interior. In Spain, by the conquest of the old kingdom of Tartessus, she had made herself master of the south-west of the country, and in a treaty with Rome, probably to be dated to 348 B.C., she was in a position to exclude the Romans from trading in Spain or Sardinia.

During the war with Pyrrhus, in 279 B.C., Rome and Carthage concluded a treaty of mutual aid, re-enacting at the same time the terms of their earlier treaty. At this time the two cities were united in resisting the penetration of Greek power into the western Mediterranean, but after the failure of Pyrrhus this threat receded, and one of the strongest bonds linking Rome and Carthage together—fear of a mutual enemy—was loosened. There was, in fact an ominous incident after the final withdrawal of Pyrrhus from Italy. The Romans were besieging Tarentum, the city whose attack on their fleet had first sparked off the war, and were close to reducing it, when the Carthaginian fleet appeared in the harbour. The Carthaginian government swore, in reply to a vigorous Roman protest, that it had only come to assist the Romans in accordance with the terms of their recent treaty. But there arose in the minds of the Romans the fixed suspicion that the real purpose of the Carthaginians had been to steal a march on Rome and get Tarentum into their own hands. This suspicion was probably justified.

Internally, too, there had been changes. At the end of the 5th century Carthage had been dominated by the family of Mago, who based their power on control of the office of Suffetes and the various military commands, which they gained by lavish bribery among a restricted electorate. But during the 5th century, as a result of military reverses in Africa, Sicily and Sardinia, the real power passed to a Board of One Hundred (or One Hundred and Four) Judges, to whom all generals and executive offices were made accountable; they held office for life and recruited new members by co-optation. As a result the State became a self-perpetuating oligarchy.

1

The First Punic War

EARLY IN THE 3RD CENTURY B.C. a force of Campanian
mercenaries who had been serving under the Sicilian war-lord
Agathocles seized the rich Greek town of Messana on the
Straits of Messina, killed some of the inhabitants and drove out
others, appropriated their wives and property, and made themselves masters of the surrounding countryside. Backed by
another gang of Campanians that subsequently gained possession of the town of Rhegium on the Italian side of the Straits,
they gained control of large parts of Sicily and caused great
trouble to the other two important powers, the Syracusans and
the Carthaginians. However, after the Romans had recovered
Rhegium in 271 B.C. the Mamertines—as the occupants of
Messana were called—were forced back on the defensive, and a
defeat that they suffered at the hands of the Syracusans under
Hiero in 268 made their position precarious. Accordingly, in
264, the Mamertines begin to look for outside aid; one party
was for appealing for help to Rome, another to the Carthaginians. The latter, being closer at hand, were able to make a
prompt response and got possession of the citadel of Messana.

The Romans found themselves placed in a dilemma by the
Mamertines' appeal, and the conflicting feelings that affected
them are described by Polybius (I, 10). From a purely moral
point of view they should reject the appeal with scorn; the
Mamertines were land pirates who had seized Messana by
violence and had made it a base for acts of brigandage. Since the
Romans had only recently overwhelmed a similar band in
Rhegium and executed the survivors, they would be acting
illogically if they took the Mamertines under their protection.

1

But logic carries little weight against expediency. A party at Rome was afraid of the Carthaginians. They realized that if the Carthaginians got possession of Messana they would have little difficulty in overcoming the Syracusans and so would gain control of the whole of Sicily. If that happened, their occupation of Messana would pose a direct threat to Italy from across the Straits, which at this point were only a few miles wide. The Romans were faced with the same problem of foreign policy that for many years exercised the minds of English statesmen with regard to the Low Countries—and American statesmen with regard to Cuba and other Caribbean islands—the need to prevent a strong and potentially hostile power occupying a position so close to their frontiers that it could be used as a vantage-point for attack.

There was a more positive reaction, too. Now that Rome had extended her power to the sea-coasts of Italy, some of her leading men had begun to extend their horizon beyond those sea-coasts, and viewed with concern the fact that Carthage already held Sardinia and Corsica and was soon likely to hold all Sicily too. The emergence of this wider outlook as well as the more immediate threat from across the Straits helped to propel the Romans towards intervention on the Mamertines' behalf.

The Senate was undecided, so the supporters of the alliance with the Mamertines brought their proposal before the Popular Assembly, probably the Comitia Centuriata. Here they appealed to the people's material interests, and held out hopes that profits to be won from a war in Sicily would make up for their recent losses in the struggle against Pyrrhus. What these anticipated profits were cannot be easily seen, as Rome was not in the habit of imposing tribute on conquered enemies. Possibly it was the prospect of booty to be obtained from the wealthy city of Syracuse. But it is likely that this aspect was deliberately over-exaggerated by leading Romans anxious to bring about a war for the promotion of their own military glory. Appius Claudius, the consul, who was given the command in Sicily and must have been one of the most active supporters of the war, belonged to a family that pursued a traditional policy of expansion to the south. It is interesting to note that the consuls of 263 and 261 were Manius and Titus Otacilius Crassus. They must have been particularly influential at this time, and they belonged to a

family that during the Second Punic War, in the persons of
T. Otacilius Crassus and his half-brother M. Claudius Marcellus,
had close connections with Sicily. It has been suggested that
Campanian influence at Rome played a considerable part in
turning the scales in favour of the Mamertines. Many Campanian nobles were now important members of the Senate. The

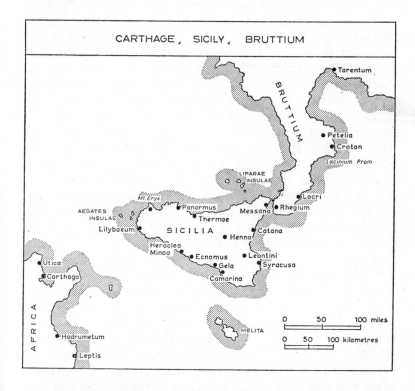

CARTHAGE, SICILY, BRUTTIUM

Otacilii were Campanians, and so were the Atilii, who held
consulships in 258, 257 and 256. Apart from their kinship with
the Mamertines, the Campanians had a national tradition of
fighting as mercenaries in Sicily. So it seems that national
arguments and personal motives, combined with opportunity,
made war inevitable.

It is asserted by Philinus, the pro-Carthaginian historian from
Agrigentum, that by crossing over to Sicily the Romans committed a breach of a treaty under which they were bound to

refrain from intervention in Sicily while the Carthaginians refrained from intervention in Italy. Polybius (III, 26) puts on record this allegation of Philinus, investigates it, and denies its truth. But Philinus has been supported by a number of modern scholars. As well as the earliest treaty, which Polybius dates, almost certainly correctly, to 509, there are records in Livy of two further treaties between Rome and Carthage, in 348, (VII, 27) and 306 (IX, 43). Diodorus Siculus (XVI, 69) states that the treaty of 348 was the first to be concluded between the two states, but his source, Fabius, had probably not searched the Record Office at Rome with the same thoroughness as Polybius. Polybius himself stated that even in his own day many eminent Romans were not aware of the existence of the Treaty of 509. It seems likely from the historical circumstances of the time that 348 was the date of the second treaty mentioned by Polybius (III, 24). That leaves the question of whether there was a treaty concluded in 306 in the terms stated by Philinus, and deliberately suppressed by the Romans at the time of Polybius's investigation because its existence showed up the Romans as the aggressors in the First Punic War. This possibility cannot be completely discounted, but it is on the whole unlikely. It is significant that in recording the treaty of 348 Livy says *foedus ictum*, while in his note on 306 he says *foedus tertio renovatum*. This indicates that the existing terms were renewed, but that no new treaty was concluded. The word *tertio* would be used inclusively, as is normal in Latin, to denote that this was the third time that a solemn agreement had been sealed between the two parties. It has been objected that the terms of the treaty of 348 would be inappropriate to the completely altered circumstances of 306; but it may have been that the representatives of the two sides were unable to agree on any new terms and had to content themselves with restating the contents of the former pact. It is interesting to note that the treaty of 279, in spite of the radical changes in the political situation since 348, confined itself to very few additional clauses, and those concerned with the immediate needs of dealing with Pyrrhus. It seems that, for nearly fifty years before the First Punic War, Rome and Carthage had found it impossible to draft any new formal clauses governing their long-term relationships and delimiting their general spheres of interest. It is therefore likely that during the negotiations in 279, apart from the conclusion of the formal treaty, certain informal undertakings were also exchanged. One of these, we can be sure, concerned the gift to the Romans of a quantity of Carthaginian silver to help finance their fight against Pyrrhus. In the circumstances, as a necessary basis to their co-operation against Pyrrhus, we can possibly assume that Rome and Carthage exchanged informal assurances to refrain from encroaching on Sicily and Italy respectively.

Meanwhile the Carthaginians had already put a garrison in the citadel of Messana, but their opponents among the Mamertines, probably with the help of a small force of Roman troops brought over from Rhegium by the military tribune C. Claudius, induced them to withdraw, and invited the consul, Appius Claudius Caudex, to take control of the city. The Carthaginians brought up their fleet and land-forces, made an alliance with Hiero, who hoped to get rid of both the Mamertines and the Romans from Messana, and with his help laid the city under close siege. But Appius Claudius got his main force of two legions across the Straits under cover of darkness, eluding the Carthaginian fleet whose commander had boasted that he would not allow the Romans even to wash their hands in the sea, and entered the beleaguered town. Appius had no wish to stand a long siege, especially with the enemy in control of the sea and able to cut him off from supplies and reinforcements. He first sent missions to both the enemy forces, proposing terms of peace. When he got no reply from either, he offered battle to the Syracusans, defeated them after a long struggle, and drove them back to their camp. Hiero, who now began to have second thoughts about the Romans, withdrew his whole army to Syracuse the following night. Then Appius made a surprise attack at dawn on the Carthaginians, inflicted heavy losses, and made them raise the siege. The Romans were now in complete control of the surrounding countryside, and no one ventured to challenge them. Appius, a bold and resolute commander, now advanced down the coast and laid siege to Syracuse itself.

At this point Hiero made a vital decision. His alliance with Carthage had been an unnatural one, forced on him by particular circumstances, and it had not been successful in producing the desired results. Under the consuls of the following year, 263, Manius Otacilius Crassus and Manius Valerius Maximus, the

Romans had completed a powerful build-up of troops in Sicily, and many of the Sicilian cities had joined them. Hiero was now convinced of the vastly superior strength of the Romans. With their help, he hoped to be able to expel not just the Mamertines but the Carthaginians themselves from Sicily. Accordingly he wrote to the consuls and offered terms of peace. An alliance was concluded under which Hiero gave back all prisoners-of-war without ransom, and paid an indemnity of one hundred talents of silver. The Romans welcomed the alliance. It would give them a safe base at Syracuse and secure their supplies. Hiero remained a loyal ally of the Romans until his death nearly fifty years later. He was one of the few foreign monarchs—Masinissa of Numidia was another—to appreciate early enough the enormous potential strength of Rome.

On the news of this alliance the Romans decided to reduce their forces in Sicily. They felt that with the help of the Syracusans, who would be able to ensure their supply position, they would be able to maintain and, if necessary, extend their bridgehead in north-east Sicily without very great effort. The Carthaginians, however, realized at once that the Roman presence in the island completely changed the balance of power that had existed between themselves and the Greeks for so many centuries. Their only hope was to bring about an immediate escalation of the war. So they enlisted a large force of mercenaries from Liguria, Cisalpine Gaul and Spain, and sent them to Sicily. It was an inherent weakness of Carthage that she never developed as a land-power in Africa on a sufficient scale to provide herself with an adequate supply of troops for her overseas wars, but had to depend on mercenaries to a dangerous extent. As a base for her counter-attack against the Romans she chose Agrigentum, a powerful city in south-west Sicily and traditionally a rival of Syracuse. It is likely that the Carthaginians had concluded an alliance with Agrigentum in 264, at the same time as they did with Hiero.

The Romans reacted vigorously. The consuls for 262, L. Postumius Megellus and Q. Mamilius Vitulus, swept down on Agrigentum in full force and encamped about a mile from the town. After an engagement between the defenders and the Roman foraging parties, in which a number of the foragers were killed, but the enemy eventually driven back to the city with heavy losses, the Carthaginians did not dare risk a pitched battle. Accordingly the Romans moved close up against the town, and built two siege-camps, one on either side of Agrigentum and connected by entrenchments, so that the city was completely beleaguered. The Romans used as their base the neighbouring town of Herbessus, and here abundant supplies of provisions were accumulated, brought in from the Sicilian towns that had joined the side of Rome. For five months the siege went on, and the garrison began to suffer desperately from lack of food. But their commander, Hannibal, was able to get messages through to Carthage about their plight, asking for help, and at last the Carthaginians responded. They sent strong reinforcements, including fifty elephants, to Lilybaeum, the Punic capital on the western tip of Sicily. The Carthaginian commander, Hanno the Elder, advanced along the coast to Heraclea, about ten miles west of Agrigentum, and at the very start of the campaign struck a deadly blow at the Romans by capturing their base at Herbessus. Cut off from supplies, the Romans in their turn found themselves besieged. Famine and pestilence took their toll, and had not Hiero, by desperate efforts, managed to get some food through to them, they would have been forced to raise the siege. While they were in this plight, Hanno moved up from Heraclea, drew the Roman cavalry into a trap, and routed them with heavy losses. Then he took up his position on a hill just over a mile from the Roman lines, and waited for the Romans to give up.

For two more months the two sides stood fast, held as it were in an interlocking grip. It was the Carthaginians in Agrigentum who were the first to weaken. Hannibal sent signals to Hanno that his men were starving and starting to desert, so Hanno gave up his policy of attrition and offered battle. The struggle was long and bitter. At last the Romans forced back the Carthaginian front line on to the elephants that were stationed in support, and the resulting confusion spread through the whole army. The Romans won a complete victory, but during the night Hannibal was able to get his troops undetected through the Roman lines and make good his escape.

The capture of Agrigentum marked the end of the first stage of the war, in which the Romans established their position in Sicily and shattered a Carthaginian counter-attack. In the second stage the Romans, convinced by this proof of their military superiority that they had it in their power to drive the Carthaginians right out of Sicily, achieved command of the sea and carried the war into Africa. This stage ended with the defeat of Regulus outside Carthage and the subsequent naval disaster off Camarina. The third stage consisted in a series of sieges and counter-sieges in Sicily, at the end of which the Romans emerged victorious because of their success in maintaining a blockade.

The Romans realized that, if they were to win total victory over the Carthaginians, they would have to gain control of the sea. The superiority of the Punic fleet meant that although many of the inland towns of Sicily joined the Romans, those on the sea-board dared not do so from fear of Carthaginian reprisals. Moreover, the Carthaginians were able to ravage the coast of Italy unchecked and unpunished. Accordingly the Romans built a fleet of one hundred quinqueremes and twenty triremes. Polybius (I, 20) tells a story of how the construction of the quinqueremes caused difficulty, since such a ship was unknown in Italy, and the Romans had to use as a model a Carthaginian vessel that had run aground and been captured while trying to prevent the original Roman force crossing over to Messana in 264. Yet Polybius himself says, in the same chapter, that the Romans borrowed quinqueremes from the Greek cities of South Italy to convey their troops across the Straits of Messina at the start of the war. It is probable that Polybius exaggerates the Roman difficulties, but their shipwrights may well have incorporated certain innovations of design taken from the captured warship. But two things are certain. The Roman fleet was crewed and manned by Romans, and the Naval Allies (*socii navales*) from the Greek cities of Italy played little part. Secondly, the Roman naval tactics, and the device they constructed to make these tactics possible, were their own. They realized that if they were to succeed at sea, they must rely on the superiority of their fighting-men to outweigh the enemy's superiority in ships and seamanship. Accordingly, their aim in any sea-battle was not to out-manoeuvre the enemy, but to get to grips, grapple, and board. Each ship was equipped with a boarding-gangway, four feet wide and with an effective length of twenty-four feet. One end of these gangways would pivot on the base of a specially constructed fore-mast; the other end would be drawn up by a pulley at the top of the mast and allowed to drop with all the force of its weight on to an enemy ship that came within reach; a sharp iron spike underneath this end would be driven into the deck of the enemy and fix fast—it was this spike that gave the whole apparatus its name *corvus* (crow); then the Roman marines would charge across the gangway, protecting each other by linking shields. Once aboard the enemy ship, the superior weapons, armour, and discipline of the Romans gave them the upper hand. It is significant that during the course of the war, the only time the Romans were defeated at sea was the fault of an incredibly bad commander.

The first experience of the Romans with their fleet was thoroughly ignominious. Cn. Cornelius Scipio Asina, one of the consuls for 260, sailed to Messana with an advance party of seventeen ships. Then he was induced by an offer of surrender to sail to the neighbouring town of Lipara. Here he was blockaded by a squadron of twenty Carthaginian vessels, his crews deserted, and he himself had to surrender without striking a blow. The rest of the Roman fleet reached Sicily, and was put under the command of the other consul, C. Duillius, who originally had been allotted the land forces. Duillius sailed along the north coast to Mylae, where he heard the Carthaginian fleet was ravaging the countryside. Here he encountered Hannibal's fleet, probably slightly superior to his numbers. The *corvi*, and the valour of the Romans, did their work, and the Carthaginians were defeated with the loss of fifty ships. After this victory the Romans landed in western Sicily, and relieved Segesta, which had revolted from the Carthaginians and had been besieged. They also captured the neighbouring town of Macella. In this way they began to close in upon the important Carthaginian stronghold of Panormus. But Hamilcar, the Carthaginian commander who had been sent to replace Hanno after the capture of Agrigentum, made a successful sortie from Panormus against the Romans' Sicilian allies, inflicting heavy losses. At the same time, the success of their fleet enabled the Romans to start operations against Sardinia. Here they again encountered Hannibal, who had brought fresh ships from Carthage. They blockaded him in harbour and destroyed part of his fleet. As a result he was arrested by his Carthaginian officers and crucified. This early interest in the island is significant in view of its ruthless annexation by Rome in 238.

The next few years were comparatively uneventful. The Romans gained some successes, capturing Hippana and Myttistratum, and recovering Camarina, but they failed in a rather half-hearted attack on Panormus, and fought an indecisive battle at sea near Tyndaris, off the north-east coast of Sicily. In 256, however, the Romans had completed their preparations for the invasion of Africa, and sailed down the east coast of Sicily with 330 ships and round Cape Pachynus to Ecnomus, where their land forces were concentrated. There they took on board nearly forty thousand troops and set off for Africa. Meanwhile the Carthaginians had realized the purpose of the Romans' preparations, and had themselves got ready a fleet of 350 vessels, which was lying in wait at Heraclea, ready to bar the way to Africa. The Romans put to sea, adopting a simple and uncomplicated formation. Their fleet consisted of four squadrons, drawn up in the form of a triangular wedge. The first two squadrons, commanded by the consuls M. Atilius Regulus and L. Manlius Vulso, formed the sides of the wedge, coming to a point at the two flag-ships. The third squadron formed the base of the wedge, in a single line, towing the horse-transports. The fourth squadron, the 'Triarii'—the name had been adopted from land-warfare—formed a reserve, in a single line that overlapped the line in front. The consuls planned to drive their wedge through the enemy line and press on to Africa. The Carthaginians, commanded by Hamilcar, who had been involved in the fighting off Tyndaris the previous year, and Hanno the Elder, employed more sophisticated tactics. Three-quarters of their ships were drawn up in a single line facing the enemy with their right wing stretching out towards the open sea. Their left wing was drawn up in a single line astern, close in to the shore.

The consuls led their ships in a charge against the enemy centre, expecting to punch their way through, but Hamilcar deliberately retreated until he had drawn the Romans on and separated the sides of their wedge from its base. For the third squadron were moving slowly, held back by the horse-transports they were towing, while the Triarii dutifully kept their position in reserve. When a big enough gap had been opened up, Hamilcar wheeled round and encircled the Romans. Meanwhile the extreme right wing, under Hanno, swooped down from out to sea upon the Triarii and threw them into confusion, while the Carthaginian left wing, sailing up along the shore, encircled the third squadron and made them let slip their tow-ropes.

For their skilful tactics, the Carthaginians deserved to win. But, in an age before the use of missiles at sea when battles were fought by ramming, they could not destroy the Roman ships without coming within range of the *corvus*, and if once the Romans could grapple, the superiority of their soldiers gave them the upper hand. This was how it turned out. Hamilcar's division was not strong enough to hold the two squadrons under the consuls, and after a long struggle it broke and fled. Then, while Manlius completed mopping-up operations, Regulus sailed back to the help of the hard-pressed Triarii. Hanno's ships, caught between two fires, hurriedly broke off the battle and took to the open sea. Meanwhile Manlius, too, had come back, and with his colleagues surrounded the Carthaginian left wing, which had penned the Roman third squadron up against the shore but had not dared to close with them for fear of being grappled. Altogether the Romans destroyed more than thirty enemy ships, and captured sixty-four, for the loss of twenty-four sunk.

After this victory, the Romans returned to Ecnomus to refit, and then sailed without incident to Africa. They disembarked near Clupea, captured it after a short siege, and set about ravaging the country. Winter was now coming on, and in obedience to orders from Rome, Manlius left forty ships and fifteen thousand men with Regulus to hold on until the spring, while he himself took the rest of the fleet and the army, together with all the captives and booty, back to Italy.

Up till now the tide of success had set strongly for the Romans. They had carried on the war for nearly ten years without experiencing any major disaster. This was due not to mere good fortune but to the calibre of their commanders, who had conducted their campaigns not only with courage and resolution but with thoughtfulness and prudence as well. But now, as a result of a series of culpable blunders on the part of their generals, the Romans were to suffer a number of calamities that would wipe out the hard-won gains of the last few years.

The figure of Regulus passed into the aura of Roman patriotic legend. His courage in refusing to support the enemy's plea for peace excited the admiration of future generations of his countrymen, his miserable end was to arouse their pity. But the true picture is more sombre. It was the stupidity, arrogance, and vainglory of Regulus that shattered the Roman hopes in Africa.

The Carthaginians recalled Hamilcar from Sicily, and he brought with him five thousand infantry and five hundred cavalry. He was associated in the command with the two Suffetes (the chief executive officers of the State), Hasdrubal, son of Hanno, and Bostar, and they determined to oppose the Romans in their systematic devastation of the countryside and try to protect some of the Carthaginian towns. At this time Regulus was attacking a fortified town called Adys. The Carthaginians moved towards him and encamped on a hill that commanded the Roman positions. They were strong in elephants and cavalry, but allowed the Romans to take the initiative and attack them on the hill-top, before they could come down on to the level ground where they could use their superiority in cavalry and elephants to full effect. The Romans drove them off the hill in disorder and destroyed their camp. From that time they overran the countryside without meeting any resistance, capturing Tunis and using it as their base for future operations against Carthage itself.

Regulus now became fired with the ambition to bring the war to a successful conclusion before the spring came and his successor arrived with reinforcements. He wanted to have for himself the undivided credit for the victory. The Carthaginians were also suffering from attacks by the Numidians, who were ravaging the countryside and driving the people to take refuge in the city. Accordingly when Regulus invited them to discuss terms of peace he did so in the firm conviction that the city was capable of being captured in a very short time. The terms he proposed were harsh, and when the enemy representatives asked him to modify them he refused with great arrogance. There are no reliable sources for the nature of the terms he proposed, but the first version given by Dio Cassius (XI, 22) is not improbable: the Carthaginians should give up Sicily and Sardinia, restore all Roman prisoners, ransom their own, pay Rome the costs of the war, and furnish a yearly tribute. Faced with these conditions, the Carthaginians felt that they had nothing to lose by continuing the struggle.

Regulus felt that Carthage was ready to drop into his hand like a ripe plum. What he did not realize was that at this critical moment the Carthaginian high command had undergone a radical change. Among the mercenaries recently arrived from Greece was a Spartan named Xanthippus, a professional soldier of great experience gained in the Greek wars, with a natural flair for the art of warfare. He was soon put in effective command of the Carthaginian forces. The Romans were eager for a decisive battle, and Xanthippus was confident that he could now defeat them in the field. His forces were of about the same size as the Romans', but he had two great advantages—four thousand cavalry against Regulus's five hundred, and nearly a hundred elephants. (Elephants, like tanks in modern warfare, could be used with devastating effect against troops who had not learnt the technique of dealing with them.) The Carthaginian elephants drove in the Roman centre, which was drawn up in a narrow, deep formation, in the hope of preventing them from breaking through. The Carthaginian cavalry swept aside the Roman cavalry and attacked their infantry in the rear, while those of the Romans who avoided the elephant-charge found themselves up against the unbroken ranks of the Carthaginian main body. Completely encircled, the Romans were crushed. About two thousand on the left wing had missed the elephants, and had been engaged with the Carthaginian right wing, which they had put to flight. These made their escape to Clupea. Five hundred, including Regulus, were taken prisoner. The rest perished.

The Roman disaster was due to bad generalship. Regulus made a mistake in not waiting for reinforcements when he knew that the Carthaginians had been able to build up their forces. He made no attempt to co-operate with the Numidians. He made an error of judgement in joining battle with an enemy greatly superior in cavalry and elephants on ground deliberately chosen by the enemy because it was favourable to those arms in which they had the advantage. Finally, he adopted a formation that inevitably enabled the elephants to cause the maximum amount of damage to his close-packed front and allowed the

Carthaginian cavalry to encircle his position and attack his rear.

The Romans manned a fleet to take off the survivors. A Carthaginian fleet, greatly outnumbered, intercepted them off the Hermaean Promontory, the headland on the eastern end of the bay in which Carthage stands, just north of Clupea. The Romans won a decisive victory, embarked the survivors of Regulus' army, which had been besieged in Clupea, and set sail back to Sicily. The consuls, Servius Fulvius Nobilior and M. Aemilius Paullus, decided to use the fleet to reduce some of the towns on the south coast of Sicily. The coast was dangerous and harbourless. It was July, a month when southerly gales were frequent. The pilots warned them again and again of the risk of being caught in a storm off a lee shore. The consuls paid no attention. Off Camarina a violent storm arose, the fleet was driven on the rocks, and out of three hundred and sixty-four vessels only eighty survived. The Romans found to their cost that the qualities of stubborn courage that served them so well against human enemies were of little use in contending with the forces of nature. This lesson, as Polybius points out (I, 37), the Romans often experienced, but never learnt.

The scene of the war now shifted back to Sicily. On hearing of the wreck, the Carthaginians recovered their morale completely, and sent Hasdrubal with all their available forces, including a hundred and forty elephants, to win back possession of Sicily. He sailed first to the impregnable Carthaginian base at Lilybaeum and there began training his men. The Romans too showed their enormous powers of resilience. They hurriedly built two hundred and twenty ships, to which they added the survivors from last year's disaster. Then the consuls for 254, A. Atilius Calatinus and Cn. Cornelius Scipio Asina, attacked the strongly-fortified Carthaginian city of Panormus, situated on the north-west corner of Sicily. They threw up their siege-works on two sides of the town, brought up their battering-rams, and stormed a tower that overlooked the sea. This made a breach in the defences, through which they forced their way in. Part of the town was stormed, the rest surrendered.

During the next two years, however, the Roman morale sank to a very low ebb. In the first place, a large-scale naval raid on the north coast of Africa had been a fiasco. The ships had run aground in the neighbourhood of the Lesser Syrtes, and had only been refloated with difficulty, at the cost of jettisoning their heavy equipment. Then, on the voyage home, they rashly attempted the direct passage from Panormus to Italy instead of coasting along to the Straits; they ran into a storm and half the fleet was lost. As a result, the Romans found it necessary to conserve their resources, and they abandoned control of the sea to the Carthaginians. On land, too, the Romans were in the doldrums. The legionaries were afraid of the Carthaginian elephants. The story of how the elephant-charge had shattered Regulus's army, crushing his troops underfoot, had taken root in their minds. Hasdrubal had one hundred and forty elephants at Lilybaeum, and these gave him complete command of the open country. The Romans dared not even come down on to level ground, and their only successes were in reducing Thermae and the island of Lipara. But neither on land nor at sea were they in any position to challenge the Carthaginians in a major engagement.

L. Caecilius Metellus, consul for 251, was left behind in Panormus at the end of the year, while his colleague took half of the army back to Rome. It was the chief task of Metellus to protect the harvest that was just then becoming ripe. Hasdrubal was sure that if he could destroy the harvest without the Romans daring to protect it, he would detach from Rome many of her Sicilian allies. So he marched in full force towards Panormus, cutting down the crops as he went. Metellus regarded it as his most vital objective at that time to put an end to his men's fear of the elephants. Accordingly he kept his troops behind the walls of the town, to convince Hasdrubal that his army was rife with cowardice. Full of confidence, Hasdrubal moved his army across the river that lies in front of Panormus. Then Metellus put his plan into action. First, he sent relays of light-armed troops to harass the enemy and provoke them into making an attack. As he had hoped, the elephants led with a concerted charge which drove the light-armed skirmishers right back against the walls of the city. Here they ran into a hail of arrows and javelins poured down upon them from archers and light-armed troops drawn up along the walls and the edge of the moat and furnished with an abundant store of weapons. The wounded elephants, maddened with pain, turned upon their own lines and threw them into disorder. At this point Metellus, who had kept his main body in reserve at one of the city gates opposite the enemy's left wing, charged the Carthaginians in the flank. The victory was complete. Ten elephants were captured complete with mahouts; the rest, that had run wild, Metellus was able to corral. None of them had been able to get back across the river.

The victory was a result of brilliant generalship, thoroughly in keeping with the founder of the most famous plebeian family in Rome, who frequently featured the elephant on their coins. Metellus himself went on to be consul a second time and Pontifex Maximus, and was blinded fighting a fire in the Temple of Vesta.

The next year, 250, marks another Roman offensive. The Romans had recovered from their losses at sea, and their morale had been raised by Metellus' splendid victory at Panormus. Under the new consuls, C. Atilius Regulus and L. Manlius Vulso, they launched an attack by land and sea on Lilybaeum. This impregnable stronghold had been built in 396 after Dionysius had destroyed the older Carthaginian bases in western Sicily at Motya. Lilybaeum had successfully defied Pyrrhus when he had captured all the other Carthaginian towns in Sicily, and its possession was now of vital importance for the future of the war. If the Romans succeeded in taking it, they would not only have won Sicily, for Drepanum was the only town of any size still in Carthaginian hands, but they would be able to use it as a convenient base from which they could launch another invasion of Africa over a short and uninterrupted stretch of sea.

The Romans came very close to success. They built a camp on each side of the town, connecting them with fortified lines. Then, starting at the point where they stretched down to the sea, they began progressively to reduce the fortifications, pushing their siege-works further and further into the town. Himilco, the Carthaginian commander, was tough and resolute; he fought back against the Romans with sallies and counter-mines, and whenever the defences were pierced he at once built new fortifications to block the attackers' advance. The fighting was prolonged and savage, and there were heavy losses on both sides.

The Romans met with three serious disappointments in the

course of their attack. First, they nearly persuaded the commanders of the Carthaginian mercenary forces in Lilybaeum to
betray the town. But while they were at the Roman camp discussing details of the scheme, Alexon of Achae, one of the
mercenary officers and a man of great loyalty and integrity,
found out about the plot and informed the Carthaginians. By
exhortations and promises they persuaded the rank-and-file of
the mercenaries to remain loyal, and when the traitors returned
from the Roman camp, they were driven away from the walls
with volleys of missiles and not given the chance to speak to
their men.

The second disappointment that the Romans had was their
inability to maintain an effective blockade from the sea. The
waters around Lilybaeum had many shoals, so that the block-
ading fleet could not stand in too close. The Carthaginians had a
number of ships that were faster than the Romans', and more
manoeuvrable, while their pilots knew channels into the harbour
and would hide behind one of the off-shore islands until the wind
was in the right quarter and then come sailing in under full
canvas right into the harbour. The first to do this was Hannibal,
son of Hamilcar. He was sent from Carthage with fifty ships and
ten thousand men, under strict orders to get this convoy into
Lilybaeum at all costs. He waited off the Aegatian Isles until the
wind was exactly right, then dashed full-speed for Lilybaeum
and swept into the harbour under full sail, with armed men
lining the decks and the Romans afraid to intercept him in case
their ships got carried on into the harbour. After this, on
numerous occasions during the year blockade-runners took
their ships in and out. The most famous of them—and in fact
the first to run the blockade after the arrival of the Carthaginian
reinforcements—was Hannibal 'the Rhodian', a brilliant sea-
man with a very fast ship that could out-distance and out-
manoeuvre the more heavily-built Roman galleys. The Romans
tried to block the harbour mouth, but the water was too deep
and the movement of the water too strong. At last they constructed an underwater mole at a point where the sea was
shallow. On this one of the blockade-runners went aground and
was captured intact. This ship was fast enough to enable the
Romans to out-sail and capture Hannibal. After this they were
able to intercept most of the blockade-runners.

It was on land that the Romans suffered their greatest set-back. Early in the siege Himilco made a savage attack on the Roman siege-works. The Romans were waiting for him and a pitched battle raged all day the whole length of the besiegers' lines. Then, at various points, the Carthaginians sent in fire-parties to set light to the Roman siege-engines. This attempt nearly succeeded, but Himilco saw that he was suffering such enormous casualties that he called off the attack. But at the end of the summer Himilco had an even better chance. A storm wrecked a number of the Roman towers and blew down the wooden mantlets that protected the battering-rams. While the Romans were trying to repair the damage, he sent in his fire-parties. The timber in the siege-works had by now become like tinder, and the strong wind fanned the flames. As the Romans struggled amidst clouds of smoke to put out the fires, Carthaginian archers, standing well back from the blaze, poured volleys of arrows into their midst. The siege-works were completely destroyed, so the Romans now abandoned all hopes of carrying the town by assault and settled down to the lengthy process of starving it into surrender.

It was probably just after this that the Carthaginians sent a peace-mission to Rome. According to the famous legend, of which the earliest mention is in Livy and Horace, the captured Roman general Regulus was sent with the Carthaginian envoys to urge a settlement, or, if the Senate refused to consider peace, to help bring about an exchange of prisoners. Regulus, however, persuaded the Senate to reject these proposals, and was taken back to Carthage and executed. The veracity of these details is extremely doubtful, but it is likely that an attempt was made to end the war, and the winter of 250–249 would be a probable time; both sides were evenly balanced with little prospect of either of them getting the upper hand in the near future.

At the beginning of 249 the new consul, P. Claudius Pulcher, arrived to take command at Lilybaeum. He belonged to a family that had a reputation—no doubt in some cases well-deserved— for an overbearing type of arrogance, and he himself is described as a brutal martinet. The best-known story about him is that, before the battle of Drepanum, when the sacred chickens refused to eat—a bad omen before a battle—he threw them into the sea so that they could drink. But stories of this type bear a strong similarity to those told a generation later about Flaminius and other enemies of the 'establishment' in the Hannibalic War, and are most likely derived from the propaganda put about by their political opponents (see pp. 51, 61, 64).

During the fighting around the siege-works at Lilybaeum the Romans had suffered heavy casualties among their ships' crews, and Claudius brought with him a newly-raised force of nearly ten thousand sailors to make the fleet operational again. For Claudius had decided to make a surprise attack on Drepanum, now the Carthaginian headquarters in Sicily, where their commander-in-chief, Adherbal, was stationed. Claudius's plan was excellent in its conception but poor in execution. By putting it into action at once he achieved the element of surprise, since Adherbal did not realize that the Roman fleet was yet fully manned, but he put himself at a disadvantage in that his new crews were still untrained. Claudius set sail at midnight, and was off Drepanum by dawn, and the Carthaginians were still almost unprepared when the Roman fleet began sailing down the narrow channel into the harbour. But Adherbal acted with speed and resolution. He got his ships together and led them out on to the open sea by a channel on the opposite side of the harbour. Claudius suddenly saw that he was likely to be trapped, and ordered his ships to get back out of the harbour without delay. In the confusion some of them collided or lost their oars, and by the time the Romans were out of the harbour and in some sort of formation again the Carthaginians had got to seawards of them and had them penned up against the shore. At first the battle was evenly balanced, but gradually the Carthaginians got the upper hand. Their ships were faster and more easily handled, their crews were better trained and more skilful, and their position to seawards of the Romans gave them more opportunity for manoeuvring. The Romans found themselves being driven into the shallows, and ship after ship ran aground. Seeing the desperate situation, Claudius left the rest of his fleet to its fate, and made his escape with about thirty ships. The rest, ninety-three, fell into the enemy hands.

Claudius was recalled to Rome, and his colleague, L. Junius Pullus, was sent out with a very large supply-fleet to revictual the Roman camp at Lilybaeum. Junius collected some ships from Messana, and then sailed on to Syracuse with eight hundred supply vessels convoyed by one hundred and twenty warships. From here he sent off half the supply ships to Lilybaeum under the command of his quaestor, with a small escort, while he himself remained to load corn that had been brought in from the inland districts of Sicily.

The Carthaginians had been informed by their spies of the approach of these supplies, and a hundred ships under Carthalo, one of Adherbal's officers, who had just come from Carthage, were lying in wait off Heraclea. But the Roman squadron learnt from their scout boats that he was coming to cut them off, so they put into a sheltered bay near Phintias, dropped anchor, and when Carthalo sailed into the bay they drove him off with fire from catapults erected on the beach. So Carthalo, after towing off a few of the grain-ships, moved along the coast to a favourable anchorage in the estuary of a river and lay in wait. Eventually he sighted Junius and the other half of the supply-fleet. Junius realized that he was hopelessly outnumbered, so he came in as close to land as he dared—the coast at that point was rocky and dangerous—and dropped anchor. Carthalo did not want to risk an engagement so close to land, so he drew off and took up his position at a point between the two Roman fleets, neither of which felt strong enough to move out from its anchorage. It was now, it seems, July, the season for storms in this part of the Mediterranean. The Carthaginian pilots knew the weather-signs, and warned Carthalo that a gale was threatening. He weighed anchor, and raced to safety around Cape Pachynus. The Romans caught the full force of the storm; on the savage, exposed coast their ships were either sunk or rendered unusable.

Junius escaped from the wreck and made his way to Lilybaeum, where he took command; corn was brought to the Roman camp from other parts of Sicily, thanks to the energy of Hiero. Junius determined to do something to make up for his recent débâcle. It was still part of the Roman strategy to transfer the weight of their attack to Drepanum, and Junius was able to seize Mount Eryx, which lies just inland from that city. This is a mountain over 2,000 feet high, now Mount San Giuliano, on the highest point of which, at the extreme eastern edge, was an ancient temple dedicated to the cult of a goddess

20

variously worshipped as Aphrodite, Astarte, and Venus. The site is now occupied by a Norman castle, but traces of the temple's massive walls still remain. At a lower point was a town, whose inhabitants had been removed to Drepanum earlier in the war. The Romans occupied the temple of Venus on the summit and the town of Eryx that lay just beneath it. They also posted a strong force to guard the foot of the mountain, at the point where the road comes up from Drepanum.

Shortly after this, in 247 (or 246—the exact year is uncertain) the Carthaginians hit back. They appointed as their commander-in-chief a man who was to prove himself the most brilliant soldier of his generation, Hamilcar Barca. He belonged to a family whose policy it was to support Carthaginian expansion in the Mediterranean rather than in continental North Africa. It was this policy that was to bring Carthage once again into a head-on clash with Rome. The adoption of the rival policy would not have made the clash any less inevitable, but it would have given Carthage the solid power needed to face Rome on equal terms.

Hamilcar adopted an entirely new strategy. He occupied Herctae (now Monte Pellegrino), a 2,000-foot mountain situated only a few miles from Panormus, with a flat top extensive enough for grazing cattle and growing crops, precipitous sides with only three steep and difficult paths of access, and in the Bay of Santa Maria a natural deep-water harbour which could be reached from the summit. From this impregnable base he would take his fleet to ravage the Italian coast as far north as Cumae, for after the disasters in 249 the Romans had given up all attempt to oppose the Carthaginians at sea. Hamilcar hoped that by this method he would induce the Romans to agree to a negotiated peace. But the Romans were not to be overawed. They moved their forces from Panormus up to a camp near the foot of Mount Herctae, barely half a mile from Hamilcar's positions, and for three years the main forces of the two sides were engaged in a fierce, though static, struggle. There was no major engagement or pitched battle. Both sides were too evenly matched, and their defensive positions were too strong. But there was continual skirmishing, patrol activity, ambuscades, and raids. The situation that developed was in many ways similar, on a limited scale, to trench warfare.

21

After this struggle had been going on for three years, Hamilcar began to realize that his efforts were not being sufficiently productive. He was, strategically, being kept on the defensive and was not doing anything to make the Romans more amenable to peace. To take a more positive part in the war, he would have to be in a position where he could interfere with the Roman's operations against Lilybaeum and Drepanum. Accordingly, he transferred his troops to Mount Eryx. Avoiding the enemy guard-post at the foot of the mountain, Hamilcar seized the town of Eryx and proceeded to besiege the Roman garrison in the Temple on the summit. Here he maintained himself for more than two years, drawing off the main Roman forces from Drepanum. They were unable to dislodge him, as his position was too strong, or to starve him out, as he controlled a road down to the sea and could have supplies brought in from Carthage.

The Romans realized that they would not capture Drepanum while Hamilcar held this dominant position in their rear. It also became clear to a growing number of people at Rome that they would never make any real progress in the war as a whole by their efforts on land alone. It is likely that there had always been some opposition to the idea of Rome becoming a naval power. This opposition had been stifled by the victories at Mylae and Ecnomus, but had been resuscitated when the fleet was wrecked off Camarina, and the débâcle at Drepanum followed by the destruction of the supply-fleet under Junius Pullus had given it the upper hand. Since then it had been the official policy of the Senate to revert to Rome's traditional strategy of relying on her heavy-armed legionaries, and such operations as there had been at sea had been in the form of privateering enterprises, of which the most successful was a raid on the North African port of Hippo. But now it was obvious that this strategy had failed, and the Romans were no nearer victory than they had been six years before. The war had been dragging on for twenty-two years. The cost in money and materials had been heavy. Polybius talks about the crippling effect of the continued drain on the Roman treasury. The cost in manpower had also been very great. The total of Roman citizens counted in the two successive censuses of 252 and 247 had dropped by forty thousand, though part of this figure may have been caused by failure to register troops serving in Sicily at the time. The losses of the Latin and Italian allies are not known, but they would be approximately equal to the Roman casualties, and the fact that immediately after the end of the war Rome had to deal with the revolt of Falerii indicates that a protraction of the struggle in Sicily may well have led to a series of uprisings in Italy.

By 242 the Romans were faced with two possible alternatives. One was to try and negotiate peace with Carthage on terms that would enable them to keep most of their gains in Sicily. They would have to withdraw their forces from the western tip of the island, and it is likely that before agreeing to peace the Carthaginians would insist on the return of Panormus. This would leave the Romans sharing the eastern half of Sicily with Hiero, forced to maintain adequate garrisons in the various towns they held to prevent them being surprised by a sudden Carthaginian attack. They could not afford to withdraw from Sicily completely, for it was now necessary to maintain some military presence there to prevent the Carthaginians using the Sicilian ports as bases for raids on Italy. But there was a slight prospect that, if a satisfactory equilibrium could be established, the two sides could maintain, for some years at any rate, a state of non-belligerence.

The other alternative was to make a supreme effort to win the war. The main argument in favour of this policy was that more than once in the past Rome had been on the verge of victory. But the course of the war had shown that to gain a decisive advantage Rome had to have command of the sea. This lesson had been learnt, unlearnt, and now had to be learnt again. The supporters of this policy got their way, but, like Scipio nearly forty years later, they had to accept a compromise. Either because of lack of funds in the Treasury, or, more probably, because some concession had to be made to allay political opposition, the cost of the new fleet that the Romans now proceeded to build was met by voluntary contributions, offered as loans to be repaid when the war was won. The building and fitting out of each warship was financed either by single individuals or by groups of men forming themselves into syndicates.

The Roman fleet, of two hundred quinqueremes, built on the design of the ship captured from Hannibal 'the Rhodian', was put under the command of the consul for 242, C. Lutatius

Catulus. Catulus, and his brother Quintus, consul for the following year, were the leading representatives of a family that was now coming into prominence for the first time and reached its greatest influence in the last century of the Republic amongst the leaders of the Senatorial aristocracy. The Lutatii Catuli, like a number of the other 'new' families at this time, would have been active in supporting a more aggressive and expansionist policy in Sicily, for it was by their prowess in foreign wars that such families were able to push themselves to the front.

Catulus was a brave and resolute commander. He sailed for Sicily at the beginning of the summer, and found no opposition. The Carthaginians had unwisely let their fleet run down, and what warships they had in service were now back at Carthage. The Romans occupied the roadsteads at Lilybaeum, sailed into the harbour at Drepanum, and launched a vigorous attack on the town, in the course of which the consul was wounded. But this did not prevent him from keeping his attention fixed on his primary purpose, the defeat of the enemy fleet, and during the months of waiting he trained his crews up to a very high pitch of efficiency. He had learnt from Claudius Pulcher the dangers of going into battle with the men raw and untrained.

The Carthaginians had been taken by surprise, and the Romans were allowed to gain command of the sea by default. It took some months to build a fleet large enough to be a match for the Romans', and by then the winter had set in. As a result, when the Carthaginian fleet sailed for Sicily at the beginning of March 241, their troops in Sicily, especially Hamilcar's field-army on Eryx, were running short of supplies. This made it necessary for the Carthaginians to load their warships with provisions. Hanno, the Carthaginian admiral, hoped to avoid the enemy, land his stores at Eryx, and then, when he had taken on board Hamilcar and the pick of his men to serve as marines, to seek out the Roman fleet and fight it.

Hanno mustered his fleet at Holy Isle, now Maretamo, on the western edge of the Aegates (whose modern name is Isole Egadi) and then, with a strong wind behind him, set sail on his final run to the coast of Sicily, hoping to get across to Eryx before the Romans realized that he had made the crossing. But Catulus had good intelligence, and got information that the Carthaginians were at Holy Isle, so he put to sea and lay in wait for Hanno off the Aegates. When the enemy came in sight he found himself in something of a dilemma. The wind had strengthened to gale force, and the seas had got up. To put out to intercept would mean that his men would have a long row into the wind with heavy seas meeting them head-on. But the Carthaginian ships had their problems too. They were heavily laden, with only a few marines on board, almost defenceless if it came to battle. To let them get through to Eryx with their stores would be to concede a tactical defeat, as it was the whole purpose of the Roman strategy to prevent supplies from reaching Hamilcar. Catulus was sure he could rely on his crews, and gave the order to put to sea. For once the Roman contempt of the elements was justified. The well-trained oarsmen played their part, and Catulus got his ships in line full across the path of the oncoming Carthaginians. He himself was still incapacitated by his wound, and tactical control of the battle was delegated to the praetor, Valerius Falto.

The final battle of the First Punic War was a massacre rather than a fight. The Romans had better ships, their men were better trained and superior in numbers. In a short time the Romans had sunk fifty ships and captured seventy with their crews; the total number of prisoners amounted to nearly ten thousand men. Only a sudden change of wind saved the rest of Hanno's fleet. They hauled their sails up and fled before the wind to the shelter of Holy Isle. Catulus and his fleet, triumphant, sailed back to Lilybaeum.

When the remnants of their defeated fleet reached Carthage, the first reaction of the Carthaginians was to crucify Hanno. These savage penalties inflicted on their generals after a disaster were intended not so much as a punishment and a deterrent as an act of expiation. The worship of Baal was a cruel and bloody cult. Then they sent instructions to Hamilcar, authorizing him to negotiate terms of peace if he did not think it possible to carry on the war now that the Romans had command of the sea and there was no prospect of getting supplies to him from Africa. The Carthaginian Treasury was exhausted. There was not enough, in fact, to pay off in full all the mercenaries who were fighting for the Carthaginians in Sicily. It was quite impossible for Carthage to prolong the war any further: to do so would involve not merely maintaining but greatly increasing their efforts of the past few years. The fact that Hamilcar was given a free hand to decide what he thought best indicates how great was the influence at Carthage of the Barcid family, to which he belonged. This influence was to continue for nearly fifty years.

Hamilcar saw that there was no purpose in fighting on, and sent envoys to Catulus asking for terms. Catulus himself was ready to offer generous conditions. He knew that the Senate was eager for a speedy conclusion of the war. To prolong it would be to deny himself the glory of imposing terms on a defeated enemy, while the memory of Regulus must have been in his mind as an ominous warning. Polybius (I, 62) gives the heads of the agreement concluded between the two generals: there should be friendship between Rome and Carthage provided that the Carthaginians evacuated the whole of Sicily, refrained from attacking Hiero, Syracuse, or the allies of Syracuse, gave back all prisoners-of-war without ransom, and paid an indemnity of two thousand two hundred talents of silver (a talent weighed approximately 57lb) within twenty years. These terms were made subject to ratification by the Assembly of the People at Rome, with whom always lay the ultimate decision on war and peace.

The conclusion of these draft terms led to strong repercussions at Rome, where there was loudly-expressed support for the continuation of the war. This no doubt was fostered by those generals who hoped to gain military glory for themselves from further victories over an already beaten enemy. It is doubtful whether another attempt to invade Africa was ever seriously considered, but it was probably put forward by one of the more militaristic politicians. The new consul, Q. Lutatius Catulus, resisted these attempts to upset the terms agreed by his brother, and eventually a compromise was reached. The final decision should be left to the ten commissioners who, according to constitutional precedent, were sent out to implement the peace terms. Q. Catulus was sent out to Sicily with this commission, and he and his brother would have had very great influence with it. The more obnoxious additions to the terms, that Hamilcar should surrender all deserters—to be executed by the Romans—and that his men should give up their arms and pass under the yoke—conditions that Hamilcar declared he would rather fight on than accept—were allowed to drop. Instead, the indemnity was increased by one thousand talents, and the period allowed for payment cut to ten years. The Carthaginians were also required to evacuate all the islands lying between Sicily and Italy; this clause would have referred originally to the Aegatian and the Liparae Islands, though subsequently it was extended to include Sardinia. Hamilcar was able to withdraw his men from Sicily with all the honours of war, but the haggling over the ratification of the peace terms left him with a bitter resentment against Rome.

So ended the first war that Rome fought outside Italy, a war that dragged on for twenty-four years and at the end left both sides exhausted—though they both showed great recuperative powers. In this war the Romans were continually out-generalled, not only by Hamilcar and Xanthippus, but by lesser-known Carthaginian commanders such as Hanno, who fought with such skill at Agrigentum and Ecnomus, Himilco, the defender of Lilybaeum, and the admirals Adherbal and Carthalo who gave Carthage back the command of the sea. The fundamental weakness in the Roman generalship was the system of annual commands. Occasionally a successful commander would get a second consulship and return to Sicily after an interval for another campaign, as did L. Manlius Vulso, L. Caecilius Metellus, and Aulus Atilius Calatinus, but there was no continuous tenure of command, no consistent strategy, no opportunity for a general to get to know his own troops or—even more important—to get to know the enemy. The system of yearly changes in command led to the precipitate rashness of Regulus in Africa, and, with less harmful effects, it influenced Catulus in his decision to accept terms from Hamilcar rather than let a successor reap the glory. Some of the worst defects in this system were cured during the Second Punic War, when a much more sophisticated command structure was evolved (see pp. 46f.). But what gave the Romans victory was their immense superiority in numbers. The First Punic War showed, as the war with Pyrrhus had merely indicated, that the military resources of Rome and Italy were far greater than those of any other Mediterranean state in the Hellenistic world. The weakness of Carthage lay in the fact that she could not draw strength from North Africa as Rome could from Italy. Some indication of the size of Rome's reserves of manpower can be obtained from the account given in Polybius (II, 24) of the army lists compiled a generation later, at the time of the Gallic invasion of 225. At that time the grand total of men capable of bearing arms, infantry and cavalry, Roman and Italian, was just over three-quarters of a million.

2

The Origins of the Second Punic War

THE SEEDS OF THE SECOND PUNIC WAR were sown at the end of the First. As Polybius points out (III, 9–10), there were three main causes. First, the attitude of Hamilcar himself. For nearly seven years he had held out on Herctae and Eryx; he had never been defeated, and had only capitulated because of the failure of the Carthaginian government to keep him supplied. He felt that if he could face the Romans again on equal terms he would have little difficulty in reversing the decision, and he was eager for an opportunity to renew the struggle. Finally, he was embittered at the way in which the Romans went back on the terms that he had agreed with Catulus, and wanted to get his revenge.

The events of the next few years made the personal feelings of Hamilcar of even greater importance. The end of the war in Sicily saw Carthage engaged in a savage and bloody war—the 'Truceless War'—with their mercenary troops, who had revolted over a delay in giving them their pay, and with their subjects in North Africa, who had revolted in sympathy with the mercenaries. The supreme command was at first given to Hanno, surnamed 'The Great' for reasons that no historian has ever been able to discover. His military reputation rested on a number of easily-won successes over undisciplined North African tribes, and his mishandling of the situation was largely responsible for the original outbreak. Hanno seems to have represented the land-holding interests at Carthage whose policy it was to expand in North Africa and consolidate Carthaginian power on the continent. This was a policy that had been developed at Carthage in the 5th century, when, as has been

29

demonstrated by G. Picard (*Carthage*, Ch. IV), a political crisis caused by crushing defeats in Sicily combined with an economic crisis arising out of a continued unfavourable trade-balance with the outside world had driven the Carthaginians back upon their own resources. Hamilcar, on the other hand, represented the commercial interests, who were orientated towards the Mediterranean world and looked back to the older traditional policy of Carthage of establishing a monopoly in the carrying trade. This policy involved expansion in the Mediterranean, and it was Hamilcar's intention to confine any expansion in the first instance to areas where there was not much likelihood of an immediate clash with Rome.

As a result of Hanno's incompetence and lack of success, when a second army was raised Hamilcar was put in command. The course of the campaign was then marked by continuous and bitter quarrels between the two generals, until eventually Hanno was recalled and Hamilcar placed in supreme command. This marked the turning point of the war, and within a year the revolt had been completely crushed. Hamilcar now stood unchallenged as the Carthaginians' greatest general, his influence at Carthage outstripped that of any of his rivals, and for the next generation it was his family, the Barcids, and their supporters who controlled affairs at Carthage.

The second cause was the inconsistent behaviour of the Romans. During the revolt they had acted with complete propriety, and had observed the spirit of the recent treaty 'that there should be friendship between Rome and Carthage'. They encouraged merchants who were bringing supplies to Carthage, and imposed a ban on sending supplies to the mercenaries; when Utica and Sardinia, who had joined the revolt, offered to submit to Rome and place themselves under their protection, they refused to accept the offer. But in 238, after the revolt had been suppressed and the Carthaginians were preparing an expedition to recover Sardinia, the Romans intervened, seized the island, and declared war on Carthage on the grounds that the Carthaginian preparations were directed against themselves. They now claimed that Sardinia, as one of the islands between Sicily and Italy, properly belonged to Rome, and only agreed to renew the peace treaty after the Carthaginians had formally ceded Sardinia and paid an additional indemnity of twelve hundred talents.

The reason for this *volte-face* involving a completely fraudu-
lent geographical claim is difficult to determine. Clearly control
of the Senate had passed to a group that was hostile to Carthage,
probably the same people who had been behind the refusal to
ratify the peace terms agreed between Catulus and Hamilcar. It
has been suggested that the change in the attitude of the Romans
was due to the eclipse of the influence of Hanno, whom they
regarded as a friend, and the rise of that of Hamilcar, whom
they viewed as an inveterate enemy. But whatever the motives
for their action, there can be no doubt about the consequences.
This completely unjustifiable annexation of Sardinia and the
ruthless imposition of an indemnity gave the whole of Carthage
a national grievance against Rome and set it solidly behind
Hamilcar. There can be no doubt that during the next forty
years the Barcid leaders, first Hamilcar and then Hannibal, had
the consistent and whole-hearted support of the Carthaginians
in their actions against Rome. To their policies there was, however, continuous opposition from a very small group of political
enemies led by Hanno, whose partisan and utterly insupportable
plea that Hannibal was acting without the authority of the
government of Carthage was accepted as true by Fabius Pictor
and passed into the historical tradition.

The third cause was the Carthaginian conquest of Spain,
which gave Carthage a base of operations for a war against
Rome, limitless resources both in men and materials for a protracted struggle, and a sense of confidence in the superiority of
her troops. Immediately after the end of the Mercenary War,
Hamilcar was sent with an army to Spain. At that time Carthaginian power was confined to a comparatively small area in the
south-west, centred around Gades (Cadiz), but in the course of
nine years (238–229) Hamilcar extended it over most of Spain.
The former system of trading-posts, designed to develop the
commerce between Spain and Carthage to the greatest benefit of
the latter, was replaced by a colonialist system of exploitation,
based on military conquest, the imposition of tribute and the
taking of hostages. At Hamilcar's death he was succeeded by his
son-in-law Hasdrubal, who, using diplomacy rather than war,
consolidated his conquests and built a capital for the new
province at Nova Carthago (now Cartagena), situated in a
splendid position a little way up the east coast. But it must be

remembered that Carthaginian power was always confined to the coastal strip and the river valleys, and never penetrated to the central mountain range.

The Romans had not let Hamilcar's operations in Spain pass unobserved, and in 231 a deputation arrived at his headquarters to try and ascertain what his real objectives were. Hamilcar entertained them politely and sent them away empty-handed, apart from the plausible excuse that his Spanish conquests had been forced on him by the need to pay the war-indemnity to the Romans. The sending of this mission indicates a hostile attitude on the part of the Romans, and the people at Rome behind it were probably the same people who ten years before upset the terms agreed between Hamilcar and Catulus. But although the Romans watched events in Spain, they did not adopt any consistent policy towards the Carthaginian conquest, and their next intervention showed a more conciliatory attitude. In 226, just before the Gallic invasion, they concluded a treaty with Hasdrubal by which it was agreed that the Carthaginians would not cross the River Ebro 'for the purpose of waging war'. Polybius, who quotes this treaty on two occasions (II, 13; III, 27) and probably had seen a copy of it in the Record Office at Rome, states specifically that no mention was made of the rest of Spain, and so implicitly denies the versions of the Roman propagandists that the treaty contained a clause guaranteeing independence to the town of Saguntum, Hannibal's attack on which was later taken as a *casus belli*. Polybius does not mention any concessions made by the Romans in return, but these were probably contained in a separate part of the agreement that was preserved at Carthage, and it is likely that in return for Hasdrubal's promise, the Romans agreed not to carry out any armed intervention south of the Ebro. If this was so, it would mean that Rome now recognized the whole of Spain south of the Ebro as a Carthaginian province. It is likely that at the time of this treaty the political situation in Rome had changed, and the dominant group in the Senate favoured a less aggressive policy towards Carthage.

In 221 Hasdrubal was murdered, and Hamilcar's son, Hannibal, now a young man in his mid-twenties, was elected Commander-in-Chief by the acclamation of the army. The appointment was promptly confirmed by the Popular Assembly at Carthage. Hannibal at once began to reduce the remaining tribes south of the Ebro. By the end of 220 the only place remaining independent was the rich town of Saguntum, situated on the east coast of Spain about mid-way between the River Ebro and Nova Carthago. Hannibal deliberately avoided any aggression against Saguntum because of Roman interests there, since he did not want to provoke a clash with Rome, for the time being at any rate.

It seems that after the Gallic menace had receded the Romans began to renew their interest in Spain, and they formed some sort of diplomatic relationship with Saguntum. The date of this is uncertain, but it was probably just after the end of the Roman offensive in 222. The object of the Romans was to secure Saguntum as a bridgehead for possible future operations in Spain against the Carthaginians, and they set about establishing a pro-Roman party securely in power. They soon had their opportunity. Early in 220—the exact date is conjectural, but at the end of that year it was described as 'a short time before'— they were invited to act as arbitrators in an internal political disturbance in Saguntum, and in this capacity they decided in favour of the party more likely to serve their interests, placed them firmly in power, and disposed of the leading members of the opposing faction by putting them to death.

During the latter part of 220 the Saguntines kept sending missions to Rome, to give the Senate up-to-date information about Hannibal's conquests in the interior and to put before them their own growing fears that, now that the rest of Spain south of the Ebro was in Carthaginian hands, an attack on Saguntum itself could not be long delayed. For many months they got no response. Although there was an influential section in the Senate that favoured an aggressive policy, the majority of the Senators wanted to keep well back from the brink. But during the winter there occurred one of those swings that make Roman foreign policy so difficult to follow on any logical basis. An embassy was sent to Nova Carthago with peremptory instructions to Hannibal not to interfere with Saguntum, as it was under the protection of Rome, and not to extend his conquests north of the Ebro, in accordance with the treaty with Hasdrubal. Hannibal reacted very strongly to this ultimatum, accusing the Romans of the unjustifiable execution of the leaders of the opposing faction in Saguntum a short time before and declaring his intention to protect Saguntum against the treacherous interventions of the Romans. Getting no satisfaction from him, the envoys went on to North Africa, to repeat the demands to the Carthaginian government, to whom Hannibal had already reported that the Saguntines were interfering with the Torboletai, a neighbouring tribe that was subject to Carthage.

It is likely that Hannibal was not yet ready for a war with Rome. One can conjecture that his intention was to consolidate his hold on Spain, and win the friendship of the important tribes in southern and indeed in Cisalpine Gaul, where there was bitter hatred of the Romans as a result of their northward expansion and their victories, before provoking any conflict. But the Roman ultimatum constituted a challenge which, if ignored, would weaken his authority in Spain and foster disaffection among the tribes, and encourage the Romans to increase their support for Saguntum; they might even send troops, confident that he would hold off. On the other hand, he could attack Saguntum at once; there was a good chance that they were bluffing. Accordingly at the start of the campaigning season of 219 he launched a full-scale attack on Saguntum.

The surprising thing is that, despite their recent ultimatum, and its reception, which made it probable that they would have to back their warning with a show of force, the Romans immediately got themselves embroiled in a petty colonial war in Illyria. It may be, as Polybius suggests, that the Senate, anticipating a long and hard struggle in Spain, wanted to make their eastern flank safe. It may be that, remembering how long towns like Lilybaeum and Drepanum had held out during the war in Sicily, they expected that Saguntum could stand a siege for several years, not realizing the comparative weakness of the town's natural defences. It is likely that the party in the Senate that was opposed to a renewal of the war with Carthage deliberately committed the main Roman forces to Illyria that year to prevent any Roman intervention in Spain on behalf of Saguntum. But when the news arrived that Hannibal had taken Saguntum by storm after an eight months' siege, there was a violent emotional reaction at Rome, and the war party gained the upper hand. The sudden ending of the war in Illyria left

their opponents in a weakened position, and gave an un-
deserved confidence in the Roman military leadership. After a
debate in the Senate (that there was such a debate is well
attested by contemporary evidence, in spite of Polybius' denial)
it was decided to send an embassy to Carthage with instructions
to present a final ultimatum, that the Carthaginians should
surrender Hannibal and his staff to Rome on pain of immediate
declaration of war. The Carthaginians advanced arguments to
show that Hannibal was not guilty of any breach of treaty by
his attack on Saguntum—the nature of the arguments they used
has been so distorted and overlaid with propaganda that they
cannot now be ascertained—but the Romans would not listen.
The leader of the embassy, M. Fabius Buteo, who had been
consul in 245 and was the oldest living ex-censor, put his hands
in the folds of his toga and said, 'I carry here peace and war.
Choose which you wish.' The Carthaginian Suffete replied:
'Give us what you will.' Then Fabius answered: 'Then I give you
war,' and made a symbolic gesture of declaring war by bringing
a stone out of the fold of his toga and throwing it on the ground
in front of the Carthaginians.

So began the Hannibalic War. In spite of the sustained efforts
of their propagandists, and the natural tendency for war-guilt to
settle on the shoulders of the losers, there is little doubt that the
Romans were in the wrong. There is absolutely no evidence that
Saguntum was an ally of Rome. There is no evidence for the
existence of any treaty between Rome and Saguntum. In fact,
Polybius, when setting out the case for war made by the
Romans, makes it clear that the pro-war party had to infer from
the Roman arbitration at Saguntum that the city had previously
placed itself under the protection of Rome (III, 30). Recent
examinations of the problem by Professors E. Badian and A. E.
Astin show that the relationship between Rome and Saguntum
was one of *fides*—an informal relationship which put the
Romans under a moral obligation not to injure Saguntum
themselves but did not lay them under any binding obligation to
protect her from third parties—especially if Rome had already
promised the third party concerned, as she probably had done
in the treaty with Hasdrubal, not to carry out any armed intervention in the geographical area in which Saguntum was
situated. It is even doubtful whether the relationship of *fides* had

35

in fact been established. There was probably some dispute at Rome on this point, and the war party would have had to argue that such a relationship between Rome and Saguntum did really exist. Their arguments, since they were successful, passed into the authoritative historical tradition.

That the Romans themselves knew how weak their case was over Saguntum is shown by the efforts of the Roman propagandists to claim that Hannibal was guilty of a breach of the treaty between Rome and Hasdrubal. This piece of special pleading probably arose out of the fact that the final Roman embassy did not return home directly, but followed a circuitous route through northern Spain and southern Gaul, rallying support against Hannibal and trying to ensure that the Roman expeditionary force that would soon set out for Spain would march through friendly territory. They probably did not reach Rome and formally report the declaration of war until after the arrival of the news that Hannibal had crossed the Ebro. In the belief that Hannibal's war-guilt lay in the fact that he had violated this treaty, later Roman historians interpolated a clause specifically guaranteeing the independence of Saguntum (as Livy, XXI, 2, 7), or cut the Gordian knot by placing Saguntum *north* of the Ebro (as Appian, *Hispanica*, II, 7). It is interesting to note that Roman historians from Livy onwards wrongly believed that Saguntum was a Greek city, colonized from the island of Zacynthus off western Greece. This theory originated from the similarity of names, the Greek word for Saguntum being Zacantha, but it gained popular credence during the first half of the 2nd century, when it was an axiom of Roman propaganda that Rome went to war to protect her Greek allies.

Technically the Romans were in the wrong in declaring war on Carthage because of Hannibal's capture of Saguntum. But on the longer view they may have been justified, provided that the party at Rome that suspected Hannibal and believed that he intended to renew the war were correct in their assumptions. Though one cannot be certain, it is probable that they were correct. The story that, as a child, Hannibal was made to swear undying hatred of Rome is likely to have been a fiction, made up deliberately by Hannibal to counteract the suspicions of his enemies at the court of Antiochus the Greek. It was then that he first told it (Polybius, III, 11). During his campaign in Italy he openly disclaimed any notion of being engaged on a war to the death with Rome, and the terms of his treaty with Philip V of Macedon in 215 (Polybius, VII, 9) clearly envisage the continued existence of Rome as an independent power in Italy. Hannibal's personal bitterness towards Rome began after the war, when the Romans hounded him from Carthage. But even when the story of his undying hatred is rejected, there can be no doubt that Hannibal inherited from his father a firm resolve to take his revenge on Rome and recover Sicily and Sardinia. This he would not do by a direct attack on Sardinia—as his enemies at Rome probably anticipated—but by striking at the heart of Rome's power, in Italy itself. Trained in the principles laid down by the great Greek generals of the Hellenistic age (he himself could read and write Greek), he understood that a comparatively small, well-trained, well-armed force, led by a professional commander, could defeat greatly superior numbers of local militia—for that was what most states put into the field —commanded by amateurs. Looking back on the history of his own country, and seeing how foreign invaders like Agathocles and, more recently, the rebellious mercenaries, were quickly joined by the subject-allies of Carthage, he expected that as soon as he had entered Italy and had decisively defeated the Roman army in the field, the Italian subject-allies of Rome would at once throw off the yoke and join him. It is likely that he wanted a little more time to prepare his plans, establish alliances with the various Gallic tribes through whose territories he would pass, and gain further and better information about the Alpine passes. But the challenge that the Romans threw down over Saguntum made him move before he was ready.

3

Hannibal's March

AFTER THE FALL OF SAGUNTUM Hannibal, with the prudence of a good general, assumed that war was inevitable and made his preparations. He sent the Spanish troops home on leave for the winter, discussed the problems of governing Spain with his younger brother Hasdrubal, whom he was leaving in charge of the province, and sent to North Africa a force of nearly fifteen thousand Spaniards, to serve both as garrison and hostages, replacing them in Spain by an approximately equal number of Libyans and Numidians. He also sent out missions to make contact with the Gauls both in the Alps and in North Italy and to get the fullest possible information about the Alpine passes.

About the end of March 218 he heard that the Romans had demanded his surrender at Carthage, the Carthaginians had refused, and war had been declared. Soon after this he received satisfactory reports from the reconnaissance parties he had sent out to make contact with the Gauls, and was now in a position to reveal his plans. His troops gave the announcement an enthusiastic reception, and some time towards the end of April Hannibal moved out of his winter quarters in Nova Carthago. His original force amounted to 90,000 infantry, 12,000 cavalry and 37 elephants, composed of men from Carthage and her dependencies, Numidia, Spain and the Balearic Islands. His first task was to conquer and secure the territory between the Ebro and the Pyrenees, and in particular to overawe the Bargusii, who were friendly to Rome, and the powerful tribe of the Ilergetes, who under their princes Indibilis and Mandonius were to play a stirring part in the affairs of Spain for nearly twenty years. This was accomplished in a very short time, though

38

not without some losses; then he left Hanno with 11,000 men in charge of the territory north of the Ebro and put in his charge the heavy baggage of the rest of his troops. None of them ever came back to claim it, so it did not matter that it was captured by the Romans later in the year (see p. 95). With the remainder of his army, now at its peak of efficiency and physical condition and numbering 50,000 foot and 9,000 horse, as well as 37 elephants, he crossed the Pyrenees at a point near the Mediterranean coast and headed for the Rhône.

Hannibal had little difficulty getting across southern France. Those tribes that were not friendly were easily intimidated. Yet it seems that from the time he crossed the Ebro to his arrival at the Rhône there were numerous desertions, and these continued until the actual ascent of the Alps. He reached the Rhône at a point about four days' march from the sea. This would be about fifty miles upstream from the river mouth, probably just north of Orange, above the confluence of the Rhône and the Aygues, a point far enough away to escape interference or observation by Rome's allies in Marseille. Here the natives were friendly; Hannibal purchased from them a large supply of barges and dug-out canoes, and his soldiers set to and made themselves canoes by hollowing them out of tree-trunks. But the Gauls on the opposite bank were hostile, and gathered to oppose his crossing. So he sent off a detachment under Hanno, son of the Suffetes Bomilcar who had shown himself a staunch supporter of Hannibal when the Romans had demanded his surrender, and gave him orders to cross the river on rafts some twenty-five miles upstream, lay up for a day to give him time to get his preparations completed, and then to make a diversionary attack in the enemy's rear.

On the fifth day after reaching the Rhône Hannibal began the crossing. The infantry were in their canoes, the cavalry and some of the horses on the barges, with three or four additional horses being towed along on either side of the stern. A smoke signal from a hill on the other side of the river told them that Hanno was moving in to the attack, and they pushed off from the bank. The Gauls on the other side stood waiting, shouting their war-cries. Then flames leaped up from the Gallic camp as Hanno's men set fire to their tents. The Gauls turned to meet this new enemy, and Hannibal landed almost unopposed.

39

Quickly forming up his men, he attacked the confused and disordered Gauls. Caught between two fires, they broke and fled, and the rest of the army was brought over without interference.

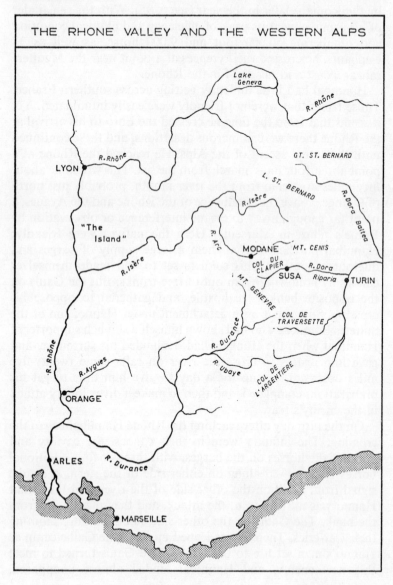

THE RHONE VALLEY AND THE WESTERN ALPS

Next day Hannibal heard that the Roman army, under the Consul Scipio, had landed at Marseille on his way to Spain. Had he not been delayed by a revolt in Cisalpine Gaul, which made it necessary to transfer one of his legions to the Po valley and raise fresh troops to replace it, he would have met Hannibal en route, and the first battle of the war would have been fought between the Rhône and the Pyrenees. Hannibal sent off a cavalry force of five hundred Numidians to find out the size, position, and intentions of the Roman army, while he himself encouraged his men by introducing a deputation from Cisalpine Gaul that had just arrived. The Gauls openly invited the Carthaginians to come to Italy and join them in their fight against Rome; they promised to guide them by a safe and direct route through country well-stocked with supplies. The words of the Gauls dispelled many of the doubts of Hannibal's men, some of whom were getting more and more apprehensive as they drew nearer to the Alps, but the meeting had hardly broken up when the survivors of the Numidian cavalry patrol arrived in great disorder. Not far from the camp they had run into a similar reconnaissance force sent out by Scipio, and after a fierce tussle had been driven back with the loss of more than half their number. Hannibal at once broke camp. He got his infantry on the move northwards, posted the whole of his cavalry downstream as a covering force, while he brought across the elephants, towing them over on rafts. Then, with a strong rear-guard of cavalry and elephants, he moved off after his main body.

Three days later Scipio arrived in full force, and was amazed to find Hannibal gone. He had presumed that Hannibal's strategy was to secure Spain from attack by gaining control of southern France, and had never believed that he would attempt the difficult and dangerous task of invading Italy by way of the Alps. He returned to Marseille in something of a dilemma. As consul, it was his duty to organize the defence of Italy against Hannibal, especially since his colleague Sempronius Longus was now in Sicily preparing for an invasion of Africa. Yet he realized the vital importance of Spain, and he saw that if Hannibal was to bring the war into Italy it was essential to deny him supplies and reinforcements from there. This appreciation was a vital factor in the strategy not only of Scipio himself but of the party of which he was now a leader. On his return to the coast he took a decision that made a great contribution to Rome's eventual victory. He sent his fleet and army on to Spain under the command of his elder brother Gnaeus, while he himself took ship for Italy to meet Hannibal as he came out of the Alps.

After four days' march Hannibal reached a district known as 'The Island', formed by the junction of the Rhône and one of its tributaries, almost certainly the Isère. The land was occupied by a branch of the Allobroges, and at that particular time the chieftainship of the tribe was in dispute between two brothers. Hannibal helped the elder brother to secure the throne and drive out his rival. In repayment, he provided the Carthaginians with supplies of food, new clothes, and new weapons, and agreed to give them an escort for the first stages of their journey through the foothills.

For ten days Hannibal marched up the Isère, covering a distance of nearly one hundred miles. Then his escort left him, and he began the real ascent, leaving the course of the Isère and turning up its tributary, the Arc, that was to lead him to the Col du Clapier. At once he ran into difficulties. The road was narrow, steep, and bordered by precipices. The Allobroges, now that he was no longer under the protection of their fellows from 'The Island', regarded him as fair prey, and occupied points of vantage all along the route from which they could attack and harry the Carthaginians. Hannibal found out their plans— Gauls in those days could never keep a secret—pitched camp just before he reached the danger zone, and waited till nightfall. Then, when according to their normal custom the Gauls had left their ambuscades and withdrawn to the near-by villages for the night, he took a picked force and seized the positions on the heights that they had just left. Next day he sent his army along the road, winding its way in a long, slow-moving line. This was too great a temptation for the Gauls, who attacked and caused great havoc in the baggage-train, with wounded or terrified animals going over the edge into the depths below. Hannibal did what he could to stop the disaster by attacking from above, but the turmoil of the fighting caused even more confusion among the pack-animals, until at last the Allobroges broke and fled. While his baggage-train and cavalry were making their way slowly on to safer ground, he rallied what men he could and attacked and captured the neighbouring village that the Gauls had used as their base. Here he found a large number of horses and beasts of burden, and enough corn and cattle to feed his army for two or three days. The next battle took place somewhere near Modane. Although the inhabitants of that area had sent him hostages and cattle and offered to provide him with guides, they suddenly attacked him in full force just as he was passing through a gorge. But Hannibal had not taken their protestations of friendship at their face value. As soon as he realized that the enemy were massing, he sent the more vulnerable part of his force, the cavalry and the baggage-train, on in front, so as to place the solid mass of his heavy-armed infantry between them and the expected direction of the attack. His manoeuvre succeeded, for the infantry was able to hold the Gauls at bay; but some of them got past this covering force along the heights overlooking the gorge and rolled boulders down upon the baggage-train from above, or pelted them with volleys of rocks. Night fell, and the Carthaginian army was split up. Hannibal encamped in the gorge, occupying a natural defensive position behind a projecting spur, while the cavalry and the pack-animals pressed on through the night till they got on to safer ground. Next day Hannibal and the infantry caught up with the rest of the army, and they made their way up the final stage of the Col du Clapier. They had little trouble now with the Gauls, apart from sporadic attempts to pillage the baggage-train. On the more open ground the elephants gave valuable protection, for the tribesmen were afraid of them and dared not come anywhere near them. They reached the head of the pass that evening, having taken nine days on the ascent, and Hannibal camped there for two days, to rest his men, to allow the stragglers—both human and animal—to catch up with them, and to encourage his dispirited troops by pointing out to them the view of the plains of North Italy that, to those looking down from the top of the pass, stretched as far as the eye could see.

It was now late September and the snow had begun to lie deep on the mountain tops, so Hannibal lost no further time in starting the descent. He did not have to face any more human enemies, but his struggles with the terrain and the forces of nature made his journey downwards just as hazardous and

costly as the way up had been. On the Italian side of the Col du
Clapier the road descended in a series of steep zig-zags. The road
itself was narrow, and now was covered with snow. At one point
it had been carried away by a landslide, for a distance of nearly
three hundred yards. At first Hannibal tried to make a detour,
but when the Carthaginians left the line of the road and tried to
push their way through the snowdrifts they ran into unexpected
difficulties. The newly-fallen snow was soft and gave way easily
beneath their feet, but underneath it stretched a hard layer of
old snow, left there since the preceding winter and frozen so
that its surface was like ice. On this their feet slipped and
slithered uncontrollably, and once they lost their balance the
steepness of the slope would send them headlong, without any
chance to save themselves. The beasts of burden, as they fell and
struggled to rise, would cut through this lower layer with their
hoofs and get them trapped in the ice. Hannibal realized that a
detour was impossible, so he cleared a place of snow, pitched
camp on the mountain-side, and prepared to rebuild the road.
According to one story, he made the huge boulders easier to
split by lighting fires and then pouring sour wine on the hot
rocks. At the end of a day's work a road had been made wide
enough to pass the horses and pack-animals down to a camp
below the snow-line, where he let them roam in search of forage,
but it took three days of unremitting toil before the road was
wide enough to take the wretched, half-starved elephants. After
another three days he reached the plains, five months after
setting out from Nova Carthago. Of the 38,000 infantry and
8,000 cavalry with which he had crossed the Rhône, enemy
action, desertion, and the rigours of the journey had taken their
toll, and when Hannibal moved down the Dora Riparia into the
territory of the Taurini he only had 20,000 infantry and 6,000
cavalry.

After his men had recovered from their ordeal, Hannibal
determined on a show of strength. The Taurini were enemies of
his friends, the Insubres. He invited them to surrender—nomin-
ally, to become his friends and allies—and when they refused he
attacked their chief city, stormed it after three days, and put the
defenders to the sword. This display of force won him the
support of the neighbouring tribes, but the Gauls living in the
plains of the River Po were cut off from him by the Roman

army that Scipio, on learning of his arrival in Italy, had brought up from Parma with unexpected rapidity. Accordingly, to challenge the Roman control of Trans-Padane Gaul, Hannibal moved south towards the Po.

Hannibal's bold sweep through the Alps did more than out-flank the Roman army at the mouth of the Rhône. It under-mined Roman strategy for the conduct of the war, which must have been planned before Rome pushed Carthage into a declara-tion of hostilities. The disposition of the two consular armies in 218 B.C. reveals the main outlines of an offensive strategy: while Scipio took his army to Massilia, a force of equal size under Tiberius Sempronius was sent to Sicily. Understandably, Rome planned to fight the Second Punic War in the light of lessons gained from the First. She would expect to reassert naval supremacy, and Regulus had shown how Africa could be invaded. It looks as though this southern army had the major offensive rôle. Scipio's task was to pin down Hannibal, either in Gaul or Spain. But a decisive success could not be won in that theatre of war. The shortest way to the vitals of Carthage was to strike through Sicily to Africa, where supplies could be poured in once a secure footing had been gained. Hannibal's audacity turned these plans upside down. It was he who made the thrust at the enemy's vitals, and it would be many years before Rome could conduct an offensive in the Italian peninsula where for the next fifteen years the major campaigns of the war were to be fought.

It is at this point that the historian must make a choice. Shall he give an annalistic account of a war conducted over much of the western half of the Mediterranean world, or a continuous narrative of each of its main theatres? Clarity seems better served by the second method, and the next chapter is devoted to the war in Italy.

4

The War in Italy

HANNIBAL IS SUPPOSED TO HAVE REACHED the summit of the Alpine pass in the third week of September, and it must have been early October before his battered and depleted army came down to the valley of the Po. Ahead of him lay three hectic months of manoeuvres, battles, and diplomacy. Rome had made a start on the conquest of Gallia Cisalpina, but had yet to tighten her grip on the land. On the east she was well placed, with a colony and advance base at Ariminum (Rimini) to stop any penetration into Italy along the Adriatic coast. Friendly relations with the Veneti, a non-Celtic people of Illyrian origin, sealed off the Po estuary and the north-eastern plains towards the Julian and Carnic Alps. But with the Celtic peoples of the middle and upper reaches of the Po relations were very different. Roman armies had operated beyond the Po and reduced the powerful Insubres near the modern Milan: the Boii in the lands around Bologna had lost heavily in the last independent Gallic attack on Italy in 225. Rome had newly-planted colonies at Cremona and Placentia (Piacenza) to secure the Po crossings against an enemy from the north-west. Between them and Ariminum ran a line of communication, predecessor of the Via Aemilia. But Cisalpine Gaul seethed with anti-Roman feeling which Hannibal's diplomacy had already turned to good use (see p. 34). He would appear there as a liberator, and the Celts were ready to rise against Rome when the hour was ripe. In Cisalpine Gaul he would find provisions, horses, and mercenary soldiers. Under Hannibal's command the Celts were again to invade Italy, to find plunder and revenge for the defeat at Telamon. But they were playing their own game, and not

46

that of either of the great powers. Hence desertions and betrayals, and loud laments of Celtic fickleness in Polybius and Livy. Hannibal would treat his Celtic troops as expendable. For the Romans, who had failed to bring Hannibal to battle in the valley of the Rhône, there were still good hopes of bringing him down on the line of the Po.

The Punic crossing of the Alps has overshadowed two notable instances of rapid movement by the Romans. One was that of Publius Scipio, who returned from the Rhône with a small staff to take command of the troops in the Po valley. His original plan, according to Polybius, was to engage Hannibal at the foot of the Alps; could he have done this, the prospects of victory over the tired and depleted Punic forces must have been good. But the Roman troops in the Po valley were entangled with a revolt among the Boii, and the best Scipio could do was to extricate them and march them west to Placentia. It was a good choice of place, for there he could dispute the river crossing with Hannibal, and by his presence discourage the Celts from joining the Carthaginians in large numbers. The second feat was accomplished by the army which Ti. Sempronius Longus had concentrated at Lilybaeum for the invasion of Africa. When the Senate heard of Hannibal's invasion of the Po valley, it decided that the African project must be abandoned, and these troops, the only substantial reinforcement available, be sent to support Scipio in the North. Polybius says that the soldiers took an oath 'to assemble before lights-out on a certain day at Ariminum'. He implies that they travelled in small groups, and reached the rendezvous after forty days' continuous march. Livy sends them by sea, but a voyage through the Adriatic in late October or November does not sound plausible. Perhaps the transports took them to Messina or Rhegium—or even to Puteoli—and their long march began from an Italian port of disembarkation. Certainly Tiberius Sempronius and his legions are described by Polybius as passing through Rome, to what all assumed would be another victory for the irresistible Roman infantry. Though the troops mustered at Ariminum on the appointed day, they were too late for the first series of encounters between Scipio and Hannibal.

The key to the battles which followed in the last few weeks of 218 lies in the strategic possibilities offered by the Po and the tributaries which join it on either bank, usually at right angles. The most important of these are the Ticinus (Ticino) on the north bank, and the Trebia on the south. Scipio, with his main base at Placentia on the south bank of the Po, and another at Cremona to the north, was better placed than Hannibal, who had to get to the south bank of the Po, and might have to face a disputed river crossing unless he could lure the Romans on to open ground.

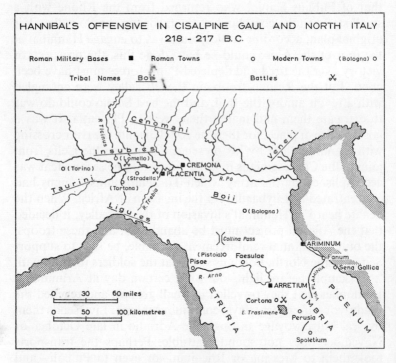

HANNIBAL'S OFFENSIVE IN CISALPINE GAUL AND NORTH ITALY
218 - 217 B.C.

Roman Military Bases ■   Roman Towns   o   Modern Towns   (Bologna) O

Tribal Names Boii   Battles ✗

Scipio's first plan seems to have been to engage Hannibal west of the Ticinus, but the battle that bears the name of that river was not a full-scale engagement but rather a cavalry action, fought near the modern Lomello. After hard fighting Hannibal's Numidian cavalry gained the upper hand and drove the Romans off the field. Scipio was severely wounded, but managed to get his unprotected legions back over the Ticinus, though the rear guard left to protect the pontoon bridge fell into the enemy's hands. Scipio led the legions safely back to Placentia, and

Hannibal declined to follow him at the risk of two river crossings. Instead, he withdrew two days' march to the west and made an unopposed crossing of the Po, near Tortona. The next phase is hard to interpret, but it is possible that Scipio now advanced on the south bank from Placentia westward to hilly ground near Stradella, hoping to wait there until his colleague came up with the army from Ariminum. In this he was frustrated because of the desertion to Hannibal of 2,000 Celtic cavalrymen serving with the Romans. At the same time all the Celtic peoples west of Placentia also went over to what looked like the winning side, and the Roman store base at Clastidium surrendered through treachery. Scipio re-crossed the Trebia to protect Placentia and wait for Sempronius.

The arrival of Sempronius with some 20,000 men changed the picture, and, in the event, for the worse. There were always difficulties when two consular armies fought side by side. Since consuls were equal, each commanded on alternate days—the principle of collegality taken to its logical but absurd conclusion. But now, with Scipio seriously ill, command fell to Sempronius, though there were many conferences between the two men which failed to resolve their basic disagreement. Scipio was for avoiding a general action with the season so far advanced. Sempronius was full of fight, and his confidence was enhanced by a cavalry action in which he got the upper hand—perhaps Hannibal was content to let it appear so. On 1 January Sempronius' command would run out, and he was anxious to win his victory first. The result was the disastrous battle of the Trebia, fought on ground carefully chosen by Hannibal.

The Trebia battle, fought near the modern Casaliggio, was the first major engagement of the Italian campaign, with some 40,000 men on either side. In it Hannibal showed to the full his qualities as a general. He assessed the opposing commander and divined his intentions: Sempronius could be relied upon to come and get him. He extracted every possible advantage from the topography of the ground. The River Trebia was made to work twice in his favour, once when the breakfastless Roman troops waded through its icy flood-waters on a bitter winter's morning, and again at the end of the day when their broken ranks were driven up to it and slaughtered. He exploited brilliantly a watercourse, which ran through the middle of the battlefield, to conceal a task force of 1,000 cavalry and 1,000 infantry, picked men under the command of Mago. (Polybius gives his readers one of his occasional lectures on the tactical possibilities of such places.) Finally, Hannibal's handling of his troops in action was masterly. While his heavy infantry, Spaniards, Celts, and Africans, engaged the legions in the centre, the cavalry, strengthened by elephants on either flank, drove in the Roman wings. The desperate struggle in the centre was resolved when the task-force in the ambush fell on the Roman rear. Even so, 10,000 Roman legionaries broke through the Celts and made their way in safety to Placentia. All the rest of Sempronius' troops were killed or taken prisoner.

This overwhelming victory brought to an end the fighting of 218. Hannibal went into winter quarters at Bologna, in the territory of the Boii, Rome's most powerful enemy among the Gauls. Here he would have a choice of passes across the Apennines for the invasion of Italy proper in the spring of 217. Meanwhile he was master of Cisalpine Gaul, except for the Roman forces pinned down within the walls of Placentia and Cremona. These isolated outposts now had to be provisioned by river from the main base of Ariminum. But Roman confidence remained irrationally high, for they had yet to take the measure of their terrible enemy. Sempronius, making full use of the break-out of the 10,000 Roman infantry, claimed that only storm and floods had robbed him of victory. The claim was too much to swallow whole, and Roman military opinion attributed the defeat to Sempronius' recklessness. Less justifiably, confidence in the superiority of the legions, given a fair chance, remained unimpaired. As so often in war, such illusions could only be shed the hard way.

The Roman dispositions for 217 attest confidence and the offensive spirit. No fewer than eleven legions were raised. The garrisons were reinforced in Sicily and Sardinia. Publius Scipio, the best general of the day, was sent on to Spain. The new consuls, Cn. Servilius Geminus and C. Flaminius, each with the usual two legions, were given the task of confronting Hannibal when he broke out of the Po valley. The election of C. Flaminius to a second consulship was a political triumph for the People over the Senate. Moreover, he could fairly be regarded as a

North Italian expert. In 223 he had defeated the Insubres beyond the Po: he had been responsible for the distribution of lands taken from the Senones on the Adriatic coast round Sena Gallica: in 220 B.C. he constructed the great strategic road which still bears his name—Via Flaminia—between Rome and Ariminum (a distance of 209 miles). His election must have seemed a sound choice at the time, though in the event he suffered disaster at the hands of Hannibal, and his memory has been blackened in the Roman historical tradition. The broad outline of Roman strategy seems clear. Servilius at Ariminum was to block the approaches to the Adriatic coast and hold the north end of Via Flaminia. Flaminius at Arretium (Arrezzo) could watch for a break-out from the upper Arno valley into southern Etruria. Two legions were kept in reserve at Rome under the praetor M. Pomponius Matho. Which of the consular armies would be the first to move would depend on Hannibal's choice of a route across the Appenines.

As the invader Hannibal had the initiative, and he put it to good use by careful reconnaissance of the ground ahead. He was anxious to get on the move, for his Celtic allies were restless. But first he must make sure that the passes were clear of snow (and it is pertinent to note that in some years skiing in the higher Apennine resorts such as Abetone can go on into May). His choice of a route can be identified with fair probability from Polybius, who describes it as 'admittedly difficult, but a short cut, and one likely to take Flaminius by surprise'. He also calls it 'the route through the marshes into Etruria'. The short cut suggests the road from Bologna over the Collina Pass (3,040 feet) to Pistoia, a matter of sixty miles: the marshes will have lain in the valley of the Arno and its tributaries between Pistoia and Florence. The crossing of the mountains seems to have been made without undue difficulty, but the marshes were far worse than anticipated. The Arno was in flood with the melting snow and spring rains—and we have learned recently what an Arno flood can do. If Polybius and Livy are right, it took the Punic army four days and three nights to cover the 21 miles from Pistoia to Faesulae (Fiesole). Most of the baggage animals were lost in the marshes, and the horses, which had wintered out in the Po valley, developed scurvy. Hannibal had a severe bout of ophthalmia which cost him the sight of one eye.

51

But eventually they won to solid ground and had a few days for rest and reconnaissance.

According to Polybius, Hannibal learned two things; that the country ahead of him was rich in booty, and that Flaminius was a self-confident fool who could easily be trapped. His next moves aimed at exploiting both factors to the best advantage. From Faesulae he slipped past Flaminius' position at Arretium as far as Cortona, ravaging the fertile Campi Etrusci and plundering stock as he went. From Cortona he turned east along the north shores of Lake Trasimene. Flaminius, in a high state of excitement—'What will they say at Rome if he ravages the land and we sit here in Etruria?'—turned a deaf ear to the advice of his staff and followed Hannibal into the trap prepared for him. So says Polybius, who will not allow that Flaminius' tactics had any basis in sense. But it is easy to suppose that Flaminius did not attack Hannibal as he passed Arretium because he wanted to bring other Roman forces into any battle, and because as yet he did not know Hannibal's objective. Until Hannibal reached Cortona it was possible to suppose that he was advancing on Rome. As for the ravaged lands of the allies, Flaminius' reaction was not mere petulance. This was one of Hannibal's most formidable weapons. Rome—and the allies—could stand only so much of it, even in worse conditions than obtained in the early summer of 217. Once Hannibal turned east to Cortona towards Perugia, Flaminius seems to have felt his way clear to follow. He may even have seen himself as leading Hannibal towards the army of Servilius. This would make sense on one condition—that he knew at all times exactly where Hannibal was. Only a complete neglect of reconnaissance will explain why Flaminius, on a June morning of low mist, led his army in column of march through the narrow Passo di Borghetto and into the deadly trap sprung by Hannibal on the north shores of Lake Trasimene.

Polybius describes the battle of Lake Trasimene in some detail (though not with clarity) based evidently on one of those personal inspections of the ground in which he took such pride. Precisely for this reason, few battles have given rise to so much controversy among modern scholars. The key to Polybius' description is a flat-bottomed valley (αὐλὼν ἐπίπεδος); this is flanked by high hills on either side; 'opposite' on the broad axis is a steep ridge; 'behind' is the lake. The hills come close to the shore at the entrance to and the exit from this valley, leaving what Polybius calls 'narrows' (στένοι). Scholars have produced at least four candidates for the flat-bottomed valley, and there is a recent variant which emphasizes the change in the shores of the lake due to medieval drainage. The well-marked valley between the east end of Passo di Borghetto and Montigeto with a 'narrows' extending eastwards along the lake shore to Passignano seems the best suited to the battle, though it is not easy to place on the map the general features described above. At least Polybius' account of the phases of the action is clear. During the night Hannibal had placed his troops in ambush all along the hills surrounding the valley. As soon as the Roman army was committed to the western narrows, their rear was cut off, and when they emerged into the valley they were attacked from all sides. From the start their position was hopeless. Because of the mist they could not see what the enemy was doing nor where he was coming from. Caught in column of march, they were unable to form any battle line. Flaminius fell at an early stage, killed, it is said, by Insubrian Gauls who thereby won revenge for their people's defeat. From then on in Livy's words, 'each man was his own commander', and Polybius pays tribute to the courage with which the Romans refused to flee or to quit their ranks. Even so, some 15,000 men were killed in the valley. Those who were caught in the narrows suffered most. Driven into the lake, they were either drowned by their armour or cut down by the Punic cavalry if they tried to wade to safety. It was a Dunkirk, without the ships. It is true that some 6,000 Roman troops broke through the defile and pushed on to high ground, but these were later surrounded by Punic troops under Maharbal, and laid down their arms under promise of safety. At the end of the day Flaminius' army was destroyed, with losses of perhaps 15,000 killed and 2,000 taken prisoner. Hannibal's losses were said to have been no more than 1,500, 'most of them Celts', 'but few of name', in fact, and only thirty of any note. Again Hannibal, as the self-proclaimed 'liberator' of Italy, sent the allied prisoners back to their homes. The Romans, after listening to a bitter invective, were kept under close guard.

When news of this disaster reached Rome, its enormity defied propaganda. Making the announcement from the Rostra, the

praetor simply said, 'We have been defeated in a great battle.'
It is odd that this is sometimes quoted as an example of Roman
fortitude, for it was nothing of the kind. It produced consterna-
tion, Polybius says, among a people grown unused to defeat:
they were quite unable to bear it with moderation and dignity.
Only the Senate kept its head and took thought for the future.
A few days later came news to shake even their sang-froid.
Servilius, unable to bring up his whole army to join Flaminius,
had sent 4,000 cavalry ahead. Somewhere near Assisi, a Punic
force under the command of Maharbal intercepted them, and
killed or captured them all. Roman strategy had broken down
completely, and new methods would have to be found if Rome
was to survive. For such emergencies the appointment of a
dictator was the traditional measure, though it had lapsed (in
the proper form) for thirty years. A dictator was normally
appointed by the Senate on the motion of one of the consuls,
and he then chose a deputy called the *Magister Equitum* or
Master of the Horse. In him were vested all the powers of the
magistracy, and he held office for six months, during which he
was expected to have resolved the crisis—military or political—
that had brought him to power. But now circumstances made it
impossible to follow this pattern. One consul lay dead on the
field of Trasimene, the other was 200 miles away at Ariminum
with the Punic army in between. So the Senate left it to the
People meeting in the Comitia Centuriata to nominate a
dictator. Their nominee must have seemed irreproachable—the
elderly and influential Senator Q. Fabius Maximus Verrucosus,
with his long record of distinguished service to the state. Fabius
Maximus had already held two consulships, and had won a
triumph for his victory over the Ligurians. An ancestor,
Q. Fabius Rullianus, had a brilliant military record against the
Samnites and Etruscans in the previous century. Fabius Maximus himself had in full measure the virtues and the limitations
of the Roman aristocracy of the day. But an addendum to their
choice was less gratifying. Wholly without precedent, the People
themselves chose the Magister Equitum—M. Minucius Rufus, a
man of humble origin who had reached the consulship in 221
B.C. as a popular candidate. Thus the rivalry between Senate and
People was perpetuated even in the Dictatorship, which was
clearly to be one of an unusual kind. Fabius Maximus at once

put in hand these measures, human and divine, which the situation demanded. Events had shown all too clearly how badly Rome stood in relationship to the gods: the first thing was to carry out the ceremonies which would re-establish a *pax deorum*. Polybius, uninterested in such matters except in so far as they were a Roman peculiarity, uses three words to say that he sacrificed to the gods. Livy gives a long description of ceremonies involved and deities invoked. They included an inspection of the Sibylline Books, a banquet for the Twelve Gods of Olympus, and the building of a temple for Venus of Eryx, and also for Mens, or Intelligence. The first of these divinities from her shrine at Erice might avert a Carthaginian invasion of Western Sicily, the second endow Roman commanders with qualities in which they seemed lacking. On a more practical level, measures were taken to put Rome itself in a state of defence by strengthening the fortifications, bringing in more troops, destroying strategic bridges, and so on.

In fact, Hannibal was in no condition to march on Rome. He had won most of his victories so far by his mastery of cavalry tactics, but now his horses were unfit for battle. The crossing of the Arno floods and marshes had been bad for their hooves, and lack of forage and proper grooming had caused them to develop what Polybius called 'hunger-mange'. Polybius, himself an old cavalryman, had an eye for these things. Hannibal was like a modern tank commander, who has won a victory but outrun his petrol supplies and sustained many casualties. He must pull out of the battle to refit and repair. So Hannibal marched leisurely eastward for ten days through Umbria to Picenum. He ravaged the land as he went, but failed to capture the walled city of Spoletium. Reaching the Adriatic coast early in July, he paused to rest the men, cure the wounded, and bring the horses back into condition. Picenum abounded in old wine, which he used to bathe the horses—alcohol will have been a good antiseptic for their sores. By the end of the month he was able to move away south for a late summer–early autumn offensive. Polybius' continuous narrative does not extend beyond 216, and we are left to speculate on the problem of how Hannibal maintained his cavalry in good condition through the years he spent in Italy without reinforcements. Especially does this apply to the Numidians, the best cavalry of their day. Their cutting edge depended on the close understanding between rider and horse—the latter the magnificent 'Arab' or Berber horses. Did he bring enough stallions and brood mares to keep the strain pure? Or did he have to cross them with Italian breeds, with a dilution of their qualities? And a cavalry trooper also grows old; he does not charge with the same élan at thirty as at twenty. There could have been some loss of efficiency in the Punic cavalry as the war dragged on. But if so, in 217 and the following year it did not appear.

During this pause in Picenum Hannibal sent back an official report by sea to Carthage. He could claim a spectacular and unbroken run of military success. But this was not matched on the diplomatic side. The cry of 'Freedom for the Italians!' had fallen on deaf ears: so far, not a single community in Etruria or Umbria had forsaken Rome and gone over to Hannibal. Further south prospects were better. There was plenty of anti-Roman feeling among the Samnites, as also among the Greek cities of southern Italy. And the scorched-earth policy might also give good results. If Rome could not protect the rich lands and cities of Campania from the ravages of Hannibal, what would happen to her prestige in Italy? So Hannibal moved south into Apulia, laying waste the lands of Luceria and Arpi on the way.

By now Fabius Maximus had worked out his tactics and could put them to the test. He would follow Hannibal's army, always taking advantage of the ground, refusing to fight in conditions that favoured the enemy, but losing no chance to cut off his forage parties and deny him supplies. These are the Fabian tactics with which his name has been associated ever since. Abrasive of the enemy if consistently applied, they might be even more so of the morale of his own army. Fabius took with him four legions to dog the movements of Hannibal, two of which Gnaeus Servilius had brought up from Ariminum, and two freshly raised. Moving along the Via Latina, perhaps as far as Teanum or Cales (Calvi) Fabius crossed the Apennines through Samnium into Apulia. Hannibal was at Arpi near Foggia in the plain of the Tavoliere, then the richest grainlands of Italy. Fabius took up a position on the easternmost edge of the hills at Aecae, the modern Troia, some twenty miles away.

At once Hannibal moved up to provoke a battle, but Fabius would have none of it. This was country Fabius knew well, for he had estates in the district. Hannibal made several attempts to lure him out, but Fabius stuck resolutely to his policy, marching parallel to the Punic army along the hills, and cutting off their foraging parties whenever he could. Already the Magister Equitum was angered by this apparent timidity, and began to spread disaffection among the troops. Worse was to follow. Hannibal moved west into Samnium, ravaging the lands of the Roman colony of Beneventum. Fabius followed, a day or two's march behind, still refusing a general battle. The boldest part of Hannibal's plan unfolded next. Reaching Cales by a roundabout route, he advanced into the plain of Campania itself and ravaged the famous Ager Falernus, the 'Campania Felix' of the Romans, and the Terra di Lavoro of modern times. This land of vines and olives had been ceded by Capua to Rome in 340 B.C. First Maharbal and the Numidian cavalry scoured it as far as the Baths of Sinuessa, almost on the coast. Then Hannibal and the main army followed, and villages and farms went up in smoke throughout the lower valley of the Volturnus. The whole operation involved a fifty-mile drive into enemy-held territory, and the devastation of the richest lands held by Roman citizens in Italy. The lands of Capua itself were carefully avoided: Hannibal already had a fifth column in that city, and there were hopes that it would fall by treachery. But the effect on the malcontents in Fabius' army was infuriating. They urged Fabius to hasten to the rescue of Campania, and for a time he did move with more than his usual deliberate speed. But once again he stopped at the edge of the hills—the Mons Massicus of Livy (Monte Massico)—and refused to come down into the plain. The anger and shame of his men comes through in the pages of Polybius, as in the speech which Livy puts into the mouth of Minucius. The plain of Campania is a great theatre: Hannibal is providing the action on the stage: the Roman soldiers are compelled to be idle spectators. More specific, for the mountain lands to which they were confined, 'We lead our army like a flock of sheep through trackless pastures and by remote drovers' tracks.' A flock of sheep, and an indolent shepherd. But Fabius, as ever, was following a rational plan. His tactics did not exclude a battle, if it could be fought on terms favourable to himself. And the opportunity would surely come when Hannibal had to lead his army, burdened with plundered cattle and loot, back through the mountain passes into Samnium.

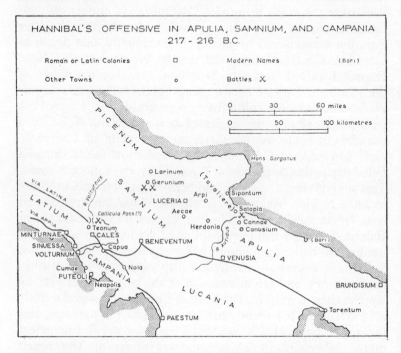

How Fabius set his trap, and the stratagem by which Hannibal avoided it, is vividly described by both Polybius and Livy. They locate it at 'Mons Eribianos' or 'the Callicula Pass', place-names not found elsewhere. This has given rise to much controversy, but by far the most convincing theory is the one that places the action north-east of Teanum. The 'Callicula Pass' is then the Borgo San Antonio, and 'Mons Eribianos' the range of hills represented by Monte Caievola (1,690 feet) and its flanking heights (see map). On this interpretation, Fabius had to watch two possible exits for Hannibal into the Volturnus valley—by the Via Latina to the north, and to the north-east through the narrow Borgo San Antonio, which Polybius calls a narrow pass. With his main army encamped on Monte San Angelo, he was ready to move either way, and a force of 4,000

58

men was sent to block the narrow pass. When Hannibal encamped 'under the hill' (San Felice?) he appeared to have walked
into the trap; Fabius now saw the problem as to how best to use
his advantage of ground for the battle next day. But there was
no battle next day. Hannibal slipped through the pass unopposed during the night by perhaps the most brilliant of all his
improvizations. Its happiest feature was the way in which he
turned to advantage the handicap of his large number of stolen
cattle. The commissariat was ordered to collect as many faggots
of dry wood as possible, and to select 2,000 plough-oxen from
the booty. The object would be, once the signal was given, to
drive these beasts at the best possible pace to the top of a slope
flanking the pass. The soldiers of the main army were given an
early supper and sent to bed. At 3 a.m. the order was given to
bind the faggots to the horns of the oxen and set them alight.
The terrified beasts plunged up the slope, goaded on by army
servants and spearmen sent with them. Seeing the lights of this
strange array moving up the hill, the Roman task-force in the
pass thought Hannibal was on the move; they left their positions to investigate. At the top of a ridge they found themselves
in the middle of a cattle stampede. Not unnaturally, they withdrew and waited for the dawn. Fabius was of course far too
sound a general to get involved in a night action—as Hannibal
had calculated he would be. Meanwhile Hannibal had slipped
through the pass with his entire army and all the rest of the
booty. Indeed, he did more. At dawn he sent some Spanish
troops to reinforce his spearmen on the ridge; as a result, about
1,000 of the Roman task-force were killed. Hannibal had taken
every trick in this exchange. (One would be ready to believe—
though no authority says so—that he recovered most of the
2,000 plough-oxen, and took them to Apulia, to provide beef
for the winter!) Fabius was left to wrap himself in his virtue, and
to reflect that he had been right all along. But he may have been
a little shamefaced as he followed Hannibal back to Larinum in
Apulia.

The closing stages of the campaigns of 217, fought in Apulia,
are very hard to interpret. They involved much skirmishing and
two major battles, neither of which can be placed on the map
with any certainty. On the Roman side these months were
bedevilled by the rivalry between Fabius and Minucius, who

held diametrically opposed views on the strategy required. This rivalry has contaminated the historical sources, for though Polybius and Livy differ from each other in detail and in scale of treatment, they both write with a pro-Fabian bias.

When Hannibal got back to Apulia it was September, and time to think of winter-quarters. A second problem was that of provisions for the troops and fodder for the animals: the latter need most acute because of the big haul of cattle made in the Campanian raid. From the plain of the Tavoliere, then the richest corn lands in Italy, these needs could be met. For winter-quarters Hannibal chose the town of Gerunium, which Polybius describes as 200 stades (35 miles) from Luceria, and which is thought to have been in the hills close to Casalnuovo di Daunia. Hannibal tried to treat with its inhabitants for the surrender of the town: when they refused, he killed them all. The buildings were spared, as ready-made granaries and store depôts. The Roman army took up a position a few miles to the north-east at Larinum.

From Larinum (it would seem) Fabius was recalled to Rome, ostensibly to take part in religious ceremonies, but really to stand inquiry into the failure of Fabian tactics, and, especially, the fiasco at the 'Callicula Pass'. Before he left, the Dictator read his Magister Equitum a lecture on the need to think of avoiding damage to his own army rather than inflicting it on the enemy. But Minucius' mind was made up: 'Even as he listened,' says Polybius, 'he was planning to stake everything on a great battle.'

Hannibal, for a time, concentrated on forage: the crops of the Tavoliere were still in the fields, and a huge store of provisions was quickly gathered in. It is in this stage, Livy tells us, that he employed the ruse of ostentatiously sparing an estate belonging to Fabius, while destroying everything round it. But the need to forage meant that the Carthaginian forces had to be divided: Minucius won several small successes and, ultimately, the chance of his big battle. Of this action, fought close to Gerunium, only two things can be said with confidence. One is that if Minucius really did as well as represented, he had good ground for believing that his tactics were correct; the second, that if Hannibal did as badly, he must have been singularly off form on that day. It may of course be that Hannibal was

THE WAR IN ITALY

deliberately trying to induce in the Roman commander an over-confidence which could be turned against him in a return engagement; he was quite capable of it. Whatever happened on the field, the battle was reported in Rome as a great victory.

The news reached Rome at a bad time for Fabius. Since his return, he had found a cool Senate and a hostile People. Now his policy met with general derision, and at a meeting of the People a bill was passed to make Minucius his colleague with equal powers (*aequatum imperium*). It was unprecedented, it nullified the whole concept of a dictatorship, and it was almost impossible to work. None the less, Fabius went back to Apulia to offer his co-Dictator the choice of command on alternate days or of dividing the army between them. Minucius chose the second, and the two armies were separated. So now there were two Roman armies, in two camps, under two commanders, one committed to attack and the other to defence. The situation was made for Hannibal, and he did not fail to exploit it. Luring Minucius to fight on broken, hilly ground, well suited for ambushes, he was on the point of crushing him when Fabius intervened and saved the day. Little more can be said of this second battle.

Livy's account reads like a morality play. Minucius' rashness leads to the brink of disaster, Fabius' steadiness almost produces a brilliant victory. Minucius begs forgiveness after the battle ('You were right, Fabius'), and asks to be reinstated as Magister Equitum. Even Hannibal was impressed. And in Rome all praised Fabius to the skies. It may be so. Certainly the two armies were re-united in a single camp. But Fabius laid down his dictatorship after the expiry of its term, and the election for the consuls for 216—long postponed and bitterly contested—reflected once again the rivalry of Senate and People and the clash of conflicting views of strategy. The new consuls were the aristocratic senator, L. Aemilius Paulus, and the People's nominee, G. Terentius Varro. So ended the long year which had brought Hannibal's army from the Po valley to Apulia.

By contrast with the previous year, events in the Italian theatre of war in 216 B.C. were concentrated on a single great battle and its consequences—the latter mostly political. Hannibal did not move from Gerunium through the late winter and early spring. He was watched by four legions commanded by Servilius and Atilius Regulus (consul 217 B.C.) who had been given pro-consular powers. There was skirmishing, which Livy makes much of but Polybius does not find worth recording. The new consuls meanwhile were busy in Rome. New levies had to be raised, and supplies sent to Spain and Sicily. New praetors were appointed to military commands—L. Postumius Albinus for Cisalpine Gaul, and M. Claudius Marcellus for Sicily. An embassy was received from Rome's loyal ally, the aged King Hiero of Syracuse. It conveyed gifts, both decorative and useful (see p. 122). The golden statue of the Victory of Syracuse was gratefully accepted by the Senate, and the goddess was established on the Capitol, in the Temple of Jupiter Optimus Maximus. There was also a force of 1,000 archers and slingers, to cope with Balearic and Moorish slingers in Hannibal's army. Even more to the point were provisions, 300,000 modii (pecks) of wheat, 200,000 of barley. One sees the advantages that Rome enjoyed, even at that point. Hannibal's army had to forage or fight for their provisions.

It was the problem of supplies that induced Hannibal to move in early June. The crops were ripening in the Tavoliere, but he had other sources in mind. Some sixty miles to the south, on the right bank of the River Aufidus (Ofanto) was a small town called Cannae. The town itself had been destroyed, but the Romans had turned the citadel into a corn-depôt and supply-base. There they stored the yield of the lands around Canusium, and sent them—perhaps by sea—to the port of Sipontum to provision the army of Servilius. Hannibal's capture of Cannae was a double gain. But it was more than that. Cannae was in a strategic position, from which routes led west up the Aufidus valley and on into Campania, or south towards Tarentum and Brundisium. Any of these might be the objective of Hannibal's next campaign, and the Roman army at Gerunium was the only force available to intervene. So Servilius sent frequent messages to Rome to ask for instructions, warning at the same time that if he tried to follow Hannibal an open battle would be the result. We are not told of the arguments that swayed the Senate to opt for a decisive battle. Popular demand would no doubt be voiced by Terentius Varro, with Fabius Maximus and his supporters in opposition. But, the decision taken, it was to be expected that the consuls, and not Servilius, should be entrusted with command in the field. They set out with new levies to a rendezvous with the army of Servilius, perhaps at Arpi. Then the entire force—amounting to two reinforced consular armies—advanced unopposed towards the Aufidus. To borrow Livy's fine phrase (used of a later stage of the operations) they were proceeding 'to make famous, under the malign influence of Fate, the name of Cannae for a disaster to Rome'. So, after the event, might one write the name of Gettysburg. But it is human actions that determine battles. Lee might have won at Gettysburg, and the Romans might have won at Cannae.

The numbers of the Roman army at Cannae are open to doubt. Polybius is explicit—eight legions, a figure which he admits to be without precedent. His casualty figures are worked out on that basis and Livy hesitates to pronounce on the number of new levies raised (i.e. beyond the four legions of Servilius), but records some variants. One of these, four new legions, would support Polybius if accepted: another is for 10,000 new recruits in all: a third, for an additional 1,000 foot and 100 cavalry for each legion. The arguments against eight legions, making a total Roman force of over 80,000 men, seem very strong. No Roman commander had ever handled such large forces, and the problem of supplying them would have been immense. Many scholars now incline to the view that four reinforced legions took the field, together with an equal number of allies. Hannibal's forces amounted to 40,000 infantry and 10,000 cavalry: since the Romans had more infantry, their army must have been at least 45,000 strong, perhaps as much as 60,000. Before the battle proper there were a few days of manoeuvre. The Romans were still handicapped by the pernicious system of alternate days of command. Aemilius was cautious because he thought the terrain near the mouth of the river was too favourable for Hannibal's cavalry—as indeed it was. Varro and his friends were for battle, confident of the result.

As for the site of the battle—after long controversy the argument seems to be swinging decisively towards placing it on the south or right bank of the Aufidus and to the east and southeast of the hill of Cannae. The discovery in 1938 of a very large necropolis at Fontanella seemed to clinch the argument: here, it was proclaimed, are the dead of Cannae. Unhappily, it now seems that these bones belong to the medieval period, or to that of the Lombards. But a south bank site between Cannae and the sea best suits the description of the battle and its preliminaries in Polybius, still the main source despite some obscurities. These are concerned in the main with the manoeuvres before the battle, which Polybius explains with the formula 'Aemilius cautious: Varro rash.' This may not be good enough. Events begin with the arrival of the army under Aemilius 'about five miles from Hannibal's camp'. We are not told where that camp was, but a later measurement places it on or near the hill of Cannae, and probably to the south-west of the citadel. Aemilius, disliking the flat and treeless plain in which he found himself, encamped near Salapia. The next day Varro, in spite of his remonstrances, pushed forward closer to the enemy (i.e. towards the river), and was attacked while in column of march by a Punic force of cavalry and light-armed troops. The encounter was a drawn battle, broken off at nightfall. Aemilius next day encamped close to the Aufidus with two-thirds of the army, sending the rest across it by a ford to a smaller fortified camp on the south bank. The motive for this is given by Polybius as the desire to cover his own forage and watering-parties, and harass those of the Carthaginians. In fact, he may not have abandoned all hope of reaching higher ground on the north side of the river some four miles away at San Ferdinando. If so, his purpose was divined by Hannibal, who led his army across the river and encamped squarely across the Roman path. Next day Hannibal kept his troops occupied with preparations for battle: no action is recorded on the Roman side, although it was a Varro-day. Perhaps it was spent in the quarrel between the generals recorded in Livy (XXII, 45). The following day Hannibal moved along the river to offer battle. But Aemilius was in command, and he remained quiet, although he covered both camps. Later the same day Hannibal sent the Numidians up to the smaller Roman camp; they prevented the Romans from watering and rode right up to the palisades. By now Varro and the troops were not to be restrained any longer. At dawn on his day of command Varro led out his forces from both camps, and began to draw up a line of battle on the south bank. Hannibal, crossing the river at two points, did the same. It was the day of the battle of Cannae, fought according to Roman tradition on 2 August.

The Roman dispositions were simple and their tactics straightforward. Their right wing rested on the river, and consisted of the Roman cavalry, under the command of Aemilius: the left wing, commanded by Varro, consisted of the allied contingents, cavalry on the far left, infantry towards the centre. The centre proper was made up of the Roman legions—*robur legionum*, 'the might of the legions', as later writers were to call it. Their job was to attack and smash the enemy infantry. All that had been learned from Trebia and Trasimene was the need to pack a heavier weight onto a narrow front. The maniples were therefore drawn up in depth rather than in length—perhaps they were as much as 30 men deep. This all-important arm was commanded by Servilius and Marcus Minucius.

Hannibal's plan of battle was more subtle. Thoroughly familiar by now with Roman tactics, he aimed first to contain the thrust of the legions, and then to turn it against his enemies. To the Roman right wing, under the command of Hasdrubal, he opposed the Spanish and Gallic heavy cavalry. The Numidians, his striking force *par excellence* were on the right, where they had most room for manoeuvre. They were commanded, according to Livy, by that great leader of cavalry, Maharbal. The infantry in the centre, very carefully positioned, were led by Hannibal himself and by Mago. In the centre were the Celtic and Spanish infantry, who were flanked on either side by the heavily armed Africans. At first the Punic forces were formed in a straight line, but then Hannibal led out the Celts and Spaniards into what Polybius calls a 'moon-shaped' or crescent formation; horrified commentators insist that what he meant was *en échelon*. Be that as it may, it is clear that this convex formation was designed as a buffer to take the first shock of the Roman infantry attack. Polybius and Livy both give a vivid description of the Punic force before it went into action. Particularly striking were the Celts and the Spaniards. The Celts fought naked from the waist up, as Celtic troops have chosen to do down to our own times. They were armed with slashing swords, ancestors of the Highland claymore. The Spaniards, also of striking physique, wore a uniform of white tunics bordered with scarlet. Their swords—prototype of the Roman *gladius*—were for cutting and thrusting. The Africans had been equipped with the pick of the Roman arms captured at Trebia and Trasimene —'you would have thought them,' says Livy, 'a Roman battle line'. Presumably they had been trained in their use during the months of inaction earlier in the year.

The battle developed in three phases, if we disregard a preliminary and indecisive exchange of light infantry and skirmishers. The first of these was the clash of the Punic heavy cavalry with the Roman cavalry by the river. At this time the Roman cavalry were not a very inspiring body of men. The best that could be said of them, only too often, was that they were defeated but they fought well. So here. There was not much room for cavalry manoeuvre, and they soon were forced to fight hand to hand. The Romans fought bravely, but were almost wiped out. Aemilius Paulus escaped from this action and rejoined the battle in the centre.

The assault of the legions formed the second and main phase of action. They drove in the Celtic-Spanish crescent, as they were expected to do. The whole issue of the battle turned on whether they could be contained. If they broke through in the centre, the Roman superiority in infantry would assert itself, and the Carthaginians would be defeated. Fighting with unusual steadiness, the Celts and Spaniards gave ground but did not break. The Roman legions drove deeply into them: when they had gone far enough the African heavy infantry, who had taken no part in the battle so far, turned inwards and attacked the legions on either side. Meanwhile, the Numidians had kept the Roman left wing in action; before long, Hasdrubal's heavy cavalry swept across the Roman rear to support them. The allied cavalry broke and fled, the Numidians were sent in pursuit, an action in which they excelled. The heavy cavalry of Hasdrubal then fell on the Roman rear, to launch the battle into its third and terminal phase. Now the legions—fatally compromised by their tendency to bunch towards the centre— were hopelessly encircled in a killing ground. All the Carthaginians had to do was to kill. In this phase Aemilius Paulus died, after sustaining desperate wounds: there fell with him Servilius, Minucius, eighty senators, twenty-nine military tribunes, and some 25 to 30,000 legionaries. Polybius' tribute to the Roman dead is that they fell as brave men, and worthy

of their country. The battle must have begun between 7 and
8 a.m. We are not told how long it lasted, but it clearly went
on through the hottest hours, and that on the dry plains of
Apulia on an August day. Livy makes much of the sirocco, a
hot dry wind blowing into the faces of the Romans and
harassing them with clouds of dust, and this became a part of
the established Roman tradition. Meteorologically, there is
nothing against it, but it finds no place in Polybius.

There were Roman survivors of the disaster, some of whom
were to play a crucial part later in the war. Terentius Varro
with a small guard of cavalry rode to Venusia 30 miles away,
and Polybius has some harsh things to say about his cowardice.
Perhaps this was a pre-arranged rendezvous for the cavalry in
case of defeat. An unknown number of infantry reached Canusium, among them the young Scipio Africanus, then a military
tribune. They were fed, clothed, and given money by a wealthy
Apulian lady called Busa. Finally, there was the Roman force of
10,000 men whom Polybius describes as being left to guard the
Roman camp, and, if possible, to plunder that of Hannibal.
They were at this task when Hannibal himself caught up with
them, killed some 2,000, and took the rest prisoner. On the
Carthaginian side the losses are given as 4,000 to 5,700 Celts,
1,500 Spaniards and Africans, and only 200 cavalry. Once again
Celtic mercenaries had paid the heaviest price for Hannibal's
victory.

Surprise that Hannibal did not immediately march on Rome
was voiced, according to Livy, at the first meeting of Hannibal's
council-of-war after the battle. It came, appropriately enough,
from the cavalry-leader, Maharbal. The passage is famous.
'I tell you,' he is made to say, 'to help you to realize what this
battle means, on the fifth day from now you shall dine as victor
on the Capitol. Follow me: I will go ahead. They will know you
have come before they know you are coming!' And when
Hannibal asked for time to consider, 'I see,' said Maharbal,
'that the gods do not give all gifts to one man. You, Hannibal,
know how to win a victory: how to use it you know not!'
A cavalry leader, with the *élan* proper to his calling, and knowing that his men were at the peak of their form and might not
long maintain it, could well use such words. But in fact, no such
choice was open to Hannibal. He had no siege-engines to carry

a city as large as Rome by assault. For the alternative method, that of sitting down and starving it out, his army was not large enough. Furthermore, if he had possessed enough troops, it is unlikely that he could have fed them. In any case, the core of Hannibal's strategy seems to have been to render Rome impotent by smashing her grip on the Roman Confederacy. And the victory at Cannae would yield solid dividends towards that end. It is not surprising that Hannibal's next aim was to gather them in.

So, instead of marching on Rome, Hannibal paraded the victors of Cannae as an army of liberation through Samnium and into Campania. Most of the Samnite communities defected from Rome, as did those of Lucania and Bruttium. In Apulia, Arpi and Salapia were in revolt. But the biggest prize by far was Capua, the largest and richest city in Italy, which made an alliance with Hannibal in the autumn of the year. Domestic politics played a large part: the aristocracy clinging to the Roman connection as long as they could, the democracy eager for a change. The same pattern held in most of the towns of Campania. Capua was promised its autonomy by Hannibal, and freedom from military obligations. More heady prospects were dangled. After Hannibal's victory in Italy, the people of Campania would be supreme in Italy. As capital, Capua should replace Rome. Hannibal met with a rebuff at Neapolis and Nola: in general, the coastal cities of Campania remained loyal to the Roman alliance.

Livy is the prime source for events in Rome on the morrow of Cannae. His picture is of a few days of panic and confusion, and the revival of barbaric and primitive rites. Finally, the calm resolve of the Senate and the wisdom of Fabius Maximus produced a recovery of nerve. What does seem clear is that popular challenge to the leadership of the Senate abated for a time. A new dictator was appointed, Q. Junius Pera, with Ti. Sempronius Gracchus as Magister Equitum. Energetic measures were taken to continue the war. Boys under age, and even slaves, were enrolled for the legions. At the same time, an offer from Hannibal to release the prisoners taken at Cannae (for a rather steep ransom) was refused. Q. Junius Pera blocked Via Latina at Teanum. Via Appia was strongly held north of the Volturnus River. No longer was the road to Rome open to Hannibal.

Claudius Marcellus was summoned from Sicily to command the troops which Varro had collected together after Cannae. And when Varro himself reappeared in Rome—Livy would have us note—he was not crucified, as a Carthaginian general would have been in his place. Instead, he was thanked 'for not having despaired of the Republic'. It has been suggested that the thanks were ironical. More likely, Varro had done a useful piece of work in gathering together and reforming the shattered fragments of the Roman army at Cannae. They had to atone for their disgrace the hard way (see p. 90)—that was to be expected —but in the long run they did so magnificently. As for Varro, his appointment to an important command in Picenum next year showed that Rome had not lost confidence in him. So the words of thanks seem to have meant exactly what they said.

The year's disasters were still incomplete. It was soon learned that there had been a lesser Cannae in the North, where L. Postumius Albinus and his two legions had been ambushed by the Boii near Modena, and cut to pieces. Livy adds that Postumius' skull, embossed with gold, was taken to the chief temple of the Boii and used for ritual purposes, and as a drinking-cup for the priests. It must have been a connoisseurs' piece among the *têtes-coupées* of the Gauls.

Roman resilience after Cannae has always won praise. What other people, asks Livy, would not have succumbed to so great a disaster? More cogently, Polybius chooses this moment for his famous excursus on the virtues of Rome's constitution, and the order and discipline of the Roman armies. A mixed constitution, such as that of Rome, with its blending of the qualities of monarchy, aristocracy, and democracy, is the best guarantee of stability in the commonwealth. The Roman Army, with its high standards of practice in discipline, organization and training, complements the political virtues of the State. A striking tribute to both, in their darkest hour. And the hour was dark indeed. Roman casualties in Italy and Cisalpine Gaul had been calamitous: even worse, the repeated underlining of Hannibal's superiority in the field. The treasury was nearly empty, yet a gigantic effort was needed to keep up the army and fleet. Complaints were received from the forces in Sicily and Sardinia about arrears of pay and shortage of provisions. The Sicilian difficulties were made good by Hiero of Syracuse—the last of the old king's many services to Rome (see page 122). Loyal allies did the same in Sardinia. At Rome taxes were doubled, the first instalment being demanded at the beginning of the year. For the campaigns of 215, forces were provided at the same level as in 216, though now there were no commitments in Cisalpina.

On strategy, there was no room for debate. It was Fabian methods or surrender, and Q. Fabius Maximus and his supporters took charge of the Italian theatres of war. In the long run there were grounds for hope. Roman resources in manpower were still greatly superior to Hannibal's—always providing he was not reinforced from outside. The heartland of the Roman Confederacy—Latium, Etruria, Umbria, Picenum— remained steadfast. In Campania and Apulia there were still loyal allies, Roman colonies, strategic roads. Hannibal had yet to win a major port. And his successes had a reverse side; there were now allies to be protected, and the number of troops he could spare for garrisons was strictly limited. In the new warfare of fortified positions his weakness in siege-equipment and methods was to tell. Supplies were a constant anxiety, and probably hampered his mobility even more than appears.

In the late autumn of 216, Mago reported the achievements of the year to the Carthaginian Senate. The chances of victory seemed rosy. Spain could be regained, together with Corsica and Sardinia. Syracusan loyalty to Rome would not long outlive King Hiero, and then Sicily could be won. As for Italy, the gold rings taken from the Roman dead at Cannae, and emptied by the bushel onto the floor of the House, attested the mastery of Hannibal and his army. But, according to Livy, the peace party asked why the conqueror should want more troops, more provisions, more money? Now was the time to make peace, for a stronger bargaining position would never be attained. Not surprisingly, these doubts did not prevail. Carthage prepared to exploit success. Three new expeditionary forces were fitted out, two for Hannibal, one for Sardinia. In the event, Roman successes in Spain (see p. 97) led to the diversion of one of the Italian forces (the larger) to the Spanish theatre. The force which Hasdrubal took to Sardinia achieved little (see p. 120). And Hannibal, who could have used troops to the best advantage, got only the small reinforcement of 4,000 cavalry and 40 elephants which Bomilcar got through to Locri.

Other observers rated the Carthaginians' prospects high, notably Philip V of Macedon. The treaty whose terms Polybius has preserved (see pp. 120f.) was made with Hannibal on his diplomatic initiative in the summer of 215: whether it was formally ratified by Carthage we do not know. Essentially, it bound Hannibal not to make peace with Rome on terms unfavourable to Macedon. Provision is made for Macedonian intervention in the war, but the help given is to be 'of such a kind as we [the Carthaginians] have need, or as we may agree upon'. It reads like a compact made by two canny bargainers, each waiting on the event. The alliance of Hannibal and Philip might mean much or little. The Roman Senate, in 215 B.C., could be excused for fearing it meant much.

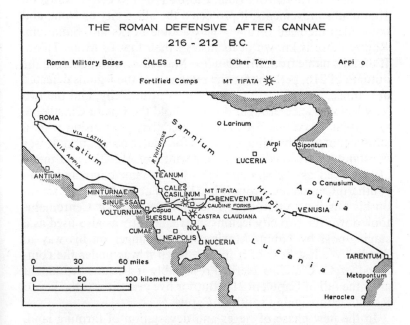

When the campaigning season of 215 got under way, Hannibal's objective was to extend his hold on Campania and, especially, to win a major port. Puteoli would have been the richest prize: failing that, Neapolis: Cumae would do at a

71

pinch. The disposition of the Roman armies (see Map 5) shows their objectives at a glance. They aimed, first, to prevent Hannibal breaking out from Campania into Latium, then, to protect the coastal cities, and third, to defend loyal allies in southern Campania such as Nola. The great fortified camps constructed by both sides show that the war had entered a new phase. The camp of Hannibal was on the Mons Tifata (Monte Virgo), north-east of Capua, whose high plateau tops 1,800 feet. The place offered many advantages. Close to Capua, it commanded the plain towards the west, and the Volturno valley eastwards leading to the passes into Samnium and Apulia. Invaluable as an offensive base, its broad summit and high pasture made it a supply-base and a grazing ground for horses and pack-animals. Some twelve miles away to the south-east was the corresponding Roman base—the Castra Claudiana on the hill (Cancello) above Suessula. Close enough to keep a watch on Hannibal's movements, it protected the allied city of Nola, and controlled the road through the Caudine Forks into Samnium. Rather more is known of its history than that of Mons Tifata. It took its name from M. Claudius Marcellus, who built it in the autumn of 216, perhaps for the remnants of the legions defeated at Cannae. In 215 these troops were sent to Sicily, and the two 'city legions' were brought down to hold the Castra Claudiana. Q. Fabius Maximus occupied it later that year, using it as a store-depôt, and building barracks for winter occupation. It was constantly garrisoned through the winter of 215–214, and thereafter served as the summer base for Roman commanders in southern Campania. From it in 214 Q. Fabius Maximus set off on his mission to devastate Lucania. Gn. Fulvius Centumalus took down the two city legions in 213, and it was also used as a staging-post by Fabius Maximus the Younger on his way to Apulia. We last hear of it in 212, when it was under the command of C. Claudius Nero. Presumably it became redundant after the fall of Capua in 211. But for five years it was the key to Roman campaigning south of Capua.

In the new phase of sieges and devastation of farming land, Hannibal achieved very little in 215. No coastal city fell to him, though he attacked Neapolis three times in all. Inland, he captured Casilinum and Nuceria, but Marcellus foiled him repeatedly at Nola, although he had a fifth column in the city.

But a second Punic army, under Hanno, overran practically the whole of Bruttium, where there were virtually no Roman troops to oppose them. Few of the allies were able to resist, though the little city of Petelia stood a long siege to the limits of endurance. By the end of 215 only the Greek city of Rhegium was not under Punic control. In the later stages of the war Bruttium was to provide Hannibal with his last redoubt in Italy: immediately, the native Bruttii were available for recruitment to his army. On balance, the years fighting in Italy might be said to have gone in favour of Rome, in so far as Hannibal's main aims had been foiled and the Fabian strategy had been successful. But the death of Hiero early in the year threatened the opening of a new and dangerous theatre in Sicily (see pp. 122f.).

For the campaigns of 214, as many as twenty legions were raised. Hannibal's main offensive was again launched in Campania, where he threatened in turn Cumae, Puteoli, and Nola. If he had been joined by a force of some 20,000 men which Hanno brought from Bruttium, more might have been achieved. But Hanno's army was heavily defeated near Beneventum by Ti. Sempronius Gracchus, and forced to retreat. Hannibal then moved south-east to threaten Tarentum and the other Greek cities along the Ionian sea, without capturing any of them. Meanwhile, Roman armies picked up some useful gains in Campania and Apulia.

The most important aspect of these grim years was the systematic devastation, by both sides, of farming-land in enemy-held territory. At the beginning of 215 Q. Fabius Maximus ordered that all grain crops had to be brought in to walled cities by 1 June: if any man failed to do so, his farm would be laid waste, the farm-buildings burned, and the slaves sold at auction. This order applied to Roman and allied territory. For enemy territory there were no limits. Later that year Marcellus ravaged the territory of the Hirpini and Samnites so savagely as to revive memories of their sufferings in the previous century, and to prompt an anguished (and unanswered) appeal to Hannibal. In 214 Fabius Maximus himself showed in the same area how his policy should be applied. He burned the crops in the Caudine territory, carried off the cattle, and killed or captured 25,000 people. In 214 Hannibal ravaged the lands of Neapolis and Cumae in the spring; in the autumn he made a large haul of grain from Heraclea and Metapontum, and carried away 4,000 horses to be broken in for the cavalry. These are only samples of a continuing process that was to eliminate the peasant farmer over a large part of the South. Truly 'the dragon of the destruction of Italy' worked for both sides.

For 213 twenty-two legions were put into the field, but in spite of this the war went, on balance, in favour of Hannibal. Apulia saw most of the fighting, and the Romans began well with the capture of Arpi, an important centre of roads which had served Hannibal as a winter base. The colonies at Luceria and Venusia had shown their value in this theatre, and the Roman position was strengthened further by the construction of a fortified camp near Herdonea. But these gains were far outweighed by Hannibal's success, during the winter of 213–212, in capturing Tarentum. He had threatened it the previous year, but now its capture was achieved by collusion with a group of disaffected Tarentine nobles. The accounts in Polybius and Livy make it clear that Hannibal showed all his cleverness in the planning, co-ordination and timing of the assault. Tarentum was the largest city captured by him during the war, and with it the Greek cities of the Ionian shore abandoned Rome. But a Roman garrison still held the citadel, and the Tarentine ships were bottled up in the minor harbour (Mare Piccolo, see Plate 11). The citadel could not be gained immediately, so Hannibal built fortifications to block it off from the city. But the ships could, and he showed the Tarentines how. Wheeled trucks were built, the ships hauled up onto them, and the trucks were dragged through a broad and flat street which led across the peninsula— in fact, an emergency slipway was constructed. Rome's hold on the heel of Italy was now reduced to the naval base of Brundisium.

At Rome the events of 213 led to renewed impatience with Fabius Maximus' direction of the war. He seemed to be getting nowhere slowly: nothing had been done to bring Capua to heel; the Roman force of four legions in Apulia had done nothing to interfere with Hannibal's capture of Tarentum. This discontent prevailed at the elections for 212–211, which swept the Fabian faction from command and made Appius Claudius and Q. Fulvius Flaccus consuls. Twenty-five legions were raised, and both the consuls were sent to Campania, with their main object the reduction of Capua. But Capua did not fall until 211, after two eventful seasons whose campaigns ranged over most of Italy south of Rome.

The siege of Capua was to be by blockade, not assault. The Roman plan was to concentrate armies large enough to surround the city, cut off its supplies, and starve it out. These armies would need to be protected against a counter-assault by Hannibal. The war of supplies had begun the previous autumn, when the Romans prevented the Campanians from sowing their crops. An important action took place early in 212, when Hanno was ordered up from Bruttium to run supplies into Capua before the main Roman armies appeared. Livy's account contains some curious statements which we lack the means to correct. Hanno brought his army to the neighbourhood of Beneventum, and fortified a hill some three miles from the town at Apollosa. This he intended as a distribution-point for supplies he had collected from the nearest allied towns. The Capuans were ordered to bring wagons and pack-animals to transport it, on a given day, under escort to Capua. Their response was feeble: only 400 carts and a few pack-animals were sent. Livy ascribes this to 'the usual Campanian negligence and idleness'; in fact they might well have had doubts about an assembly-point so close to the Roman colony of Beneventum. This first inadequate convoy got through. Hanno delivered a harsh rebuke to the Campanians, and named a second day. This time more than 2,000 wagons appeared from Capua. But the Beneventines had informed the Roman consuls at Bovianum (Pietrabbondante) where they were mustering their legions. By night, Fulvius took a force some fifty miles to Beneventum. By night, again, he moved up to Apollosa, and attacked at dawn. After bitter fighting, the Romans overran the camp, inflicted heavy losses on the garrison, and won a huge haul of supplies. Hanno, who had been away on the day of the attack, got through to Capua with 2,000 men. Supplies would have been more useful.

For their own supplies, the Romans built and fortified a base at the mouth of the Volturno river, to receive cargoes from Sardinia and Etruria. The materials for the blockade were assembled at Casilinum. But as two consular armies were closing in on Capua, Hannibal appeared with a relief force. And now his shortage of supplies came into play. The Roman armies withdrew. It was useless for Hannibal to take his troops into the city—they could not have been fed. All he could do was to follow Appius Claudius into Lucania. The Roman general gave him the slip, and got back to Capua. At the end of the year three Roman armies (six legions) invested it, and throughout the winter they worked on the construction of a double ring of fortifications, facing inwards and outwards.

Elsewhere things did not go so well for Rome. Ti. Sempronius Gracchus, on his way to Beneventum, had been ambushed and killed. When Hannibal returned to Apulia, he fell upon a Roman army near Herdonea and inflicted on it a resounding and disgraceful defeat. The Roman general, Gn. Fulvius Flaccus, brother of the consul, seems to have panicked and abandoned his troops; he was later brought to trial in Rome and sent into

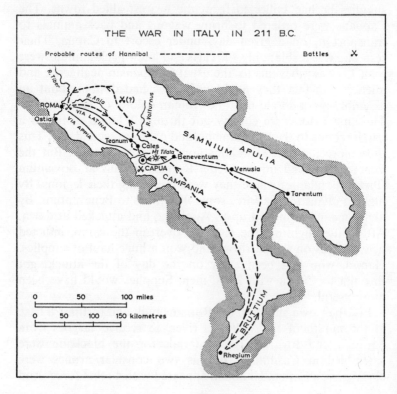

THE WAR IN ITALY IN 211 B.C.

Probable routes of Hannibal -----------   Battles   X

exile. Nothing more could be attempted in Apulia that year; Tarentum went unrelieved; but Hannibal failed to take Brundisium in a surprise attack.

The eventful year 211 opened with the same enormous Roman forces in the field, but the new consuls, Gn. Fulvius Centumalus and P. Sulpicius Galba, were to be employed in Apulia. Fulvius Flaccus and Appius Claudius were left to complete the strangulation of Capua. It was foreseen that Hannibal would intervene, but not that his intervention would take the dramatic turn it did.

Hannibal had wintered in Bruttium, and from that base led a picked force of cavalry and infantry to Capua. The last time he had appeared in front of the city the Roman armies had withdrawn. But that was before the double line of circumvallation, now garrisoned as a huge fortress by six legions, apparently under the supreme command of Appius Claudius. The next ploy tried by Hannibal was to lure the Romans out to battle by frequent skirmishes. Appius declined. Polybius comments that the strategic factors remained unchanged: the Carthaginian cavalry were masters of the open field, but Hannibal could not carry a defended position. Probing assaults confirmed that this was so at Capua. Hannibal then decided on perhaps his boldest —certainly his most spectacular—stroke of the war, a march on Rome. Several bonuses might accrue. At the best, a surprise appearance *might* enable him to capture part of the city. It could fairly be expected that some of the forces round Capua would march to the relief of the capital; they could be defeated en route. With the investing armies weakened and divided, Capua might be relieved. The problem was to keep up Capuan resistance while he was away, without the whole plan leaking to the enemy. A Numidian took a secret message through the Roman lines and into the city. Then Hannibal, leaving all his camp fires burning, set out by night. The stakes were high—at best Rome, at worst Capua.

Ancient authorities could not agree on the route he took, and it is still a matter of controversy. Livy says that the Via Latina was used for the later stages of the march, but he also makes Fulvius Flaccus take a relief force along Via Appia and reach Rome ahead of Hannibal. Far more likely is the account of Polybius, who makes Hannibal take a wide swoop through

Samnium on an unidentified route, and come down on Rome, it would seem, from the north-east. At any rate, Hannibal finally encamped on the Anio only three miles from the city. It is easy to understand the panic that seized the people. Memories of the terrible disasters were revived by the mere sight of Hannibal. Again, there was the fear that his presence must mean that the legions round Capua had been destroyed. Strategically, the position was more alarming than dangerous. The fortifications were strong, and by good luck the consuls were still in the city, and with them two legions—perhaps even four. Instead of assaulting Rome, Hannibal plundered and devastated the surrounding countryside, whose people must have felt exempt from such things. Livy notes that he robbed the rich shrine of Feronia, near Capena, of its gold and silver, and archaeological traces of its sacking have been found in modern times. Hannibal gave sufficient time for a relief force to set out from Capua, and then started south. Sulpicius Galba disputed the Anio crossing, recovering some of the booty and killing 300 of the enemy. He then followed Hannibal, 'keeping to the hills'. After five days' march Hannibal learned that no Roman army was moving up from Capua: he had lost another big prize. He turned back to savage Sulpicius Galba in a night attack, and then went after other game, abandoning Capua to its fate. Somehow—and the route recorded by Polybius seems incredible—'through Daunia and Apulia'—he reached Bruttium and was at the gates of Rhegium before anyone could have expected him. The city did not fall, but it was a near thing. Perhaps Hannibal made a feint at Tarentum, in a last attempt to relieve pressure on Capua, and then attacked Rhegium with fresh troops who had wintered in Bruttium. Hannibal had given a wonderful display of speed and flexibility, and Polybius—in a rather parochial way—compares it with Epaminondas' well-known march on Sparta. The comparison flatters the Greek. But for all his dash and virtuosity, Hannibal had achieved nothing. Roman pertinacity was about to achieve the downfall of Capua.

The failure of Hannibal to raise the siege deprived the Capuans of their last hopes. The decision to surrender was opposed by only twenty-eight senators, led by the intransigent Vibius Virrius. When the vote went against them they dined together for the last time, and then took poison. The next day the gates were opened to Roman troops under Fulvius Flaccus. The question now was what form of punishment would be inflicted on Capua. Fulvius was for harsh treatment: Appius Claudius for milder, but he had been wounded and died shortly after. In the end seventy of the most compromised senators were executed, together with certain other leading citizens. (It should be recalled that they were all Roman citizens, guilty of collusion with an enemy of the state.) The city was not sacked, and its lands and buildings became the property of the Roman people. As a political entity, however, it ceased to exist. A Roman praetor took charge of justice. As quickly as possible, the fertile lands of the Ager Campanus were brought into production, but now for the benefit of the Roman conquerors.

The fall of Capua, and the treatment of its people, marked a turning-point in the Italian theatre of war. The central fact was that Hannibal had been unable to rescue his most important ally. The vision of a federal Italy, independent of Rome, lay shattered. The same summer also saw the brilliant victories of Marcellus in Sicily, and the fall of Syracuse (see pp. 128f.). But these successes in Italy were almost outweighed by the disaster in Spain (see pp. 101f.). Unless the position there could be reversed, there was still a possibility that Hannibal could be reinforced overland. Hence the insistence which in 210 B.C. the people showed for power to be given to P. Cornelius Scipio, young as he was, to continue the work of his house by an aggressive policy in Spain.

After the events of 211, the tempo and scale of the war in Italy were reduced. It is hard to give a coherent picture of 210–208 (for most of which we lack Polybius), or to discern the general strategy of the two sides. Both, it seems, were trammelled by their own limitations. War-weariness and defeatism were rife on the Roman side. Its most alarming symptom was the refusal of twelve of the thirty Latin colonies to furnish their quota of troops for the campaign of 209. Livy preserves their names on a list of dishonour, and, in contrast, those of eighteen colonies that honoured their obligations. At one point, disaffection at Arretium reached the point of open rebellion. In Rome the raising of sufficient rowers for the fleet met public opposition: in the end it was achieved only because the Senate set the example of private subscription. In 210, the number of legions was reduced to twenty-one, of which thirteen served in Italy.

Hannibal had the standing problem of supplies to cope with, and a sharp deterioration in relations with his allies. It was unlikely, after the fall of Capua, that he would attract any others— it was increasingly difficult to retain those he had. Two instances from Apulia will show up his problems. Salapia was taken by the Romans in 210, partly through internal political rivalries. It was garrisoned by 500 Numidian cavalry, of whom 450 were killed in the fighting. So Hannibal lost one of his most effective cavalry units. In 209 he tried to retake the city by a ruse, but he failed. Salapia had to be written off. After defeating Fulvius Centumalus in 210 outside Herdonea, Hannibal removed the whole population of that city to Metapontum and Thurii, lest they should go over to Rome. Perhaps, also, he could neither garrison nor feed them. His reputation as a general was still formidable, and he was still invincible in the open field. But if the Romans would not meet him there, there was really nothing he could do. It is notable that all his moves during these years were in response to Roman initiative. In short, the military situation in Italy had reached a stalemate which only two things could break. One would be the arrival of reinforcements large enough to restore Hannibal's freedom of action. The other would be the appearance of a Roman general who could beat Hannibal by his own tactics.

It remains to note, against this general background, the most important events of these campaigns. 210 was an unrewarding year for Rome. The second disaster at Herdonea cost the life of the consul, Flavius Centumalus, and the loss of at least 7,000 men. Marcellus opposed Hannibal, and held his own. Nothing was done to relieve the Roman garrison at Tarentum, and when the Tarentine fleet defeated a Roman escort flotilla the arrangements for its provisioning broke down.

209 saw the fifth consulship of Q. Fabius Maximus and his first victory in an offensive action—the recovery of Tarentum. In a carefully planned operation, Marcellus held off Hannibal, while Fabius besieged Tarentum with the aid of legions released from Sicily. After its capture the city was sacked, and the people treated with great harshness. Its days as one of the great cities of the Hellenic world were at an end. Hannibal's failure to prevent its capture was another blow to his prestige.

In 208 fortune swung his way. Marcellus, in his fifth consulship, again operated in Apulia, his colleague Crispinus in Lucania. That summer the long and brilliant career of Marcellus came to an inglorious end. He rashly exposed himself to an ambush near Venusia, where his small force was annihilated and he was killed. The only Roman general who had consistently and successfully operated against Hannibal, his death removed any prospect of driving Hannibal's army out of Italy. Crispinus, the other consul, was wounded in the same action, and died soon afterwards at Capua. Never before had both consuls been killed on active service during their year of office. A Roman attempt to besiege Locri had to be abandoned when Hannibal intervened. A gloomy year for Rome ended in the knowledge that a fresh crisis was impending. Hasdrubal was reported to have entered Gaul from Spain. Next year he would bring a second Punic army across the Alps to the relief of Hannibal. After all that Rome had suffered and endured, she might yet be defeated in Italy.

Much care was taken over the election of consuls for the crucial year ahead. The choice of experienced commanders was not large. Scipio was in Spain, Marcellus was dead, Fabius Maximus and Fulvius Flaccus were old. There was Gaius Claudius Nero, who had done good service at the siege of Capua, and under Marcellus in Apulia, and who had held the Ebro line in Spain at the critical time after the defeat of the Scipios. For his colleague they chose a man who had long been under a shadow—M. Livius Salinator, who had distinguished himself in Illyria in 219 B.C. After his return he had been accused of peculation, and had withdrawn from Rome after a *cause célèbre*. He had to be persuaded to lay aside both his bitterness against the state and his personal hostility to Claudius Nero, who had been one of his accusers. In the end the two men agreed to work together in the interests of Rome. Claudius was given the Southern Command, with four legions in Lucania and Bruttium, two in Apulia, one in Campania. Eight legions protected Northern Italy under Livius, two in Etruria, two in Picenum, two in Umbria, and two near Ariminum. For the first time since the passage of Hannibal, the northern front was to be the more important. But the armies of Etruria and Picenum had played a vital role in preventing Gallic reinforcements from reaching Hannibal, and keeping under Roman control indispensable sources of men and supplies.

Hasdrubal, after the defeat at Baecula, had taken his army west of the Pyrenees and into Gaul (see p. 110). The Celts gave him a friendly welcome, and he was able to recruit both Celtic

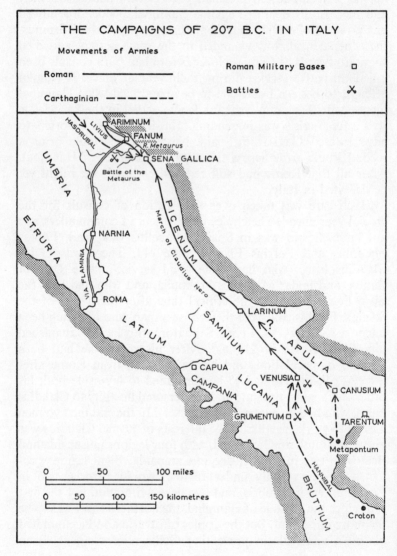

THE CAMPAIGNS OF 207 B.C. IN ITALY

Movements of Armies

Roman ——————

Carthaginian — — — — —

Roman Military Bases ▫

Battles ✗

and Ligurian volunteers. Leaving winter quarters east of the Rhône early in the spring of 207, he crossed the Alps (Appian says by the same pass as Hannibal, but see p. 110) and reached Italy in two months, against Hannibal's five. This took everyone by surprise. The Romans had hoped to engage him as soon as he entered Cisalpina: Hannibal was slow to move north from his own winter quarters in Bruttium. The Carthaginian problem was how to effect a juncture of the two armies, the Roman, how to prevent it. But first, the Romans had to discover the Carthaginian plan.

The main concentration of Roman forces in the south was at Venusia, with other troops at Tarentum and Capua. Moving from Bruttium, Hannibal made for Grumentum in central Lucania. Here he was met by Claudius Nero, and there was a sharp fight which Livy claims as a Roman success. A few days later Hannibal slipped away unobserved and got as far north as Venusia, where Claudius Nero overtook him and fought again. Hannibal then turned aside to Metapontum, marching by night along mountain roads. His object was to collect reinforcements before he marched north again, but the move had a fatal consequence. From Placentia Hasdrubal had sent six cavalrymen—four Celts and two Numidians—with a letter for Hannibal; they had ridden the whole length of Italy undetected, but in trying to follow Hannibal to Metapontum they missed the way, and fell into the hands of Roman foragers near Tarentum. The all-important letter was taken under seal to Claudius Nero at Canusium. He read it and sent it on to the Senate in Rome. According to Livy, it said that Hasdrubal would meet his brother 'in Umbria'; Appian adds that it gave the number of troops he had brought into Italy. It was then that Claudius Nero conceived his bold plan—the most audacious carried out by any Roman commander in Italy in this war. He would detach part of his forces, leave the rest to mask Hannibal, and join his colleague to grapple with Hasdrubal. If successful, he could be back in Apulia before Hannibal noticed his absence. If he failed —but Nero refused to talk of failure. The need was to organize supplies and transport for the 240-mile dash along the Adriatic coast road to Sena Gallica. So he sent messengers to the lands of Larinum, the Marrucini, the Frentani, and the Praetutii asking for provisions, ready to eat, to be brought down to the road, and for vehicles, horses, and mules to enable exhausted men to keep up.

These details remind us that we know much of the Roman plans, little of the Carthaginian. Livy says two things, that the two generals were to meet in Umbria, and also that 'the two Punic generals were encircling Rome: whichever of them first won a victory would in a few days join his camp with the others'. The first comes from Hasdrubal's letter, the second was common talk in Rome as the consuls set off for the field. They are not readily reconciled. 'In Umbria' means almost certainly the Adriatic coast, between Ariminum and Ancona. The movements of Hannibal and Hasdrubal, and indeed of the Roman commanders, are entirely consistent with this view. But it does not seem likely that Hannibal would lead the bulk of his army so far north, and thus risk the loss of all his bases in Bruttium. Far more likely that he would lead it as far north in Apulia as possible, leave there a force large enough to hold down the southern Roman army, and himself take a picked force to join Hasdrubal and take over the army in the north. The same plan, in fact, as that of Claudius Nero. But Claudius Nero was the better placed, and put his plan into action.

Livy has a splendid passage on the northward march of Claudius' picked force—six thousand infantry and one thousand cavalry, the flower of the southern army. Men and women poured out from the farms to watch them pass, calling them the champions of the state, who would win freedom and safety for themselves and their children. They showered gifts on them, implored the gods for their success. (Those who saw the British and American troops move down to the Channel ports before the Normandy landings of 1944 will know the feeling.) Old soldiers and young men joined their ranks as they marched. The soldiers pressed on, marching night and day. So they came 'ad Senam', where Livius Salinator had his camp, with Hasdrubal only five hundred yards away.

'Ad Senam' is often taken to be the town of Sena Gallica, as Appian explicitly says. But Sena is also the name of the river (modern Cesano) a little north of the town, and many difficulties diminish if we suppose, with Pareti and other Italian scholars, that the river flowed between the Roman and the Carthaginian camps. Hasdrubal had clearly by-passed Arimi-

num and also Fanum, where Via Flaminia reached the coast.
Lucius Porcius, in charge of the troops at Ariminum, hung onto
his flanks and harassed him. When Hasdrubal had passed
Fanum, and was clearly advancing along the coastal road,
Livius and Porcius barred his way. They would join battle as
soon as Nero came up from the south. Every conceivable pre-
caution was taken to hide the arrival of Nero's force: there was
a night entry to the camp, the men were crowded into the existing quarters. The next day both sides deployed for battle.
Hasdrubal was uneasy. There were shields he had not seen
before, some of the horses looked very lean, the enemy numbers
seemed greater than usual. But there were two camps, as before,
the earthworks had not been enlarged, there were no extra
tents. Then came a report that two trumpets had sounded in the
camp of Livius. Hasdrubal deduced that both consuls were
present. He was probably outnumbered: worse still, what had
happened to Hannibal? Had his despatch got through? Per-
plexed and alarmed, Hasdrubal sounded the recall to camp.
That night he ordered the army to pack and march—a night
march through unknown country in the face of the enemy
towards the Metaurus River and Via Flaminia.

From this moment everything went wrong for Hasdrubal.
His native guides deserted. When he reached the Metaurus, he
could not find the fords: the army wandered in circles round the
windings of the river; men got lost in the darkness, others fell
out through exhaustion. At daybreak, when he hoped to find a
crossing, the river was flowing between high banks, which got
steeper as he went inland. As he was trying to fortify a camp on
a hill above the river, the Romans caught up with him, first Nero
with the cavalry, then Livius with the infantry, ready for
immediate battle.

Such is the prelude to the decisive battle of the Metaurus,
most controversial of all battles of the Second Punic War. Livy
and Polybius give conflicting accounts of the dispositions of the
two armies. Modern scholars have failed to agree on the site:
there are at least five sitings on the north bank of the Metaurus,
six on the southern. If we accept that the original camps were on
the Sena, and that Hasdrubal failed to find a ford across the
Metaurus, then the battle must have been fought on the
southern or right bank. There is still the problem of what

Hasdrubal meant to do if he had reached Via Flaminia. He could have marched north-east and then back into the Po Valley, but this is not very likely. Probably he intended to turn left towards Rome, by-pass the Roman armies at the Sena, reach friendly communities in Etruria or Umbria (see pp. 79, 91) and then find out what had happened to Hannibal.

A battle, then, on the south bank, and the steepening banks of the river suggest a site west of Montemaggiore towards Fossombrone. Perhaps one should not try to be more precise. The salient features of the battle are that Hasdrubal recognized it was all or nothing, and staked everything on a heavy concentration on the right against Livius. Here his Spanish veterans, who had fought and beaten Roman armies in Spain, were engaged in a desperate battle. Hasdrubal's ten elephants (used like tanks in the centre) caused confusion in both armies. On the left, Nero detached himself from a cramped position, rode round the rear of his own army, and fell unexpectedly on the Punic right wing. This move turned the battle into a rout. Hasdrubal, having done all a general could, saw that the battle was lost, and rode into the thick of the fighting to die. The Romans killed perhaps 15,000 of the enemy, took some 10,000 prisoners, and won immense booty. Their own losses were about 8,000 men. The northern arm of the Carthaginian pincers had been utterly destroyed, and the threat removed from Rome and Central Italy.

Claudius Nero rode back, 'faster than he had come', and reached Larinum, where Hannibal had finally halted, in six days. Here he flung Hasdrubal's head into the enemy outposts. It had been carefully preserved, and the features were recognizable (a touch that foretells certain of the later emperors of his line!). Hannibal withdrew into Bruttium: he was scarcely to leave it again until he embarked for Africa.

After the deliverance at the Metaurus, tension in Rome relaxed. Euphoria followed, although Hannibal was still in Italy. When the victorious consuls returned to Rome, it was noted that Claudius Nero was given the greater acclaim in their joint triumph. The disbandment of four legions showed that no great projects were in view for 206, and indeed nothing more was achieved, save keeping Hannibal bottled up in Bruttium.

1a Portrait of Hannibal on Punic coin of Nova Carthago,
with African elephant on reverse

1b Portrait of Mago on Punic coin of Gades, with prow
of galley on reverse

1c Portrait of Masinissa, King of Numidia, on Numidian
coin, with galloping horse on reverse

1d Helmeted head of Scipio on Roman *denarius* (c. 105
B.C.), with Jupiter, Juno and Minerva on reverse

2 Punic masks from Carthage

3 Carthaginian oil flask in the shape of a salamander

4 Saguntum, showing acropolis and theatre

5 Nova Carthago (Cartagena), with view of harbour

6 Aerial view of the battlefield of Cannae (left centre – the hill of Cannae)

7 Lake Trasimeno seen from Monte del Lago

8 Syracuse – aerial view of the harbour

9   Syracuse – fortress of Euryalus (reconstruction)

10   Syracuse – for-
tress of Euryalus

11 Harbour at Taranto (Tarentum)

12 Crotone – Temple of Hera

13   Carthage – view from Byrsa Hill looking towards the Gulf of Tunis

But in the autumn of that year Scipio returned from Spain, and a surge of popular enthusiasm carried him to a consulship for 205. It would clearly be under his auspices that Rome would make the last effort to end the war. But where that effort should be directed was still to be settled.

Livy presents the issue as polarized in a debate in the Senate between Q. Fabius Maximus and Scipio. The gist of Fabius' speech is: 'First peace in Italy, then war in Africa!' It contains also historical examples, Greek as well as Roman, of disasters incurred by the invasion of enemy territory, warnings of the un-trustworthiness of Syphax and the Numidians, with whom Scipio had negotiated earlier in the year, and underlying all this, the implication that Scipio was more concerned for his own *gloria* than for the good of the State. In reply, Scipio takes his stand on military advantage: 'I shall meet Hannibal, Quintus Fabius, but I shall pull him after me: not let him hold me back. I shall force him to fight in his own country, and the prize will be Carthage, not the half-ruined hill-forts of the Bruttii!' As for faithless Africans, they would be faithless to Carthage. And for *exempla*—'if you want Greek fairy-tales'—there are plenty that point the other way. But as for *gloria*, 'Yes, Quintus Fabius, I do wish to attain the praises you have won: if possible, to exceed them.'

Livy gives this pair of carefully balanced, antithetical speeches; modern scholars deduce a conflict of principles. Fabius and his followers favoured an agrarian, purely Italian policy for Rome. Any expansion would be limited to completing the interrupted conquest of Cisalpina. Scipio stood for expansion: already, he had an imperial vision: looking back over his career, Scullard says that 'because of the torch which he kindled, the shadow of the Empire fell athwart the Republic'. It may be so, and the invasion of Africa could be the first kindling of the torch. Equally, the conflict in 205 between Scipio and Fabius (who had with him the majority of the Senate) may have arisen from short-term considerations, and from the renewed ferocity of political rivalries within the Senate. The cult of *gloria* was relentlessly pursued by the great aristocratic families, and by none more avidly than the Scipios, as their epitaphs attest. And what glory would attend the victor of Carthage and his friends, tangibly expressed in wealth, honours, patronage, and office? Indeed, for fifteen years after Zama Scipio Africanus held a position in the State without precedent in the history of Rome. Much of this could well have been foreseen by Fabius and his friends when they opposed Scipio's grand design for Africa. It comes out later, when the consuls Gn. Servilius (203) and Tiberius Gracchus (202) tried to deprive Scipio of the glory of making peace with Carthage. In 205, Scipio obtained Sicily as his province, with the option of proceeding to Africa if he thought fit. The Fabian party next turned to hampering his plans for an adequate invasion force.

If peace in 205 would have suited Fabius and his friends, as has been suggested, the military situation argues strongly that it would have suited Carthage even better. Why were negotiations not begun? Once again, we do not know the minds of the Carthaginians at this juncture. Livy gives no account of a debate in the Carthaginian Senate: perhaps Polybius did, in one of the books now lost. To understand their motives we need to know what hopes they attached to what seemed an ill-conceived and belated venture—the expedition of Mago to Liguria and Cisalpina. Livy does say expressly that Mago undertook this at the orders of the Carthaginian Senate, who instructed him to proceed from Gades to Italy 'there to hire as many young Gauls and Ligurians as possible, to join with Hannibal, and not to allow a war to languish which had begun with great energy and even greater good fortune'. In other words, the main hopes of the war party at Carthage were pinned on this expedition.

The plunder of all the temples around Gades—and that of Hercules was enormously wealthy—gave Mago plenty of funds. After wintering in Minorca (206–205) he took 12,000 infantry and 2,000 cavalry to the Gulf of Genoa. He captured and destroyed Genoa itself, the chief centre of Roman influence on the Ligurian coast, and then made an alliance with the Ingauni, a powerful Ligurian tribe with a fleet of their own. With Savo (Savona) as his main base he was in a strong position, commanding the Gulf of Genoa and with good communications into Cisalpine Gaul. The Romans naturally thought that he would follow Hasdrubal's example and invade Italy; they prepared accordingly. This interpretation is followed by Livy. But Mago's actions in the north do not suggest the copying of a policy which had already led to disaster. The convoy of eighty Carthaginian ships captured that summer off Sardinia by the Romans represent the first signs of his intentions. They were laden with grain and provisions, on their way to Hannibal. Later that year, Mago received reinforcements from Carthage, 25 warships, 6,000 infantry, 800 cavalry, 7 elephants, and a large sum of money to hire auxiliaries. He also received instructions that 'relying on these resources he was to move closer to Rome and join up with Hannibal'. The latter is probably Livy's gloss. The real point of the reinforcements—which he also discloses—was to deter Scipio from invading Africa.

On the arrival of the fleet, Mago held a great council of Ligurians and Gauls to recruit for war on Rome. He repeated what Hasdrubal had said, and Hannibal before him, that he was come as the champion of their liberties. Officially, the Gauls were cautious. An open move would bring Roman armies upon them. The Ligurians, they pointed out, ran no such risk. The Ligurians asked for two months' delay to raise levies. Unofficially, Mago's recruiting agents were busy among the Gauls: volunteers came in in great numbers, as did supplies. But Mago's activities were not confined to Gaul and Liguria. In 204 Livy reports a series of judicial investigations in Etruria, 'where practically the entire land was inclining towards Mago, in the hope that political change might be brought about through him'. These resulted in the condemnation of many Etruscan nobles, who had either gone in person to Mago or reported to him on disaffection in their own communities. Others went voluntarily into exile, and were condemned in their absence. Two years earlier, Livius Salinator had investigated communities in Etruria and Umbria who had assisted Hasdrubal with supplies or in any other way. Here, surely, and not in any junction with Hannibal, was Mago's real threat to Rome. Discontent in Etruria had been smouldering: if he could set it ablaze, Rome could hardly mount an expedition to Africa. For in Spain, also, the Roman position did not look impregnable. Mago is said to have attached strong hopes to the nationalist uprising of the Ilergetes in 205. On his way from Gades, he had attacked Nova Carthago, thinking it lightly held by the Romans, with a prospective fifth column in the city. If Carthage could establish a firm hold on Liguria and Cisalpina, might not the Romans be forced to draw off forces from Spain? And then, at the least, Carthage would be in a position to negotiate favourable terms. Such—if we have guessed them correctly—were the hopes that might have been entertained.

The sources for accounts of Mago's expedition are scrappy and discontinuous. The only action reported against the Romans was in the late summer of 203 B.C. in the land of the Insubres, that is, beyond the Po near Milan. Some historians doubt the whole story, mainly because of the location of the battle. What was either party doing so far to the north-west in Cisalpina? But it does not follow that Mago was ready to mount a full-scale invasion of Italy, on the pattern of Hannibal or Hasdrubal. His object could have been to draw the Roman armies into Cisalpina, and thus open the way to an attack on Etruria, led perhaps by anti-Roman Etruscan nobles. Livy reports the battle as a bloody one on both sides. Mago, who received a severe wound, withdrew to Liguria. There he found instructions from Carthage, ordering withdrawal: two armies in Italy were now beyond her power to support. As the homeward-bound armada was passing Sardinia, Mago died of his wounds. Yet even now, Carthaginian agents were left behind in the north. One of them, Hamilcar, is heard of in Liguria some years after the peace with Carthage. No wonder that Rome then found it necessary to win control of Liguria and Cisalpina, though it involved bitter fighting so soon after a hard war. And had Carthage been the victor, she would probably have established herself in those parts much as she did earlier in Spain.

The main purpose of Scipio's going to Sicily was to use it as an invasion base. Lilybaeum offered a good harbour and the shortest crossing to Africa. The only troops in the province were the two legions made up from the survivors of Cannae, but who had been strengthened by Marcellus' veterans. The Fabians may have consoled themselves with the thought that these were an unsuitable nucleus for the expeditionary force: Scipio thought precisely the reverse. Scipio had shared the disaster with these men, and rallied them afterwards. He knew how they felt. They longed for a chance to redeem themselves, and bitterly resented the humiliations they had been made to endure. Those who survived were hardened soldiers. Marcellus' veterans included men who had served at the capture of Syracuse and were siege-specialists. Training and good leadership could make such men into an unbeatable army. For further troops, supplies, oarsmen and ships, beyond the 30 warships already assigned, Scipio had to rely on voluntary effort throughout Italy. He got it in good measure. Livy gives a valuable list of the communities that helped. The Etruscans took the lead. Caere sent grain and provisions, Populonia iron, Tarquinia linen for sails, Volaterrae grain and interior fittings for ships. From Arretium came a generous and extensive contribution—3,000 shields, 3,000 helmets, 50,000 sets of javelins, short spears, and lances; axes, shovels, sickles, baskets, and hand mills to equip 40 warships; 120,000 pecks of wheat; supplementary pay for petty officers and oarsmen. From Perusia, Clusium, and Rusellae came a great quantity of grain and fir for shipbuilding. (Of the twelve major Etruscan cities, the names of Vulci, Volsinii, and Cortona, are missing; this *might* be a pointer to where disaffection lay. Certainly the other Etruscan cities seem to have a need to attest their loyalty.) Umbria and the Sabine country sent soldiers: the Marsi, Paeligni, and Marrucini came forward in large numbers for the fleet. Caemerinum sent 600 men, armed and equipped. Scipio took with him to Sicily a force of 7,000 volunteers. Livy notes the speed with which his ships were built: 20 triremes and 10 quadriremes were equipped and launched, fully rigged and equipped, forty-five days after the timber had been brought from the forests.

Early in the spring of 204 all the troops in Sicily, and all merchant ships, were concentrated at Lilybaeum. Forty-five days' rations—including cooked rations for fifteen days—were placed on the ships, together with water-supplies for men and beasts. Scipio in person checked with representatives of each ship that the supplies had been loaded. Embarkation was fixed for the next day. Before an immense crowd of spectators, Scipio recited a solemn prayer 'to all the gods and goddesses of land and sea' for success for himself and his army, and a happy issue for the war. Then the armada set sail, 40 warships escorting 400 transports. Livy describes the scene in terms which recall Thucydides' description of the departure of the Syracusan expedition from Athens in 415 B.C. But Scipio was sailing to a very different destiny.

In the late autumn of 203 B.C. another army was transported from Bruttium to Africa. It was that of Hannibal, recalled for the defence of Carthage. Since his retreat into Bruttium after the Metaurus disaster, it had been all he could do to maintain himself in Italy. In 205 his armies had been able to operate as far as Thurii in one direction and Locri in the other, but later his movements were further hampered by shortage of supplies and by an epidemic which afflicted the Roman army in Bruttium as well as his own. For the last two years before evacuation he held little more than a strip extending from Croton, his main base, to the Lacinian Promontory and the Gulf of Squillace as far as Catanzaro. His chief strategic object must have been to retain a good port, first, in the hope of reinforcements, later, for the embarkation of his own army. This explains his quick reaction to the capture of Locri by a force sent across from Sicily in 205 by Scipio. The siege of Locri is of military interest because, briefly, it brought Scipio and Hannibal face to face, and it was Hannibal who retired. But it also illustrates the spirit in which the closing scenes of the Italian campaigns were conducted. The unhappy people of Locri had been most brutally treated by the Carthaginian garrison. When this was succeeded by a Roman one, under A. Pleminius, Scipio's legate, it was found that their sufferings had only just begun. Pleminius and his men, besides inflicting every possible atrocity on the inhabitants, also plundered the temples, including the famous shrine of Proserpina. The wretched Locrians sent an embassy to Rome, where it found a ready hearing. The reason was party politics rather than conscience.

Fabius Maximus, now in extreme old age, saw the Locrian atrocity as a stick to beat Scipio. Here was yet another instance, he complained, of the licence and indiscipline to be found among Scipio's troops. In the Senate he proposed that Scipio's command be withdrawn and that he be recalled to Rome. He added the charge that Scipio and his staff were more concerned with enjoying the delights of Syracuse than in preparing for the invasion of Africa. The proposal for recall did not command assent but a Commission of Inquiry was sent to Locri and to Sicily. At Locri the Commission ordered restitution to be made to the citizens; all the temple treasures were recovered and restored, and the rites of expiation duly performed. Pleminius,

found guilty on a first hearing, was sent in chains to stand trial
in Rome: he obliged by dying in prison. When the commissioners reached Sicily they were exposed to the full blast of
Scipio's charm. For their benefit, military and naval exercises
were performed in the harbour of Syracuse. Their advice was
asked about preparations for the African invasion. Fêted,
flattered, and enormously impressed, the Commissioners
returned to Rome. No more was heard of the atrocities at
Locri.

Hannibal, too, was charged with brutal and inhumane conduct in these last years. Some of it was inflicted on the Bruttii,
especially those who were guilty—or suspected—of disloyalty.
There may be an element of propaganda here, since the Bruttii
would do all in their power to help themselves back into Roman
favour. But Hannibal had been forced into a position where he
must look to his own army: his allies were expendable. The
garrisons that he left behind in certain unnamed Bruttian towns
were perhaps to cover his withdrawal, should it be contested.
Appian gives the fullest account of his withdrawal, but leaves
many questions unanswered. How much notice was he given?
The Carthaginians are said to have debated his recall both
before and after the battle of the Great Plains (see p. 139);
finally they sent a mission headed by the admiral Hasdrubal,
at a time when Carthaginian ambassadors were negotiating for
peace in Rome. Hannibal was thus able to withdraw under
cover of an armistice. But he must have made his preparations
well in advance: Hasdrubal's arrival was the equivalent of the
modern code-word. Where did he get his transports? Both Livy
and Appian say that he built them himself—he would have
needed some 200 transports—and Appian adds that 'Italy is
very well timbered'. In fact, Hannibal had under his control at
least part of the Sila, the finest of all Italian forests. Hasdrubal,
then, probably brought with him the warships which provided
the escort.

The Lacinian promontory was the scene of Hannibal's last
deeds in Italy. In the great Temple of Hera Lacinia on Cape
Colonna—the most famous of all Greek shrines in southern
Italy—he is said to have massacred a large number of Italian
soldiers who refused to follow him to Africa, 'lest such fine
soldiers should be later used by the Romans'. He also slaugh-

tered 4,000 horses and many pack-animals, for which there was no room on the transports. He had already composed and set up in the Temple precincts the great bronze inscription which recorded, in Punic and Greek, his exploits during his fifteen years in Italy. Then he set sail.

No Roman historian could escape conjecture as to Hannibal's emotions on leaving Italy. According to Livy, he felt bitterness against the Carthaginian Senate for lack of support, sorrow at leaving Italy 'more acute than any native going into exile', and bitterness at himself for the opportunities he had missed. On the latter, like Napoleon at St. Helena, he had ample time to brood. He had defeated so many Roman armies, but he had not defeated Rome. His own place was secure among the great generals of the world. And over a large part of Italy he had left such devastation as, some would have it, has even now not been made good.

5

The War in Spain

WHEN HIS BROTHER PUBLIUS had sailed back to Italy to face Hannibal (see pp. 41–2), Gnaeus Cornelius Scipio Calvus set out with his fleet from the mouth of the Rhône and brought it in safety to Emporiae (Ampurias), a town on the north-east coast of Spain, about one hundred and fifty miles north of the Ebro, and friendly to Rome. Gnaeus is largely overshadowed by his brother and his brilliant nephew, but he had been consul in 222 B.C. and with Marcellus had won a notable victory over the Insubres and had captured Milan. It is interesting to note that, apart from Aemilianus, who was only a Scipio on his mother's side, almost all the members of the family who achieved prominence during the 2nd and 1st centuries B.C. were his descendents. Gnaeus proceeded to consolidate Roman power north of the Ebro in a methodical manner. First he won over the support of all the towns between Emporiae and the Ebro, either by persuasion or force of arms, and secured them against counter-attack; then he advanced inland, now accompanied by numerous Spanish allies. He found the Carthaginians encamped before the walls of Cissa, the town where Hannibal's men had left their baggage to await their return (see p. 39). Scipio attacked and defeated them, and captured the town, which yielded rich booty. Among his prisoners were the Carthaginian area-commander, Hanno, and, more important, the Spanish prince Indibilis, whose tribe, the Ilergetes, dominated most of the hinterland north of the Ebro. He had been friendly to Carthage, but his capture brought the Ilergetes over to the Roman side—for the moment.

Hannibal's brother, Hasdrubal, held supreme command in

Spain. Hearing of Hanno's defeat, he crossed the Ebro with a strong column of nearly ten thousand men, with which he made a sudden onslaught on the Roman fleet. The Roman sailors and marines were caught off their guard and driven back to the shelter of the ships with heavy losses. Having somewhat restored morale by this bold stoke, Hasdrubal withdrew south of the Ebro for the winter, while Scipio, after executing some of the ships' captains for negligence and suppressing a number of insurrections among the tribes caused by Hasdrubal's raid, himself went into winter quarters at Tarraco.

Next spring Gnaeus was joined by his brother with reinforcements of ships and men. The Senate had ratified his policy of trying to deny Spain to the Carthaginians even though Hannibal was now in Italy. But even before Publius arrived, Gnaeus had attacked Hasdrubal's fleet in the mouth of the Ebro, driven it on to the land, and captured more than half the ships. Now that the Romans had been reinforced, they were in a position to take the offensive: hearing that Hasdrubal had withdrawn into the central parts of Spain to deal with a revolt among the Celtiberians (possibly incited by Roman agents), they crossed the river and marched south to Saguntum. Here they encamped about five miles from the town, close to the sea in order to keep in touch with their fleet. In Saguntum were the hostages Hannibal had taken from the Spanish tribes, to ensure their loyalty during his absence. Abelux, a crafty Saguntine noble, who had favoured the Carthaginian cause, now thought the time was opportune to change sides, and tricked the Carthaginian commander, Bostar, a rather stupid but kind-hearted individual, into giving him the hostages to take back to their own homes, with the idea of keeping the loyalty of their tribes more effectively by gratitude than by fear. Abelux immediately took them into the Roman camp. As a result it was the Romans, not the Carthaginians, who had the credit for the unfortunate Bostar's humane gesture. Nothing further is heard of Bostar. He was probably crucified.

The records of the next two years are rather sparse. It seems that the Romans concentrated on the consolidation of their power north of the Ebro, with occasional naval raids down the east coast. Gnaeus was left in command of the land forces, while Publius had charge of the fleet. At first Hasdrubal avoided making contact, feeling that his forces were no match for the Romans. Eventually, after long and vigorous pleas to Carthage, he was sent reinforcements. But before he could get to grips with the enemy, a number of his ships' captains deserted, out of resentment at the severity of the reprimands he had dealt out to them after the battle in the mouth of the Ebro the previous year. This sparked off a revolt in southern Spain. Livy (XXIII, 26.5) says that the people who rebelled were the Tartesii. In fact, they were probably the Turdetani, a powerful and comparatively advanced tribe in the valley of the River Baetis, in whose territory lay the 7th century Phoenician colony that had taken the old name of Tartessus. The uprising was serious, and Hasdrubal abandoned his plans for attacking the Romans in order to suppress it. This he accomplished only with some difficulty.

The effects of this pacification were quickly spoilt by the publication of the news that Hasdrubal had received firm orders from Carthage to take his army to Italy and join his brother there as soon as possible. Hasdrubal was furious at this breach of security, and demanded in the strongest terms that adequate troops should be sent to take his place in Spain before he set out; otherwise they could regard the province as lost. The Carthaginians refused to countermand their orders, but finally sent Himilco with a powerful army and fleet to control Spain during his absence. Hasdrubal made contact with Himilco, raised as much money as he could in the short time available—for he knew he would have to pay for the help of the Gauls—and then moved north towards the Ebro.

The Romans knew about his plans well in advance, and concentrated their forces along the Ebro to stop him at all costs. For a second Carthaginian army to get into Italy at the present time might well bring Rome to her knees. They took up their position near Ibera, a city on the south bank of the river, commanding the route along which Hasdrubal would march. Here the battle took place. Both sides were of about equal strength. The tactics of the battle are interesting. The Romans adopted the normal triple-line formation, though with the light-armed *velites* mixed in with the heavy-armed legionaries. Hasdrubal had his Africans and Carthaginians on the wings, with Spanish troops forming the centre. As soon as the Romans advanced, the

Spaniards immediately gave ground, and drew the Romans into a position in which they could be attacked from both sides by Hasdrubal's wings. These tactics were almost identical to the ones used by Hannibal at Cannae, and had probably been worked out by the two brothers before the start of the war. But the result on this occasion was different. The Romans were strong enough to force open the trap that was closing on them. They made the Spanish troops break and flee, and then crushed the Africans and Carthaginians who were trying to envelop them. Hasdrubal managed to extricate himself with heavy losses, but all hopes of his getting to Italy had to be abandoned. The situation in Italy was affected in another way, too, by Hasdrubal's defeat. His brother Mago had gone to Carthage after Cannae to procure additional troops for Hannibal (see pp. 70–1). He had now raised a force of 12,000 infantry and 1,500 cavalry, and was on the point of sailing to Italy, but when the news of this disaster arrived he was diverted to Spain.

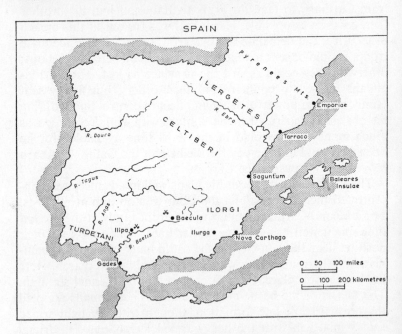

During 215 the Romans had to beat off Carthaginian attempts to recover towns that had deserted to them. The places mentioned by Livy (XXIII, 49), Iliturgi and Intibili, probably lay on or near the coast, somewhere between the Ebro and Saguntum. They would have joined the Romans in 217. All that we can be sure of is that the Carthaginian attacks were beaten off. The details of the battles, in particular the numbers involved and the size of the enemy casualties, were probably derived from Valerius Antias, whose accounts of battles are thoroughly unreliable.

In 214 Hasdrubal made a vigorous attempt to re-establish Carthaginian influence over the Spanish tribes, and at first gained some success. This drew the Romans south of the Ebro, and a desultory campaign ensued, consisting mainly of marching and counter-marching, as the Carthaginians threatened, one after another, the various cities that had joined the Romans, while the Romans kept switching their forces to protect them. The place-names mentioned by Livy are unreliable, but the fighting probably took place along the eastern coastal plain south of the Ebro. Livy's account indicates a campaign around Munda, Castulo and Bigerra, in the valley of the Baetis, but it is impossible to believe that the Romans penetrated into this area before the capture of Saguntum, which would be indispensable as a base for any advance into Baetica.

After this year's campaigning, the Romans had managed to maintain their position while the Carthaginians had exhausted themselves and suffered fairly heavy losses without having achieved very much. As a result of this improvement in their relative strength, the Romans took the opportunity the following year to carry out a sizeable advance. They penetrated as far as Saguntum once again, and this time attacked and captured the city. This gave them a base for further operations against Nova Carthago and the valley of the River Baetis (now the Guadalquivir). At the end of 213 two significant events took place. Publius Scipio had always been set on an offensive strategy, and had originally seen his expedition to Spain as the first step towards an invasion of North Africa and an attack on Carthage from the west. With this ultimate end in view, he sent three centurions as envoys to Syphax, King of the Masaesylii, who occupied western Numidia. An agreement was concluded, under which one of the centurions was to remain with Syphax and train his troops, while Syphax, for his part, would carry on war with the Carthaginians in North Africa and would send his own envoys to Spain to try and encourage Hasdrubal's Numidian troops to desert. In return, the Romans promised rich rewards from the Senate in the event of victory. It seems that a number of the Numidians were induced to desert, but in Africa Syphax was not able to give much effective help. As soon as his attacks became dangerous, the Carthaginians instigated Masinissa, the young prince of the Massylii, who lived to the east of Masaesylii, to attack Syphax. This he did with great vigour and success, at first in conjunction with the Carthaginians who had withdrawn forces from Spain, and then with his own tribal levies, leaving the Carthaginians free to deploy their troops elsewhere. The alliance with Syphax had little effect on the outcome of the war in Spain, but it brought the Romans, and in particular the Scipios, into Numidian power-politics for the first time.

It was about this time too that the Celtiberian mercenaries who had been serving under Hasdrubal agreed to switch their allegiance to the Romans for the same terms of pay. This, as Livy pointed out (XXIV, 49.8) was the first occasion that the Romans had employed mercenaries. As would soon be shown, it was not a happy experiment.

For two years there was little activity in Spain, while the Romans consolidated their position after their advance. It seems that during this period Hasdrubal himself, and certainly part of his army, had to be withdrawn to Numidia to combat the attacks launched by Syphax and his newly-trained army, who had defeated the Carthaginians in a pitched battle (Livy XXIV, 48.12). With the help of Masinissa, Hasdrubal crushed Syphax, and was able to return to Spain with reinforcements. Masinissa carried on the war by himself, and after inflicting further defeats on Syphax in Morocco forced him to make peace with Carthage. Now that the war was ended in North Africa, Masinissa was able to join Hasdrubal in Spain with a very large force of Numidian cavalry. At about the same time, it seems, Hasdrubal, son of Gisgo, was sent to Spain to join Hasdrubal and Mago, to counterbalance the influence of the two Barcids. This probably happened at the end of 212, so that when the Scipios made their plans during the winter of 212–211 they did not fully realize the extent to which the enemy had been reinforced.

The aim of the Scipios was to seek out and destroy the enemy's forces in Spain. If they succeeded, there is little doubt that they intended to cross to Africa, and, using Syphax's kingdom as their base, threaten Carthage itself. It is likely that they did not know that Syphax had been forced to make peace. The carrying out of their plans inevitably involved the division of their forces, in order to make simultaneous attacks on the two Carthaginian armies, one of which, under Hasdrubal, was somewhere near Nova Carthago, and the other, made up of the combined forces of Mago and Hasdrubal Gisgo, was in the valley of the upper Baetis, near Castulo. Had the Romans kept their forces together and crushed Hasdrubal, who was the nearer, they were afraid that Mago and Hasdrubal Gisgo would withdraw into the interior and prolong the war indefinitely. It was only by engaging the two enemy armies both at once that they had any hope of ending the war in Spain in that campaign. In the event, the decision to divide the Roman forces proved a disastrous one, but at the time when it was taken it was logical, for it was necessary to ease the pressure of war in Italy and Sicily.

It was decided that Publius should take two-thirds of the army against Mago and Hasdrubal Gisgo, while Gnaeus was to attack Hasdrubal Barca with a force consisting of the remaining third of the Roman army combined with a very powerful force of 20,000 Celtiberian mercenaries, who had joined them that winter. The Romans advanced with their forces still united as far as a town called Amtorgis, the site of which is unknown but which probably lay on the headwaters of the Segura. Then Gnaeus halted and encamped opposite Hasdrubal Barca, with their forces separated by a stream, while Publius continued on towards his destination, probably striking across towards the upper Baetis. Gnaeus had a force powerful enough to crush Hasdrubal with little difficulty, but Hasdrubal possessed an asset that gave him a decisive advantage—many years' experience of dealing with both Spaniards and mercenaries. He secretly sent some of his Spanish troops into Scipio's camp and bought over the Celtiberian mercenaries, promising them more than they would get from the Romans merely to desert Scipio and leave him at his mercy. This was a grim lesson to the Romans on the use of mercenaries. Scipio was trapped. His

Roman troops were not numerous enough to stop the Celtiberians going, he was now hopelessly outnumbered by the enemy, and it seems that, by crossing the stream, Hasdrubal had cut him off from all chance of rejoining his brother. So he had no alternative but to move back down the Segura, keeping to the higher ground.

By now Publius, too, had run into difficulties. As he entered the valley of the Baetis, not far from Castulo, he met the Numidian prince Masinissa with a very large force of cavalry. The Numidians, when well led, were the most effective light cavalry of that time, and Masinissa was one of the most skilful cavalry commanders of the ancient world. He kept harassing Scipio's advance with constant attacks, and when the Romans camped he not only prevented them from leaving the camp to forage or get wood, but kept charging the Roman outposts and keeping them in a continuous state of alarm. Scipio knew that Hasdrubal and Mago were not far away, and he now learnt that another enemy force was approaching, 7,500 Spanish tribesmen under Indibilis, the prince of the Ilergetes, who had been deposed by the Romans for his pro-Carthaginian sympathies. Scipio formed a bold plan, to slip out of camp with part of his forces during the night, when he could avoid interference by the Numidians, and meet and crush Indibilis before he could join up with his allies. The scheme nearly succeeded. Scipio intercepted Indibilis, and soon got the upper hand, but before the battle could be decided Masinissa and his Numidians were upon him, and as he rallied his men to drive off the Numidians, who were now swarming round his flanks, Mago and Hasdrubal fell upon his rear. Scipio, wounded in the side by a spear, was left for dead on the battlefield, and his men broke and fled. Many of them got back to Scipio's camp, which had been left under the command of the legate, Tiberius Fonteius.

Gnaeus realized that his brother's army had been destroyed when he saw that Hasdrubal's army, which was following in close pursuit, had now been joined by Mago, Hasdrubal Gisgo and Masinissa. He knew that his only hope lay in retreat, so the next night he broke camp while it was still dark and managed to get a long way ahead. But the Numidians caught up with him before nightfall and forced him to halt, as it had become impossible to advance under their attacks. At last Scipio got his men moving again, and they went slowly forward, trying desperately to keep ahead of the enemy's main body. When night fell, Scipio halted near the village of Lorqui, drew his troops up on to a little hill, and for a time his infantry, forming a square, was able to keep the Numidians at bay. But the countryside was bleak and desolate, utterly devoid of vegetation, so that there was no wood that could be cut to make a palisade, while the ground was like flint and it was quite impossible to use entrenching tools. In desperation, the Romans piled up a sort of rampart out of their pack-animals and baggage. Behind this, when the Carthaginians arrived, they fought for a very short time. Gnaeus was killed, either in the first attack on the hill or trapped and burnt to death in a watch-tower near by. The Romans were overwhelmed, and scattered in flight, but most of them reached the forests and got across country to join Fonteius, who was making his way over the hills towards Saguntum.

The Scipios were dead and Roman power in central Spain destroyed, but the Carthaginians had been unable to follow up their success, and about half of the two defeated armies got back to the Ebro. Here they concentrated the various Roman garrisons from Saguntum and other places south of the river, and altogether could muster some 15,000 men, enough to beat back the Carthaginians when they tried to force their way up the coast road to the Pyrenees. In spite of the presence of the legate Fonteius, supreme command was conferred, by the vote of the soldiers, on a young man of equestrian rank, L. Marcius, who had been on Gnaeus Scipio's personal staff. This choice was subsequently declared invalid by the Senate. The details of the victories of Marcius are clearly fictitious, as is the story of how C. Claudius Nero, who was sent almost at once to succeed him, trapped Hasdrubal Barca in a pass south of the Ebro but was tricked into letting him go. It seems that until the arrival of young Scipio in the following year with reinforcements—Nero probably brought very few troops with him—the Romans were just able to maintain their hold on the vital coastal strip north of the Ebro. What saved the position for Rome was undoubtedly the friction between the three Carthaginian commanders, in particular between Hasdrubal Gisgo and the two Barcids. It was this that prevented the Carthaginians making the united thrust that would have swept the Romans aside and opened the way to

the Pyrenees and to Italy. It is possible that there was an un-
resolved dispute on the fundamental strategic problem of
whether to send Hasdrubal on to Italy as a first priority or
whether to make their primary objective the destruction of the
remaining Roman forces. What was more, although Indibilis
had been restored to his rule over the Ilergetes, and could have
posed a very dangerous threat to the Romans, his loyalty to
Carthage was destroyed when Hasdrubal Gisgo demanded a
large sum of money from him, either as a war-contribution or,
more likely, as a personal bribe, and, when he refused, seized his
daughters as hostages.

The war now enters a new stage with the appointment of the
young Publius Scipio, son of the Publius who had recently been
defeated and killed, to the supreme command in Spain. He was
at this time, in 210 B.C. about twenty-five years old. He had first
gained prominence by taking part in the rescue of his father,
when he was wounded at the battle of the River Ticinus in 218
(see p. 48). In 216, after the disaster at Cannae (see p. 67) he had
been given command, jointly with Appius Claudius, of those
survivors from the battle who escaped to Canusium, and though
the credit for rallying what was left of the Roman army must
properly belong to Varro, there is no doubt that Scipio, then a
military tribune, played an important and responsible part. In
213, in spite of criticism of his extreme youth made by hostile
tribunes, he was elected *curule aedile*. The story told by Polybius
that he put himself forward as a candidate in order to help his
elder brother Lucius, and that they were both elected together,
cannot be wholly true, as his colleague is known to have been
M. Cornelius Cethegus. It is possible that, knowing Lucius (who
seems to have been a degenerate, as his later career shows) had
very little chance, he put himself forward as a candidate in an
attempt to maintain the political influence of his family. The
story told by Livy of his election to the Spanish command is also
highly suspect. The truth seems to be that the group of families
that were connected with the Scipios and supported them in
politics now made a vigorous effort to get Claudius Nero, a
member of a rival group, superseded by one of their own
number, and succeeded in getting the decision transferred to the
Popular Assembly, where they had more influence. Scipio,
though very young, was their best candidate. He had a good

military reputation and was now in line for the praetorship—
Cethegus, his colleague as aedile, was already praetor. To anyone who might protest that he was not old enough to hold a
supreme command, the answer could be given that Spain had
proved a good field for young commanders—for Hannibal had
not been much older when he won his first victories there. But
the real reason for Scipio's appointment was political. Certain
families or groups of families were associated with certain
theatres of war, Marcellus and Otacilius, his half-brother, with
Sicily, for example, the Sulpicii with Greece, and the Scipios
with Spain. Now that the Scipios had a possible candidate available they were in a position to re-assert their claim.

Scipio's real character is hard for us to discern, and it seems
to have baffled his contemporaries. The traditional portraits are
of a charlatan, who deliberately played on people's superstitious
beliefs to increase his own influence over them—this is the
rationalist Polybian view, derived from Scipio's friend Laelius—
or the national Roman interpretation that he always enjoyed the
favour of Fortune. It is likely that he was a genuine mystic,
though not above using his mysticism to impress others. But
some things are certain. He had intellectual gifts that placed him
high above other men of his age. He had a natural courtesy, a
genuine culture, and a real sympathy for people of other races.
That he stood so clearly apart from the ordinary Roman nobles
is the reason why he excited so much jealousy among them. As a
soldier his greatness is undisputed. He was one of the greatest
creative thinkers in the field of warfare, and the tactics that he
developed made the Roman army supreme for many centuries.
He was also an outstanding field commander with a wonderful
sense of timing, and could carry out complicated manoeuvres
with success in the face of the enemy.

The new pro-consul arrived in Spain at the end of 210, with
11,000 reinforcements and an experienced soldier, M. Junius
Silanus, as his chief-of-staff. He landed at Emporiae, and at once
went down to Tarraco (Tarragona) where he met the representatives of the Spanish tribes and made a very good impression by
his courtesy and quiet confidence. He then went on to visit the
Roman troops in their winter quarters, where he did a lot to
raise morale by praising the men for the successful resistance to
the Carthaginians and congratulating Marcius for holding the

line of the Ebro. It seems that his arrival filled his troops with a
new spirit, something that is a mark of a truly great commander,
whether it be a Scipio, a Cromwell, or a Montgomery.

Scipio had given careful study to the strategic problems of his
new command even before he left Rome. He realized that the
division of the Roman forces, though its motive had been to
hasten the end of the war, had been a fundamental mistake. He
saw the difficulty of having to deal with the different Carthaginian armies piecemeal, but he thought he could see a completely different answer to the problem—the capture of the
enemy base. Nova Carthago, the Carthaginian capital, was
situated on the south-east of Spain, convenient for the voyage to
Africa. It had an excellent harbour, far better than any other
town on the coast; it controlled the rich silver-mines of the
neighbouring country; it contained vast stores of money and
materials, as well as the hostages recently taken from the
Spanish tribes; and the garrison was only one thousand strong.
The city itself had strong natural defences, being built on a hilly
peninsula with the sea to the south and west and a lagoon to the
north. But, as Scipio found out during the winter at Tarraco,
the lagoon could be forded and he was able to get guides who
knew the shallows. There was also the possibility that, with a
north or north-east wind blowing, the level of the water would
drop by a foot or eighteen inches. The vital question was the
position of the three Carthaginian armies. During the winter
Mago was somewhere near the Straits of Gibraltar, Hasdrubal
Gisgo was on the west coast, around the mouth of the Tagus,
while Hasdrubal Barca was in central Spain, besieging a city of
the Carpetani. He would be the nearest to Nova Carthago, but
even so he was a good ten days' march away, and by himself he
could do nothing until joined by one of his colleagues. Scipio
knew that there was bad blood between the three Carthaginians,
and they were not likely to react with the prompt co-operation
that was the one thing that would be fatal to his scheme. In any
case, they were out of touch with him, and he would have
reached Nova Carthago almost before they knew that he had
moved at all. The one question that remained to be answered
was whether the Carthaginians would maintain their dispositions during the spring. If, as seemed likely, these dispositions
had been adopted to prevent a widespread revolt of the Spanish

tribes, there was every reason to hope that they would.

Scipio crossed the Ebro at the beginning of spring with nearly 30,000 men, leaving a force of 3,500 under Silanus to guard the river-crossing. He had sent off his close friend and companion, C. Laelius, with the fleet of thirty-five ships arranging that they should both arrive at Nova Carthago on the same day. Laelius was the only man to know their real objective—Scipio's security was always excellent. On reaching Nova Carthago he encamped on the isthmus to the east of the town, on a ridge of hills that offered good natural defences. He entrenched his camp on the outward side, but left it unfortified towards the town, with his flanks protected by the sea and the lagoon.

The next day the assault began. The fleet sailed close in under the walls on the harbour-side, to pour a hail of missiles in upon the defenders, while Scipio drew up his men outside the camp on the isthmus, ready to attack. At this moment the Carthaginian commander, Mago, rashly made a sortie. Scipio drew his men on towards the Roman camp and by prolonging the fighting encouraged Mago to commit more and more reinforcements. Eventually the Carthaginians were driven back into the town after suffering heavy losses that they could ill afford. The Romans nearly forced their way in through the gate on the heels of the fugitives, and in the confusion had little difficulty in fixing their scaling-ladders up against the walls. But the height of the walls made it difficult to take the town by escalade, for the ladders had to be so long that they often broke under the weight of the men on them; some of the climbers suffered from vertigo as they neared the top; while often a skilfully-directed baulk of timber would put paid to a whole ladder-full of men. The attack was pressed home for several hours, but as evening drew near Scipio ordered a retreat.

The defenders were cheered by their success, but their relief was not to last long. Only a small part of the Roman force had been engaged, and now Scipio threw in another wave of attackers. The garrison fought back as best they could, but they were now dispirited and discouraged—Scipio's temporary withdrawal had been a good psychological move—they had lost a lot of men, and they were running short of missiles. It was now that Scipio sent orders to a wading-party of five hundred men that he had stationed, with ladders, at the edge of the lagoon, to force their way through the water and make an escalade on the side of the lagoon, where the walls were less well fortified and at the moment, as the attention of the garrison was concentrated on the main attack, were undefended. At this very time, too, the north wind that Scipio had hoped for began to blow and lowered the level of the water in the lagoon, so that it was never more than waist-deep, and in some places knee-deep. As a result this new attack was mounted too quickly for Mago to have any time to send troops to repel it. The Romans scaled the walls unopposed. They swept along the battlements, brushing aside all attempts to stop them. They cleared a space round the gate, hacked through the bolts, and let the attackers in, while the main escalading force were now able to get a footing on the walls. Mago withdrew to the citadel, and the town itself was given up to a holocaust of slaughter, in which the victorious soldiers put to the sword every living creature that they met. To save life, and realizing that further resistance was hopeless, Mago surrendered, and the killing stopped.

Scipio gained a rich haul at Nova Carthago. Apart from the normal plunder that was divided up amongst the soldiers, he found six thousand talents of money in the public treasury, which he added to his war-chest. There were more than three hundred Spanish hostages, including the daughters of Indibilis, prince of the Ilergetes, and the wife of Mandonius, his brother. There was a vast supply of metal, food, and munitions of every kind. There were also numerous slaves. Two thousand of these, skilled craftsmen, he set to work, under Roman overseers, to construct weapons and armour. Of the rest, he enrolled the strongest to serve on his fleet, so that he was able to man the eighteen enemy ships that he captured in the harbour, and double the size of all the crews. During the next few months he employed his men in continual tactical exercises and weapon-training. It was his intention to replace the old Roman type of sword, suited mainly for thrusting, by the Spanish sword, which could be used equally well for thrusting and cutting. At the same time he wanted to move away from the old-established type of tactics, based on a frontal attack made in mass formation, to something more flexible, in which the various parts of the legion could be used independently. He also gave the fleet intensive training. Then at the end of the summer, leaving an adequate garrison in Nova Carthago, he marched back to winter quarters in Tarraco. By now Saguntum must have been recovered, if it was ever recaptured by the Carthaginians, as well as the other towns that lay between Saguntum and the Ebro. The whole of the east coast of Spain was now in Scipio's control.

The capture of Nova Carthago and the recovery of the hostages had an electrifying effect on the Spaniards. The first to leap on the Roman band-waggon was Edeco, prince of the Edetani, who lived just south of the Ebro. But the most important people affected were the leaders of the Ilergetes, Indibilis and Mandonius, who with their tribal levies were serving in Hasdrubal Barca's army. They deserted the Carthaginians in a body, and took up a position on an easily defensible hill, so as to be safe from reprisals. They at once entered into correspondence with Scipio, and when he crossed the Ebro and moved south they marched across the hills and joined him. Scipio handed over their hostages to them—as he had done with the other tribes that had joined him—and concluded a treaty of alliance with them, by which they agreed to serve under his command. It is significant that Mandonius and Indibilis fell at Scipio's feet and addressed him as king. Their loyalty was to him, not to Rome.

Hasdrubal now was in a desperate position, as all the Spaniards were deserting him. He decided to give battle once more. If victorious, he would review the situation at his leisure and either restore the position in Spain or make for Italy. If defeated, he would collect what troops he could, cut his losses in Spain, and try and join Hannibal. Accordingly he moved down into the valley of the Baetis and took up a strong position on hilly ground near Baecula (the modern Bailen), not far from Castulo and the silver mines.

Scipio had laid up his fleet during the winter and drafted nearly 4,000 sailors and marines into his land forces. He had been joined by numerous Spaniards as he marched south, and now must have had nearly 35,000 men against Hasdrubals' 25,000. But Hasdrubal was encamped on top of a plateau, with his rear protected by a river, the approaches on each flank difficult and rugged, while to his front the ground dropped in steep terraces from a ridge to the plain below. His intention was to lure Scipio into delivering his frontal attack on this strong position, so that his own lesser numbers would be made up for by the favourable nature of the ground.

Scipio waited for two days. He was afraid that if he put off the attack any longer he might be caught in a trap by the arrival of Hasdrubal Gisgo and Mago. He may, too, have been running short of water. He sent two cohorts to watch the entrances to the Baetis valley, at the point where the road and the river pass through the mountains, to give early warning of the approach of reinforcements. Then he sent his light-armed troops, supported by a picked body of heavy infantry, up the slope in front of Hasdrubal's position. The ridge at the top and the terrace below were guarded by light-armed troops and Numidian cavalry. The Romans fought their way up the terraces and got a footing on the ridge at the top. Rather than sacrifice the advantage of his position, Hasdrubal hurriedly led his army out of camp and started to draw it up to defend the ridge, expecting the light-armed men to be followed up closely by a frontal attack from Scipio's main body. But Scipio had divided his main force into two, under himself and Laelius, and they had led their troops round on each side and were advancing up the rugged slopes at the sides of the plateau. Hasdrubal, while still in the process of getting his men into line to meet a frontal attack, found himself attacked on both flanks. He realized that his position was now untenable, and at once extricated himself with as many men as he could—probably nearly 15,000 men—and made for the Pyrenees. He crossed the pass at the western end without meeting any opposition, spent the winter of 208–207 in Gaul, and in the spring of 207 crossed the Alps without any difficulty, probably by one of the more southerly passes leading out of the valley of the Durance.

Scipio took 12,000 prisoners. Most of them were probably Spaniards from the locality, who surrendered readily. These he sent back to their own homes. The Africans he sold as slaves, apart from one young Numidian who turned out to be Masinissa's nephew. Scipio sent him back to his uncle with rich gifts.

Hasdrubal Gisgo and Mago held a council of war after they heard of the battle. It was decided that Hasdrubal should take over Mago's army and keep to the west and south-west parts of Spain, where the tribes were still loyal, avoiding any conflict with the Romans. Meanwhile Mago would take a large sum of money and cross over to the Balearic Islands to raise recruits. The only offensive action was to be left to Masinissa, who was given a force of 3,000 cavalry with orders to harry the Romans and their allies in eastern Spain.

Scipio encamped on Hasdrubal's old position and waited there for part of the summer, hoping he could lure Mago and Hasdrubal Gisgo to attack him. He had prudently sent off detachments of his troops to watch Hasdrubal Barca and see that he crossed the Pyrenees. He did not want him turning back without warning and joining with his two colleagues in a concerted attack. But the summer passed without incident, and eventually Scipio led his men back to winter quarters at Tarraco. He has at times been blamed for allowing Hasdrubal to get away from Spain. But Scipio saw his main task as the destruction of Carthaginian power in Spain, and the denial of the country to Carthage as an effective base. To achieve this, he had to adopt an offensive strategy. Had he remained purely on the defensive and been content to hold the line of the Ebro, his position would have been weaker, and the enemy would have been able to develop their strength and possibly force his positions. As it was, it was a battered remnant of his original forces that Hasdrubal took out of Spain, and Scipio was probably confident that the Romans, now that Capua and Syracuse had been recaptured, would have little difficulty in dealing with him (see pp. 82–6).

The last two years of the war in Spain saw the gradual grinding down of Carthaginian military strength, in spite of all the efforts made to restore it. New reinforcements were sent, under Hanno, and he and Mago, who had returned from the Balearics, went to raise fresh troops among the Celtiberians, in the very centre of the country. They had mustered a force of about 9,000, including 4,000 heavy-armed men, when Silanus, despatched by Scipio with a flying column of 10,000 men, made a surprise attack on them. After a short, sharp battle in rough country he destroyed or dispersed the new recruits, and captured Hanno, though Mago, with his cavalry and about 2,000 of the Carthaginians troops, made his escape to Gades, where he and Hasdrubal now had their base. They now gave up all hope of meeting the Romans in the field, and determined to retain their hold on southern Spain by dividing up their forces and stationing garrisons in various fortified towns. This policy would impose on Scipio the long and wearisome task of reducing a series of fortresses one by one. Wisely, he refused to accept the challenge, but made a gesture by sending his brother Lucius, with 11,000 men, to attack Orongis, which, thanks to fertile territory and silver mines, was the richest town in that area. Its exact site is unknown, but it probably lay somewhere near the headwaters of the Baetis. Lucius at first attacked with too small a force, and was beaten back. He then attacked in greater strength, and made such headway that the local inhabitants left the Carthaginian garrison to its fate, flung open one of the gates, and rushed out in a body to surrender. Lucius, however, not realizing their intention, cut them down, and the Romans burst in through the empty gate. The town now surrendered and the lives of the survivors were spared. This was the end of campaigning for 207, though events show that Scipio spent much of the year giving his men intensive training.

At the beginning of 206 Hasdrubal Gisgo knew that hopes of success in Spain rested on himself and Mago alone. Now that Hasdrubal Barca was dead (see p. 86) there was no prospect of the pressure of war in Italy compelling the Romans to recall Scipio or reduce his forces. There was now no point in continuing the policy of attrition adopted in the previous year. The only chance of success was to defeat Scipio in a pitched battle. So he concentrated all his forces and with an army of about 50,000 infantry, 4,000 cavalry, and 32 elephants he took up his position on the edge of the plain at the foot of a range of hills. The site of his position has been disputed, because the names in the ancient authorities vary, Polybius giving 'Elinga', Livy 'Silpia' and Appian 'Carmona'. It is generally identified with the town of Ilipa, near Alcala del Rio in the valley of the lower Baetis, not far from Seville. This is supported by Appian's 'Carmona', which is in this neighbourhood, and also by the fact that subsequent events show that the battle must have taken place within reach of the sea.

Scipio prepared at once to meet the challenge, and moved down the Baetis valley with a force of 45,000 infantry and 3,000 cavalry. Of this total, just over 15,000 would have been Spanish. He was therefore faced with the daunting prospect of fighting a decisive battle not only with inferior numbers, but with an army of which one-third was composed of allies whom he could not really trust. For Scipio remembered the treachery of their Spanish auxiliaries to his father and his uncle, and held that the Spaniards felt no real loyalty towards the Romans. In this belief he was proved completely justified by his later experiences with the Ilergetes.

The solution to this problem was one of sheer military genius. Scipio evolved a plan by which he used his weakest troops, the Spaniards, to pin down the strength of the enemy line without coming into action, while he used his best troops to destroy the weaker sections of the enemy's army and leave himself in a position of immense tactical superiority that he could then exploit against the hard core of the enemy.

The fighting began with an attack by Mago and Masinissa and their cavalry on the Romans as they were encamping. Scipio had posted the Roman cavalry in reserve, hidden behind the neighbouring hills, and their surprise counter-attack beat off the Carthaginians. Then for the next few days the two armies drew up opposite each other on the plain, and there was skirmishing carried on by the light-armed and cavalry of both sides between the two lines. Both armies were drawn up in the conventional pattern, with the best troops, the Romans and the Africans respectively, forming the centre, and the Spanish allies out on the wings. But on the evening before the day he had chosen for the battle Scipio ordered his men to take their breakfast early and march out of camp as soon as it was light, with the Spaniards forming the centre and the Romans on the wings.

Hasdrubal was taken by surprise. The two armies had developed a routine of waiting in camp till late in the day. Now, with the Roman army marching out at daybreak and the cavalry and light-armed men coming right up to the walls of his camp, he at once ordered his men out and drew them up in the plain below the foothills before they had had time to get their breakfast. Having set the stage, Scipio deliberately waited for some hours to allow growing hunger and the midday heat to take their toll of the enemy's resistance. At last, a little before midday, he withdrew his cavalry and light-armed men, stationed them behind his wings, and began to advance. At first the Romans went forward in line. Then, when they were about a quarter of a mile from the enemy, Scipio ordered his centre, composed of Spanish troops, to move on forward at a slow but steady pace, and his right and left wings, where the Romans and Latins had been placed, to turn right and left in column and to move outwards parallel with the enemy, keeping up a very quick rate of march. When they were opposite the ends of the enemy's wings, they then wheeled left and right. Scipio's wings were now advancing towards the enemy in two double columns, with the infantry forming the inside of the columns and the cavalry and light-armed outside. Scipio himself was in command of the right wing, and Marcius and Silanus the left. The final stage of this manoeuvre, which must have been less complicated to perform than historians find it to describe, came when the Romans were within range of the enemy. Then, on the right wing the infantry fanned out to the left, so as to come into line facing the enemy left wing, while the light-armed and the cavalry fanned out to the right, so that they were in line in a position where they could outflank and encircle the end of the enemy line of battle. A converse movement took place on the Roman left wing, while the Spaniards in the centre held back from making contact with the Carthaginian centre. No doubt it had been Scipio's purpose that his light-armed men should attack the elephants while his cavalry should deal with the enemy cavalry, having every confidence that in a pitched battle the heavier Roman cavalry would have the advantage. But it seems that the light-armed men immediately caused such havoc with the elephants, getting in amongst them and attacking them from behind, that they were driven back on their own cavalry and put them out of action. At any rate Hasdrubal's cavalry are not mentioned as playing any part in the battle. Meanwhile Scipio's best troops were pounding Hasdrubal's weakest, who were now also being encircled by the victorious light-armed troops and cavalry, and the Carthaginian wings soon began to crumble. While this was going on, Hasdrubal's centre, where his best troops, the Africans, were, had to remain inactive, for the enemy centre facing them refused to make contact, and Hasdrubal dared not make any move to help his wings in case he invited a flank attack from the Spaniards. By now, too, the effect of the lack of food and the exhaustion caused by standing in the heat—it was an oppressive, sultry day—began to be felt. Seeing his wings being destroyed, Hasdrubal began to withdraw, hoping to retire in good order across the foothills to their camp. But the retreat soon became a rout, and though they reached their camp they would not have been able to defend it had not a torrential storm forced the Romans to break off the battle.

Scipio's victory was the result of careful planning, perfect timing, and the training of his troops to such a degree of skill that they could carry out a complicated manoeuvre in the face of the enemy. It involved an early appreciation of the fact that it was safer to station his Spanish troops, whose loyalty was suspect, in front of Hasdrubal's Africans rather than in front of their fellow Spaniards, who might tempt them to desert. The whole plan was based on Scipio's ability to seize the initiative at the very start and maintain it throughout the battle. This, in its turn, depended on a correct appraisal of the character and temperament of the opposing general. Scipio decided, and his subsequent encounters with him proved this opinion correct, that Hasdrubal was a commander who always thought in defensive terms and was always slow to take the initiative. As a result of this judgment, he had every confidence that Hasdrubal would not do the one thing that might have endangered Scipio's position: make a resolute charge against Scipio's isolated centre. While Hasdrubal waited, his wings disintegrated before his eyes and the situation passed out of his control.

During the night the Carthaginians prepared to defend their camp, but the Spanish troops began to desert, and news came that two of the towns in the locality had surrendered to Scipio. So under cover of darkness Hasdrubal extricated what was left of his army and got a good start. Next morning Scipio set off in pursuit. He tried to cut Hasdrubal off from the crossing of the Baetis, but the Carthaginians headed in a different direction and made for the west. The Romans caught up with them at last and killed or captured a large number, but Hasdrubal and Mago got about six thousand men into a strong position on top of some hills with access to the sea. Ships were brought up from Gades, and Hasdrubal was evacuated with part of his army. At this point Scipio realized that there was little he could do, and returned to Nova Carthago, leaving Silanus with ten thousand men to mop up. When the ships came back from Gades, Mago got off most of the troops that were left. The remainder either deserted or dispersed to their own homes. During this short siege Masinissa decided to change sides. By now he heard that his father, Gala, was dead, and that the chieftainship of his tribe had been usurped by a rival branch of the family, with the assistance of Syphax who had now made a treaty with Carthage. After meeting Silanus and promising his support, Masinissa crossed to Africa and plunged into the stormy whirlpools of Numidian inter-tribal politics. The meeting with Scipio, which Livy records later in the year, is almost certainly a dramatic fiction.

Having gained control of Spain Scipio now began his plans for carrying the war into Africa. His hopes were fixed on the Numidian princes. Masinissa had recently promised him his support, and had now gone to Africa to re-establish his control over his people. Syphax was now an ally of Carthage, but Scipio thought that dictates of expediency could easily win him back to his former alliance with Rome. Then an invasion in force from Sicily could be supported by the tribal levies of the two Numidian kings, possibly strengthened by Roman troops from Spain. With this end in view Scipio sent Laelius to Syphax with an invitation to re-establish his old friendly relations with Rome. It is interesting to note that when any task of difficulty or importance was involved, Scipio employed Laelius and not his brother Lucius.

Laelius was successful in his mission, but Syphax insisted that the agreement could only be ratified by Scipio in person. So Scipio crossed to Africa with two quinqueremes. In the harbour of Siga he found Hasdrubal Gisgo (also coming to woo Syphax), with seven triremes on the point of disembarking. Hasdrubal tried to get his ships out to sea to intercept Scipio, but a favourable wind carried the Roman ships into the royal harbour, where Hasdrubal dared not touch them. Scipio's courtesy and personal charm made a great impression on both Syphax and Hasdrubal. It was fortunate that the diplomatic conventions of those days did not prevent opposing enemy leaders sitting down to dinner at the same table. Scipio concluded his treaty with Syphax and returned to Spain. Hasdrubal took his diplomatic defeat with good grace—since he still had his trump cards to play. Scipio had to deal with a mutiny among Roman troops stationed on the Sucro River on his lines of communications with Tarraco (Tarragona) and suppress a revolt in northern Spain led by the princes of the Ilergetes, Mandonius and Indibilis, who resented the fact that the Roman victory did not give them sovereignty over all the other tribes in the Ebro valley. There were now two main tasks that remained for Scipio before he could return to Rome. One was the crushing of certain local centres of resistance and the paying off of old scores. One town, Ilorci, now the village of Lorqui, had been allied to Rome, but had treacherously put to death some of the survivors of Gnaeus Scipio's army after the disaster. No quarter was expected or given. Attacked on both sides by Scipio and Laelius, the town was stormed after a desperate resistance. Men, women and children were put to the sword. The buildings were set on fire, and what would not burn was razed to the ground. A second town, Castax, the locality of which is unknown, surrendered on terms. Two other places surrendered to Marcius, but the town of Astape (now Estopa), near Urso, which had always been fanatically loyal, held out to the bitter end. The defenders made a sally and were surrounded and wiped out. Then a group of warriors left in the town immolated the women and children, threw their bodies on a pyre, lit it and flung themselves upon it. The base of the pyre was composed of all the gold, silver and precious things in the town, and many of the Romans, as they burst in, got badly burned attempting desperate acts of salvage.

The other task was the reduction of Gades, where Mago was now in command. A party inside the town who were plotting to betray it had already got in touch with the Romans. Marcius was sent with a column of troops in light marching order to be on the spot when the *coup d'état* took place, while Laelius was despatched with a small squadron to provide naval co-operation. Somewhere on the Baetis Marcius ran into a recruiting party under Hanno, with four thousand Celtiberians they had just enrolled. The Romans stormed the enemy camp and broke up Hanno's force, Hanno himself escaping with a handful of his original troops. But shortly after this Marcius had a message from Laelius that made him decide to call off the expedition. Laelius had reached Carteia, just inside the Straits of Gibraltar, when he heard that the conspiracy inside Gades had been detected and the ringleaders shipped off to Carthage. He was almost successful in intercepting the ship that was carrying them, and did in fact sink two of the escorting vessels. So Laelius and Marcius returned to Nova Carthago.

When Mago heard of the mutiny among the Roman troops (see p. 116) and the revolt among the Ilergetes he sent despatches to Carthage and urged the government there to let him have reinforcements with which he could take advantage of this favourable opportunity and recover Spain for the Carthaginians. But nothing was done, and the chance was lost. It is clear that at this time there was a high-level policy debate at Carthage, and in the end it was decided to cut their losses in Spain and make a last effort to win success in Italy. Mago was ordered to embark what troops he had, sail to Italy, enrol as many Gauls and Ligurians as possible, and try to join Hannibal. Funds were sent him from Carthage to finance these operations, and he was to raise further money from Gades.

Before he left Spain Mago made one final desperate effort. He sailed round to Nova Carthago, and tried to take it by surprise. Beaten back, he returned to Gades, and found the gates of the town closed against him. His last attempt to raise money, which had involved stripping the temples as well as emptying the treasury, had been too much for the spirit of the townspeople. Mago enticed the leading magistrates into his camp, on the pretext of hearing their justification, seized them and crucified them. Then he sailed to Pityusa (now Alboran), an island about a hundred miles from the continent, took on supplies and some fresh troops, and headed for the Balearics. He was driven off from Majorca, but was able to land in Minorca and spent the winter there. Then in the spring of 205 he sailed to Liguria and captured and burnt Genoa (see p. 88).

After the departure of Mago Gades surrendered to the Romans. Scipio knew the war in Spain was over. He handed over command to Silanus and Marcius, pending the arrival of officially appointed successors, and sailed from Tarraco back to Italy. His claim for a triumph was refused, and he did not press it. The old quarrel between Livius Salinator, his supporter, and Claudius Nero, one of his rivals, whom he had superseded in Spain, had broken out afresh, and it is probable that Fabius Maximus was supporting Claudius. This was a combination that Scipio would have to break, but he would wait till there was a bigger prize at stake—the command of Africa.

6

Sardinia, Greece, Sicily, and the War at Sea

OPERATIONS IN SARDINIA were unimportant. In 217 the consul, Servilius Geminus, patrolled off the island with his fleet before making a raid on North Africa. But by 215 news of the Carthaginian successes had put the country in a state of unrest; the retiring praetor, Cornelius Mammula, reported that his successor, Mucius Scaevola, had fallen victim to a protracted fever, while his army was insufficient to meet the troubles that were now expected. Accordingly it was decided that an additional legion should be enrolled for service in Sardinia, and that a temporary governor should be appointed until Mucius was fully recovered. This command was given to T. Manlius Torquatus, now old, partly blind, but, as Livy says, a man of old-fashioned and, as most people thought, excessive toughness. He had been consul twice before, and once censor; many years before, in one of his consulships, he had subdued Sardinia shortly after it had been annexed by Rome. On his arrival Manlius was given a fortunate respite, for the Carthaginian fleet under Hasdrubal the Bald that had set sail for the island had been caught by a storm and wrecked in the Balearics.

The leader of the revolt was a local potentate called Hampsicora, the most wealthy and influential of the Sardinian chieftains. The trouble seems to have been caused by the excessive imposition of taxes in the previous year, needed to help pay for the war. Manlius beached his fleet at Carales (Cagliari), drafted the sailors and marines for service on land, and was able to raise a force of just over twenty thousand men. With these he penetrated into the interior and attacked Hampsicora's base. Hampsicora himself was absent on a recruiting expedition, but his son,

119

Hostus, who was in command, rashly gave battle and was completely defeated. The remnants of his army took refuge in a town called Cornus, the capital of that region, near Cape Mannu. Suddenly the news came of the arrival of the Carthaginian fleet under Hasdrubal the Bald. At this, Manlius withdrew on Carales, allowing Hasdrubal to join Hampsicora. Their combined forces advanced on Carales, ravaging the country as they went. Manlius met them not far from the town and gave battle. The Sardinians were soon routed, and the Carthaginians, after a long struggle, found themselves outflanked and surrounded by the section of the Roman line that had defeated the Sardinians. Hasdrubal and other Carthaginian nobles were captured. Hostus was killed, and his father Hampsicora committed suicide. The survivors fled to Cornus but Manlius captured the town after a few days' siege. Then he took hostages from the other Sardinian towns, imposed indemnities, and returned to Rome, leaving Mucius, now recovered, in charge. Sardinia took no further part in the war, apart from suffering an occasional raid by the Punic Fleet.

In Greece the fighting was more prolonged, and their intervention opened up for the Romans new worlds to conquer. But the Carthaginians played little or no part in the events, which can be described very briefly. Philip V, the restless, ambitious young king of Macedon, had been considerably moved by the news of Hannibal's victory at Trasimene (in 217), and at once brought to an end the war in Greece between himself and his allies, the Achaeans, and the Aetolians, so that, if the opportunity presented itself, he would have a free hand to invade Italy (Polybius, V, 101–105). After Cannae (see p. 71), Philip entered into direct negotiation with Hannibal, and they concluded a treaty for mutual help that was ratified some time in 215. The terms, which are given in detail by Polybius (VII, 9), included a stipulation that one of the conditions of peace with Rome should be that the Romans would surrender all their bases and alliances in Illyria.

It is at this point that a note of comic opera enters into the proceedings. The Macedonian envoys had landed in Bruttium and were making their way through Apulia towards Hannibal at Capua when they blundered into the Roman lines and were taken before Valerius Laevinus, the praetor, who was encamped at Luceria. Xenophanes, the leader of the envoys, was a man of quick wit, and at once declared they were a good-will mission from Macedon to Rome, sent to conclude an alliance between Philip and the Romans. Laevinus was overjoyed at such a touching act of faith. He sent the envoys on their way with precise information as to where the Roman positions were and where Hannibal was encamped. They reached Hannibal, concluded the treaty, and made their way back accompanied by three Carthaginian envoys to assure Philip of Hannibal's agreement. They reached their ship in safety, but as they put out on to the open sea they were seen and intercepted by a Roman naval patrol under Valerius Flaccus. Xenophanes tried to repeat his old story, but the Carthaginian dress of Hannibal's envoys aroused the suspicions of Flaccus, and as soon as he began to question them their speech gave the game away. The party were searched, the incriminating documents found, and they were sent under close guard to the Senate. One of the envoys somehow made his escape, and reported what had happened to Philip. The king sent another delegation to Hannibal to find out the exact terms of the agreement. They came and went without discovery, but by now so much time had been lost that before Philip could take any action the Romans had a powerful fleet under Laevinus guarding the Adriatic.

In the summer of 214 a report came to Laevinus that Philip, with a large fleet of light warships, had captured Oricum and was besieging Apollonia, presumably as a prelude to crossing over into Italy. Laevinus acted promptly. He recaptured Oricum. His subordinate, Naevius Crista, got a relieving force into Apollonia and, by a surprise night attack, captured the camp of the besiegers. Then Laevinus brought up his fleet, blocked Philip's ships in their harbour, and eventually forced the king to set fire to them and retreat by land. After this success Laevinus instigated Philip's old enemies, the Aetolians, to renew the war in Greece, with a modicum of Roman support. This kept Philip engaged until the danger from Hannibal was over.

In Sicily the first few years of the war were fairly quiet. In 218 an attack by the Carthaginian fleet on the Roman base at Lilybaeum was beaten off, and there were always threats of raids, either on the Roman province in the west of the island or on Hiero's kingdom in the east. But the Roman fleet under

121

Otacilius Crassus was made up to seventy-five ships and he was given permission to retaliate by raiding the African coast. On one occasion when he did this he ran into the fleet of Hasdrubal the Bald on its way back from Sardinia, and captured seven of Hasdrubal's ships. Old King Hiero proved a faithful ally, and after Trasimene sent to Rome a golden statue of victory as a sign of his confidence, as well as half a million bushels of grain and a thousand light-armed troops. After Cannae (see p. 70) he gave Otacilius, the governor of Sicily, all the money he needed to pay his troops and six months' supply of corn, at a time when in Rome the treasury and the granaries were empty. But at the beginning of 215 Hiero, the right hand of Rome, died, and was succeeded by his fifteen-year-old grandson Hieronymus, a degenerate. Under his rule a compact was made with Hannibal for the expulsion of the Romans from the island, and two brothers, Hippocrates and Epicydes, men of mixed Sicilian and Carthaginian stock, were sent to Syracuse as his emissaries. Hieronymus, however, was becoming more and more hated. Even the Carthaginians regarded him as untrustworthy, unreliable—and expendable. At the end of 215, when he was at Leontini, trying to persuade a number of Sicilian cities to expel their Roman garrisons, a conspiracy was formed and he was assassinated.

In the disturbances that followed, which involved the cold-blooded murder of the surviving members of Hiero's family, men, women, and children alike, the two envoys of Hannibal, Hippocrates and Epicydes, got themselves elected to the Board of Generals, and began to work up popular feeling against Rome. They were not strong enough to prevent the decision being taken to renew the old alliance with Rome, but the situation was very tense, and when the Roman fleet under the praetor Appius Claudius sailed into the Great Harbour the news was spread around that the city was being betrayed to the Romans. This alarm was quietened with difficulty, and envoys were sent to ratify the treaty, but the situation remained delicate, especially since it had been reported that a Carthaginian fleet was off Cape Pachynus.

Soon after this Hippocrates was sent with a force of four thousand mercenaries and deserters from the Roman army to protect Leontini. He was later joined by Epicydes, and they incited the people of Leontini not only to ravage Roman territory but also to defy the Syracusans when, at the request of the Romans, they ordered them to stop. As a result the Syracusans gave the Romans *carte blanche* to reduce Leontini and restore it to their control.

Because of the possible dangers of a major war breaking out in Sicily, the command in the island had been conferred on the consul M. Claudius Marcellus. Marcellus was a soldiers' general, of great professional competence, ruthless in imposing military law but devoted to the welfare of the troops who served him loyally. He had a type of courage that was born of a complete lack of imagination, and that bordered on sheer recklessness. In his first consulship, in 222, he had killed the Gallic general in battle with his own hand, and so had won the unique distinction of the *spolia opima*. In the campaign after Cannae, without ever defeating Hannibal in a full-scale pitched battle, he had succeeded in denying him points of vantage on the Campanian coast.

Marcellus stormed Leontini without much difficulty and, without considering the possible consequences of his action, flogged and beheaded two thousand of the enemy troops whom he ascertained were deserters from the Roman army, an act that was to have unfortunate repercussions. Hippocrates and Epicydes escaped, and were able to exaggerate and distort this ruthless action in such a way as to convince the Syracusans, both in the army and in the city, that the Romans had carried out a wholesale massacre at Leontini. By their skilful propaganda they discredited the moderate leaders, and gained control first of the Syracusan army and then of Syracuse itself. Roman envoys sent by Appius and Marcellus were either attacked or refused admittance. Marcellus brought up his forces from Leontini, and, in an attempt to bring back the city to the alliance with Rome, began to attack Syracuse by land and sea.

The war that followed was fought both around Syracuse itself and in the Sicilian countryside. Himilco, the Carthaginian admiral, had brought his fleet into Heraclea Minoa and landed a force of 25,000 infantry, 3,000 cavalry, and 12 elephants. Then he returned to Carthage, where, helped by letters from Hannibal and the personal exhortations of some of Hippocrates's officers whom he had brought with him, he persuaded the government to send another large force to Sicily in the hope of recovering complete control of the island. If this could be accomplished, the problem of reinforcing Hannibal would be solved. With these additional troops Himilco returned to Heraclea and within a short time had captured Agrigentum.

The assault on Syracuse was begun in a spirit of almost light-hearted confidence. The circuit of the walls was so long that the Romans had little doubt that they could soon force an entry at some point. Appius Claudius attacked from the landward side, at the district called Hexapylum, while Marcellus and the fleet aimed at capturing Achradina, at a point where the city walls came right down to the water's edge. Then began an historic struggle between the finest military engineers of the age.

Marcellus packed the decks of his warships with archers, slingers, and other light-armed men. Standing well off from the wall, they kept up a volley of missiles that cleared the defenders from the battlements. Then the assault-craft moved in, pairs of warships lashed together, like some gigantic catamaran, propelled by oars only on the outward side. These craft were designed to act as floating platforms that would carry enormous scaling ladders, four feet wide, equipped with side-rails and protective covering overhead, measured to fit the height of the wall. These ladders were raised and swung into position by ropes and pulleys suspended from the mast-head, and held in place by poles. At the top of each ladder was a platform protected to the front and sides by wicker shields, with room for four fighting-men. When these platforms were swung into position on the top of the city walls, the men would unfasten the shields under cover of the fire of missiles from out to sea and force their way onto the battlements, while the rest of their comrades swarmed up the ladders in support. These devices were given the name of 'harps', from the combination of the ropes and hawsers and the slanting ladder.

But the defences of the city had been prepared by the great Greek scientist Archimedes, backed with all the resources amassed during Hiero's reign. A series of catapults of various ranges had been built, so that the attackers, however close in to the walls they came, could always be brought under fire. The walls themselves, too, were loopholed with embrasures through which a deadly fire of short-range weapons could be directed at those of the attackers who were actually working the ladders. Beams that swung out on a pivot would drop huge stones or masses of lead that smashed the scaling-ladders and often went through the decks of the ships beneath. Finally, at various points along the walls were cranes that could be let down by operators concealed behind the battlements. They would fasten on to the prow of one of the attacking ships, then the counterpoise would be set in motion and the whole vessel would be lifted out of the water and dropped back from a height, causing it either to capsize or become waterlogged.

Baffled by these ingenious devices, Marcellus tried bringing up his ships by night, but with no better success, and the attack was called off. Marcellus made the wry comment that his 'harps', having come to the party uninvited, had been thrown out in disgrace. Appius Claudius had no better success in his attack by land, for the defences on that side were just as effective, and in many places the walls ran along overhanging cliffs. So the Romans gave up the idea of taking Syracuse by storm and settled down to a prolonged siege.

After the assault had been called off, the scene of the fighting moved to the open country. Leaving Appius with two-thirds of the army to maintain the blockade, Marcellus took the rest of his troops to try and reduce those Sicilian cities that had joined the Carthaginians. Marcellus tried to save Agrigentum, but he was too late. He withdrew towards Acrillae, and, being a thoroughly competent commander of great experience, was marching with his troops ready for action, in case he encountered Himilco, whom he thought was somewhere nearby with superior forces. As a result, when he suddenly came upon Hippocrates with ten thousand men busy pitching camp, the engagement that followed was somewhat one-sided. Hippocrates had left Epicydes with sufficient men to defend the city and had taken what was not needed to swell Himilco's field army. Marcellus surrounded and destroyed most of the infantry, though Hippocrates escaped with his cavalry to join the Carthaginian main body.

Now both sides began to send in reinforcements. The Romans landed a legion at Panormus, on the north-west corner of the island, and Himilco advanced across country with all his forces to try and cut it off. However, the Romans had chosen to march round the coast, where they could have the protection of their ships, while Appius Claudius went out with part of his army and, it seems, some of the fleet, to meet them at Pachynus and escort them back into Syracuse. Himilco, cheated of his prey, turned his efforts to spreading revolt among the Sicilian towns, and gained an immediate success at the Roman arsenal at Murgantia, where the garrison was betrayed by the townspeople. Meanwhile Bomilcar, with fifty-five ships, had sailed into the Great Harbour. Here he found himself in a dilemma. He had not enough vessels to be a match for the Roman fleet when it returned in full force while if he landed his men in the town they would only aggravate the shortage of food without making any worthwhile contribution to the defence. Accordingly he set sail and returned to Carthage. This was another example of the lack of initiative shown by so many of the Carthaginian subordinate commanders.

The example of Murgantia was followed by a number of other towns, which drove out or treacherously massacred their Roman garrisons. At Henna, however, the Roman commander was made of sterner stuff. Lucius Pinarius was a man of soldierly qualities who relied more on alertness combined with healthy suspicion to ensure the safety of his men than on any trust that might be placed in the Sicilians. He knew that the people of Henna had arranged to betray the town to Himilco. When they found they could not catch the garrison off their guard, they came openly to Pinarius and demanded that he should give up to them the keys of the town and evacuate the citadel. Pinarius refused, and referred them to Marcellus. At this an impasse developed, as the leaders of the townsfolk refused to accept any further delay, but insisted that their demands should be met at once. Eventually they agreed that Pinarius should be invited to a public meeting in the Theatre the following day so that he could be sure that their demands had the support of the people as a whole and did not merely come from a small clique.

During the night Pinarius made his plans, and next morning his men unobtrusively began to take up their positions above and around the Theatre and along all the roads leading to it. Pinarius was introduced to the assembly by the magistrates. At first there were just verbal demands that he should hand over the

126

keys of the town. Then, as he persisted in his refusal, saying that he had no authority to do so and that only Marcellus could make such a concession, the shouting grew, threats were made, and it was clear that the meeting was on the point of erupting into violence. Pinarius now gave the signal by raising the fold of his toga. His men saw it, drew their swords, and closed in. The townspeople, shut in on all sides, were massacred, and the town itself was sacked. The news of this disaster quickly spread throughout Sicily, and precipitated further revolts among the cities, though their defection could not in any case have been long delayed. Hippocrates and Himilco had been summoned to Henna by the leaders of the townsfolk, but arrived too late to save the town and withdrew to their bases at Murgantia and Agrigentum. Appius Claudius left Sicily at the end of the year to hold the consulship and die of a chest-wound at the capture of Capua. His successor, Quinctius Crispinus, later a victim of the reckless bravery of Marcellus, was put in charge of the naval camp and the blockade of Syracuse, while Marcellus himself moved into winter quarters a short distance away from the city.

When the spring came, Marcellus took stock of his position. A direct assault had failed. The blockade was ineffective; regular supplies of food were being brought into the city from Carthage, as the circumference of the walls was too long for the Romans to guard every point. Marcellus now turned to treachery, and managed to make contact with the pro-Roman party inside the city. Negotiations were tedious, as the defenders were on the watch for any possible act of treason, and the conspirators had to be conveyed in secret to the Roman camp hidden under a pile of nets on the deck of a fishing-boat. All the preparations had been made when a Syracusan noble found out about the plot, and, jealous that he had not been invited to take part, betrayed it to Epicydes. The conspirators were all arrested and tortured to death.

It was an accident that led to the capture of the city. A Spartan called Damippus, sent by Epicydes to get support from Philip of Macedon, was intercepted and captured by Roman patrol boats. Epicydes asked if he could be ransomed, and Marcellus agreed, since at that time the Romans were trying to enlist the support of the Aetolians, with whom the Spartans were allied. The negotiations for ransoming were conducted from the city walls, at a point near the tower of Galeagra, and involved repeated visits to the spot. During the conversations one of the Roman soldiers present, looking idly about him, formed the impression that, due to the configuration of the ground, the walls at that point, when seen from close to, were in fact much lower than they appeared at a distance. He checked this impression by estimating the thickness of the layers of brick and counting the number of layers. At that point, he was sure, the top of the wall could be reached by moderate-sized ladders. He reported his discovery to Marcellus, but as that part of the wall, being lower, was particularly well-guarded, nothing could be done at the moment.

It was some time later that the opportunity occurred. One of the pro-Roman sympathizers inside the city sent word to Marcellus that for the last three days there had been a festival of Artemis celebrated in the city, at which the shortage of food caused by the Roman blockade had been made up for by an abundant supply of wine. It did not take Marcellus long to put his plan into operation. A scaling party of a thousand men was detailed. At the dead of night the thin line of Romans crept up the slope. Absolute silence was maintained. They got their ladders in position without a sound and mounted the walls. The guards in the towers were by now nearly all dead-drunk. They were overcome without difficulty, not even giving the alarm. The Romans rushed on towards the Hexapylum, where they forced open a postern gate and gave the signal by trumpet from the walls for the supporting force to move in. The main gates of the Hexapylum were broken open, and the garrison of the Epipolae, the adjacent part of the city, were frightened into abandoning their posts. By daybreak Marcellus had all his forces inside the walls.

The very size of the city now helped the Romans, for the report of the breach in one quarter took a long time to spread to the other parts. Epicydes, hurrying across from the Island, was under the impression that the penetration had been merely local, and that only a small isolated party of Romans had got inside the walls. But when he saw the whole of the Epipolae was in enemy hands, he hastily withdrew to secure his positions in the Island and Achradina.

Marcellus hoped to get the rest of the city to surrender on terms, and sent some of the Syracusans who had joined his side to try and arrange a conference. But the garrison of Achradina, to whom he made the first move, were mainly deserters from the Roman armies. They remembered what had happened at Leontini, and knew they could expect no mercy. So they refused to allow the envoys to approach the walls. Marcellus then turned his attention to Euryalus, a part of the town built on a hill on the landward side, and commanding the main road into the interior. He opened negotiations with the Greek commander of the garrison, Philodemus, who deliberately played for time in case help might come from the Carthaginian forces outside.

However, when it became clear that Himilco would not be able to arrive in time, he surrendered Euryalus on condition that he was given a safe-conduct to join Epicydes in the Island. Meanwhile Marcellus had camped in the middle of the city, between the rich suburbs of Tycha and Neapolis. He now systematically plundered all the wealth in this part of Syracuse, though on his strict instructions no violence was done to any citizen. While everyone's attention was centred on the part of the city that the Romans had captured, the Carthaginian admiral, Bomilcar, who was in the harbour, slipped out with thirty-five ships and got away to Carthage. He reported the critical situation in the town, and was able to raise a fleet of one hundred warships, with which he sailed back to Syracuse a few days later.

Marcellus secured himself against a full-scale attack from the rear by garrisoning Euryalus, and now prepared to attack Achradina, hoping to reduce it by blockade. But within a few days the Romans found themselves forced onto the defensive. Himilco and Hippocrates arrived in full force, and, since the citadel of Euryalus was barred against them, they encamped near the Great Harbour. Then, at a signal given from Achradina, they launched an attack on the Roman naval camp, while simultaneously Epicydes led a sortie against Marcellus's lines. At the same time Bomilcar put his men ashore at a point between the city and the Roman naval camp, so that the Roman lines of communication were cut and Marcellus was unable to send support to Crispinus. But the Romans were capable of dealing with the attack. Crispinus drove Hippocrates off in great disorder, while Marcellus, a man who never lost a battle, crushed the sortie made from Achradina. Yet it was not the valour and skill at arms of the Romans that proved decisive, but disease. It was now autumn, and at the end of the long, hot summer pestilence broke out. It was particularly virulent among the men camped on the low ground near the Great Harbour. But Marcellus, always concerned for the welfare of his men, got most of the Romans into the city where the sick could be put indoors and properly treated. Even so, their death-roll was high. In the enemy camp, most of the Sicilians dispersed to their own homes, as soon as they saw the disease taking hold. The Carthaginians were not so fortunate. They had no place of refuge, and were wiped out almost to a man.

The Romans were still not out of the wood. Next spring (211) the Sicilians mustered a large army from all over the island and occupied two fortified towns a few miles from Syracuse. At the same time Bomilcar sailed back to Africa and persuaded the Carthaginian government that by making one more supreme effort they could take advantage of the awkward position in which Marcellus now found himself and trap the Romans inside the walls of Syracuse. He was given a convoy of seven hundred transports, loaded with supplies, and his own fleet was increased to one hundred and thirty warships. With this armada he sailed back to Sicily, but was prevented by strong east winds from rounding Cape Pachynus and had to lie off Heraclea, on the south coast, waiting for the wind to change. Epicydes became impatient, and was afraid that Bomilcar, a man who seemed to work by fits and starts, would abandon the attempt and sail back to Africa. So he handed over command at Achradina to some of his mercenary captains and sailed to join Bomilcar. The Carthaginian fleet considerably outnumbered the Romans, but Bomilcar did not want to go into battle against an enemy who had the wind dead astern. However, Epicydes persuaded him to put to sea. Marcellus, too, put to sea, for he knew it was absolutely vital to head off this fleet before it could get to Syracuse. To do this he was prepared to face any odds. So both fleets waited near Pachynus, ready to engage as soon as the force of the winds moderated. At last the wind dropped. Bomilcar stood right out to sea to round Cape Pachynus more easily. He saw the Roman fleet bearing down upon him, and lost his nerve. Sending word to the transports at Heraclea to get back to Africa, he made for the open sea, avoiding the Roman fleet, and headed for Tarentum. Epicydes, in disgust, not wanting to be trapped in Syracuse, sailed to Agrigentum to await events.

The departure of Epicydes and Bomilcar changed the situation in Syracuse. The leaders of the Sicilian army encamped outside sent envoys to Marcellus to ask for terms, and got his permission to enter Achradina so that a general surrender could be negotiated. With the help of the moderates in Achradina they assassinated the three officers whom Epicydes had left in charge, appointed new magistrates, and sent representatives of the new government to conclude terms with the Romans. But during their absence there was a counter-revolution. The Roman deserters, who formed the hard core of the garrison, won over the mercenaries, murdered the leaders of the moderates, massacred their supporters, and appointed their own commanders, three to take charge in Achradina and three in the Island. However, a reaction soon spread among the mercenaries, and they began to realize that their case and that of the deserters were entirely different. In this they were confirmed by the encouraging report brought back by the envoys, who declared that they had nothing to fear from Marcellus. One of the new commanders in Achradina was a Spaniard called Moericus. Marcellus got in touch with him through a fellow-tribesman serving with the Romans, and persuaded him to betray the town. Moericus had charge of a section of the walls that stretched from the entrance to the harbour to the Spring of Arethusa. Late at night Marcellus had a transport-ship loaded with troops towed round to the gate near the Spring of Arethusa. Moericus let them into the city. At daybreak Marcellus mounted a fierce attack on the walls of Achradina from the landward side, heavy enough to draw off the defenders in the Island into Achradina to strengthen the defences there. Almost deserted of its garrison, the Island fell to a surprise attack from the sea. When the Roman deserters in Achradina saw that Moericus had betrayed them, they broke and fled. Marcellus called off his attack, to give them a chance to escape. He wanted Syracuse undamaged.

The fighting was over, and the Syracusans opened the gates of Achradina and surrendered to the Romans. Marcellus was ruthless. He would spare the lives of the people of Syracuse, but he must seize the royal treasures and hand over the city to his soldiers to sack. Glory was not enough reward for a three years' siege. While the city was being systematically plundered, some Roman soldiers killed Archimedes. Marcellus claimed that it was an accident, and outwardly expressed deep regret, but he was not a man who spared his enemies.

Some fighting still went on for about a year, centred on Agrigentum, where, shortly after the departure of Marcellus to Italy, a Carthaginian force had been landed. This new force included three thousand Numidian cavalry, who, under their leader Muttines, roamed the island at will and ravaged the lands of the Roman allies. The praetor, S. Cornelius Cethegus, reduced a number of towns, including Murgantia, that had gone over once more to the Carthaginians, but the continual depredations of Muttines were more troublesome, and it had to be left to the successor of Marcellus to deal with them.

The amount of loot that Marcellus brought back from Syracuse aroused great resentment at Rome, and when Sicilian envoys arrived to complain of his ruthless and cold-blooded sacking of the city, he was driven to resign his command in Sicily, to which he had just been re-appointed on his election as consul for 209. His colleague, M. Valerius Laevinus, fresh from diplomatic successes in Greece, was appointed in his place. It was Laevinus who finally brought the war to an end. There had been growing jealousy between Muttines and Hanno, the Carthaginian commander in Agrigentum, who resented the prestige that the Numidian was gaining. Eventually he deposed Muttines from his command and gave it to his own son. Muttines immediately sent word in secret to Laevinus. On a night that had been arranged, the Numidians siezed the water-gate at Agrigentum, cutting down the Carthaginian guards, and admitted the Romans into the town. Hanno and Epicydes made their escape, and got away to Carthage in a small boat, but the rest of the garrison were cut down. The leaders of the pro-Carthaginian faction were executed, the rest of the inhabitants sold as slaves, and the town itself was sacked. This marked the end of the resistance. Within a short time the other Sicilian towns had either been captured, or betrayed to the Romans, or, in most cases, had made a voluntary surrender. Laevinus disarmed the Sicilians, transporting a notorious band of malcontents to Rhegium where they did good service raiding Hannibal's allies in Bruttium. Then he got agriculture going again in the island, so that there could be a surplus of Sicilian corn to help feed Rome and Italy, and the whole island was reorganized as a Roman province.

7

The War in Africa

SCIPIO SET SAIL FROM LILYBAEUM in the summer of 204
B.C. (see p. 91). He had two strong legions, mainly drawn from
the survivors of Cannae who had been condemned to ignominious service in Sicily and had played a glorious part in the
capture of Syracuse. With the normal complement of Latins and
Italians, this would have given him a total of between 20,000
and 25,000 regular infantry. The regular cavalry would probably
amount to 2,000 men. In addition, he would have several
thousand sailors and marines, making a total force up to
between 30,000 and 35,000 men. He had a calm voyage, though
somewhat troubled by fog, and made a landfall at the Pulchrum
Promunturium, also known as the Promontory of Apollo or
Cape Farina. This headland forms the western arm of the bay
in which Carthage is situated, and on the promontory itself is
the important town of Utica.

The Roman landing caused panic and alarm throughout the
neighbouring towns and villages. This was not a raid, such as
they had experienced from time to time during the course of the
war, but a full-scale invasion, the first since the invasion of
Regulus in the First Punic War, a little more than fifty years
before. To find out the size of Scipio's force and to interfere, if
possible, with his disembarkation, a column of five hundred
cavalry was sent out. These came up against Scipio's outposts
and were driven off with heavy losses. The Romans completed
their landing unopposed.

Soon after his arrival, Scipio was joined by Masinissa. The
Roman diplomatic schemes for North Africa had gone sadly
awry since Scipio left Spain. Syphax, King of the Masaesylii, had

134

soon been wooed away from his alliance with Rome by the lovely Sophoniba, daughter of Hasdrubal Gisgo, and her recent marriage with Syphax had firmly cemented his union with Carthage. Masinissa had been hounded out of his kingdom, and either, as one version maintains, was a powerless refugee in the remoter parts of North Africa, or, according to the other version, had regained his throne by the good grace of the Carthaginians and now ruled on sufferance; he was, following this account, actually serving with the Carthaginian forces at this moment. The next Roman success was brought about by Masinissa's cunning—or treachery. The main force of the Carthaginian cavalry was now quartered at a town called Salaeca. He lured them out into an ambush placed by the Romans in the winding folds of the hills, at a spot called the Tower of Agathocles, about four miles from Utica, where the Djebel Menzel Roul joins the Djebel Douimis. The Carthaginians were routed with heavy losses. Scipio now gave up plundering the countryside, which had yielded rich booty in recent weeks, and concentrated all his land and naval forces on besieging Utica.

The attempt to capture Utica was to prove one of the few failures of Scipio's military career. He pressed home the attack with catapults and artillery for about forty days, at the end of that time the relieving force arrived. Acting on urgent instructions from Carthage, Hasdrubal Gisgo had raised a large force himself and spurred Syphax into action. They now approached Utica and encamped in a position six miles off from which they could threaten Scipio's lines. Their numbers, as given by Polybius and Livy, 30,000 infantry and 3,000 cavalry under Hasdrubal, and 50,000 infantry and 10,000 cavalry under Syphax, are no doubt exaggerated, but the force was large enough to compel Scipio to raise the siege and withdraw into a strongly fortified camp on the nearby headland. Here he spent the winter.

Scipio was now in a difficult position. He had become penned up in his original bridgehead on the Pulchrum Promunturium, and was now so greatly outnumbered that he could not risk meeting the enemy in the open field. Moreover, the Carthaginians were now preparing a fleet to attack him from the sea. Unless he could break out of the trap, Fabius' ill-omened comparisons with the disaster of Regulus (see p. 87) seemed likely to

be proven true. Scipio felt that his best hope lay in detaching
Syphax from the Carthaginian side. The Numidian had not
acquired the reputation of being a very stable ally, and Scipio
hoped that he would regard his recent marriage-tie with Hasdrubal as expendable. But Syphax saw little advantage in joining
the Romans, as long as they were allied with Masinissa, whose
kingdom he wanted to control. Instead, he suggested ending the
war on terms that would provide for the evacuation of Africa by
Scipio and of Italy by Hannibal. This would leave the Massylii
at his mercy. These proposals were, of course, impossible for
Scipio to accept, and he would have broken off the negotiations
at once had not some of the envoys reported that the huts in the
Carthaginian camp were constructed of wooden boughs, while
those in the Numidian camp, about a mile away from Hasdrubal's, were, as was traditional, built of reeds, and in fact most of
the reinforcements that were continually flowing in had built
their huts outside the stockade. Accordingly, Scipio gave Syphax
a hint that his proposals might possibly be made the basis of a
settlement, and continued with the negotiations.

Throughout the winter the envoys went backwards and for-
wards, often staying in each other's camps for several days at a
time. The Roman emissaries were accompanied by grooms and
servants, brawny men in rough clothes who, when not attending
on their masters, passed away the time slouching around the
enemy camps with shrewd, watchful eyes. On their return to the
Roman camp they reverted to their normal dress and duties as
senior centurions, and enabled Scipio and his staff to form an
exact picture of the whole lay-out of the enemy camps.

At the beginning of the spring of 203 Scipio was ready. He
launched his fleet and renewed the attack on Utica—as a blind.
Then he sent a message to Syphax, asking whether Hasdrubal
and the Carthaginians would ratify a peace treaty based on the
terms they had been discussing, if Scipio himself should agree to
them. Syphax immediately consulted Hasdrubal, and was able
to send back an answer that peace could be concluded at once.
To this Scipio replied that he himself was ready to agree, but
there was some opposition from his advisers, who insisted that
no agreement should be concluded. In this way Scipio was able
to break off the formal negotiations without arousing Syphax's
suspicions. His behaviour was not in accordance with the tradi-

tional Roman 'image' of good faith, but in dealing with Numidians and Carthaginians he may have felt justified in using their methods.

Shortly after this Scipio made his final preparations. He had increased the pressure on Utica, to give the impression that this was his real objective. But he gave special orders at noon that as soon as the evening trumpet-call was sounded, his officers were to lead their men out of camp. The Roman force moved out at about nine o'clock at night. As they approached the enemy camps, they split into two halves, Laelius and Masinissa to attack the Numidian camp, and Scipio himself the Carthaginian. The operation was a complete success. While Laelius surrounded Syphax's camp, Masinissa took his Numidians to fire the nearest rows of huts. The fire spread through the dry buildings, and soon engulfed the whole camp. The occupants, made utterly unsuspicious by the prolonged talk of peace, thought the fire was accidental, and rushed out, some half-asleep and some half-drunk, to put it out. In the turmoil many were trampled underfoot, others burnt to death, and those whom the flames had spared perished by the sword.

The Carthaginians, too, assumed that the Numidian camp had been set on fire by some mishap, and they rushed out unarmed either to help or to watch. Scipio fell upon them, drove them back into their own lines, and set fire to their huts. Both camps were completely wiped out in this double holocaust. Hasdrubal escaped with just over two thousand men, and Syphax with rather fewer. Many of the rest made their escape in isolated groups, but the loss of life must have been terrible, possibly 30,000 men, and the two enemy armies no longer existed as an organized force.

Hasdrubal had been guilty of very bad generalship. It had been his strategy to pin the Romans down by his superior land forces and hold them in a trap. Then, when the Carthaginian fleet was ready and made an attack from the sea, the trap would be sprung. But his experiences of fighting against Scipio in Spain should have taught Hasdrubal that Scipio was not the man to wait on his enemy's convenience. It was a fundamental feature of Scipio's generalship that he insisted on holding the initiative. This was where he differed from Hasdrubal.

After the battle Scipio did not relax his efforts. He chased

Hasdrubal out of the town of Anda, where he had taken refuge with the remnants of his forces, compelled the town to surrender on terms, and then took and sacked two neighbouring settlements. At Carthage there was great alarm, and some defeatism, but thanks to the efforts of the Barcid party, aided by Hasdrubal himself, it was decided to fight on and a request was sent to Syphax to do all he could to raise an army and prepare to renew the struggle. Hasdrubal went into the interior to raise fresh troops, while Syphax, who had at one time thought of returning to Numidia, was persuaded by Sophoniba to remain loyal to Carthage. While he was collecting his troops near the small town of Abba he was joined by four thousand Celtiberian mercenaries who had been recruited in Spain and had just arrived in Africa. These were splendid fighting material, and formed a useful nucleus for the new army. In fact, when, a month after the burning of the camps, Syphax joined Hasdrubal on the Great Plains, a place on the upper reaches of the Bagradas River, 75 miles from Utica, they could muster a force of nearly 30,000 men.

Once again Scipio refused to let the enemy keep the initiative. Leaving a small holding force at Utica, he made a forced march up the Bagradas with the bulk of his army, following the strategy of 'search out and destroy'. He encamped on a hill three miles from the enemy. The next two days were occupied in skirmishing. Then the two armies joined battle. The engagement that followed provided a text-book example of the working of Scipio's tactics. The enemy cavalry were dislodged and put to flight, leaving the wings unprotected. Then, while the *hastati* kept up the pressure on the Carthaginian centre, of which the nucleus was formed by the Celtiberian mercenaries, the other two lines, the *principes* and the *triarii* were brought round independently to outflank and envelop the enemy main body. The Celtiberians fought bitterly, for they had no hope of mercy from the Romans; they perished almost to a man, but their stubborn resistance enabled Hasdrubal and Syphax to escape with most of their troops.

After the battle the Roman forces divided. Scipio, with half the force, made the rounds of the various towns in North Africa that were subject to Carthaginian jurisdiction. Some of them surrendered of their own accord, out of fear of the Romans or a desire to be free of the burdens of Carthaginian financial exactions that had been increasing over the years as a result of the prolonged wars in Spain. Others were taken by assault, with little difficulty. Then Scipio returned to Utica, and prepared to bring the war home closer to Carthage.

Meanwhile the other half of the Roman forces, under Laelius and Masinissa, had entered Numidia. The Massylii welcomed them with joy, and they pressed forward into the kingdom of Syphax. Here they came up against the full force of the Masaesylii. At first Masinissa's cavalry was pushed back by sheer weight of numbers, for the Masaesylii were a far more powerful tribe. But the Roman legionaries under Laelius came up to give support, and gradually the enemy were driven back. The critical moment came when Syphax galloped forward in a desperate effort to rally his men. His horse was killed under him and he was thrown. Before he could be remounted, the Massylii were upon him and he was captured alive. This was the worst blow that had befallen the Carthaginians since Scipio's landing. With Laelius and the infantry following in easy stages, Masinissa pressed on to Cirta, Syphax's capital. The sight of their king in chains induced the townspeople to surrender. Masinissa took possession of his rival's palace—and his wife.

At Carthage itself the disaster on the Great Plains did not break the people's spirit. But proposals for peace negotiations, that had been put forward and rejected after the burning of the camps, were now reconsidered and tentatively adopted. However, the Carthaginians determined that, if they were to negotiate they would do so from a position of some strength. Accordingly, before approaching the Romans to discuss terms, they sent urgent instructions to Hannibal and Mago to return to Africa without delay, while they gave orders for their ships to put to sea to make an attack on the Roman fleet at Utica, which they knew was in little shape to fight a naval battle. With Scipio's fleet damaged or destroyed, and Hannibal back in Africa with his veteran army, they felt that they would have a good prospect of getting acceptable terms from the Romans.

Meanwhile Scipio, with the bulk of his army, had advanced on Tunis. He seized a position near the town, and then, when the garrison fled, occupied the town itself unopposed. He was now only ten miles from Carthage, within sight of the city, and as he was pitching his camp he saw the Carthaginian fleet put out to sea and set sail for Utica. So he broke camp at once and hurried back to meet this new threat. The danger lay in the fact that, for the assault on Utica, the Roman warships had been adapted for use as floating platforms and made to carry siege-engines and scaling-towers. There would be no time to dismantle and remove all this impedimenta and get them in a fit condition for a sea-battle. Had the Carthaginians sailed straight into the attack, they would have had the Roman ships at their mercy. Instead, they sailed past Utica and anchored for the night at Rusucmon, on Cape Farina. Scipio made use of this delay to organize his defences. He withdrew the warships, encumbered as they were, close into land, and stationed his transports in front of them, in a line three or four ships deep, to act as a stockade. He linked them together with masts and spars to prevent the line being breached, leaving room for the pinnaces and light vessels to pass in and out under the interconnecting booms. A strong force of marines, well supplied with missiles, was posted on the decks of the transports. Having made these preparations, Scipio waited to beat off the enemy attack.

The battle itself was a shambles. The Carthaginian fleet drew up in battle-formation out to sea, but when the Romans did not sail out to meet them, they came in and attacked the rows of transports. At first the attackers were at a disadvantage, since their decks were far below those of the transports, and the Roman marines made their volleys fall with greater force. But when the light craft began to move out through the gaps in the lines to engage the attackers, they masked the fire of the marines. The Carthaginians closed in and attached grapnels with iron chains to the first line of transports, and began to tow them off. In some cases the connecting booms held, and a whole row of ships was drawn away together. In many cases the marines barely had time to leap back onto the ships of the second line. By evening the Carthaginians had captured and taken to Carthage about sixty ships. They had won a tactical victory, but it had done little to affect the strategic position.

Soon after the sea-battle Laelius and Masinissa returned to Scipio's camp with Syphax as their prisoner. Shortly afterwards Scipio moved the majority of his forces back to Tunis, leaving enough men to press on with the siege of Utica. It was here that he was visited by a Carthaginian deputation asking for terms of peace. The improvement in morale caused by the victory at sea had been shattered almost at once by the news of the capture of Syphax. Although it seems that Vermina was still holding out in the western parts of his father's kingdom, it was clear that no more help could be expected from Numidia. The peace party at Carthage now gained the upper hand, and it was decided to ask for terms. Scipio himself was not unwilling to conclude the war by a negotiated peace. He had already achieved enough in North Africa for glory—and for expediency. He knew that his political enemies at Rome were intriguing to succeed him, and he saw no reason why someone else should reap the credit for his own hard work. He realized that to capture Carthage itself, whether by assault or blockade, would be a difficult and dangerous task, and might involve the protraction of the war longer than the Senate would be willing to allow. Above all, and this is a point that is not usually given sufficient weight, Scipio wanted peace firmly concluded before Hannibal could get back to Africa. In this, however, he was thwarted by the obstinacy and short-sightedness of his political opponents in Rome.

The terms that Scipio proposed were moderate. The Carthaginians were to evacuate Italy and Cisalpine Gaul, and abandon all their interests in Spain. They were to give up all the islands between Italy and Africa. All prisoners-of-war, deserters, and runaway slaves were to be given up. The Carthaginian fleet was to be reduced to twenty warships. A large quantity of wheat and barley was to be supplied to feed the Roman troops. A heavy indemnity was also imposed, the exact size of which is uncertain but was probably five thousand talents. These terms were accepted at Carthage, an armistice was concluded, and envoys were sent to Rome to ratify the terms of the peace treaty. This took place in the autumn of 203 B.C.

Scipio sent Laelius and Masinissa to Rome, Masinissa to obtain formal recognition of his kingship, Laelius to sponsor Scipio's proposals for peace. As soon as the Carthaginian envoys arrived, the Senate began to discuss peace terms. Scipio's leading supporter at Rome, Q. Caecilius Metellus, together with Laelius and Q. Fulvius Gillo, who had escorted the envoys to Rome, were insistent that peace should be ratified before Hannibal and Mago could return to Africa. But there was strong resistance to

this, partly from Scipio's traditional enemies, such as Valerius
Laevinus, partly from his former allies, M. Livius and the
Servilii, who were aligning themselves with the Claudii in
opposition to Scipio. This resistance was partly based on a
genuine reluctance to conduct negotiations with an enemy
while enemy troops were still on Italian soil, partly on a desire
to prolong the war so that some of Scipio's rivals could gain a
share in the glory. The result was that the Senate refused to
open negotiations while Hannibal and Mago were in Italy.
Hannibal sailed from Bruttium late in the autumn with the
remnant of his great army, probably ten thousand in number.
He landed at Leptis, near Hadrumetum, in the Syrtes, where he
could recruit and reorganize his forces without interference
from Scipio—or from Carthage. Here he was joined by the sur-
vivor's of Mago's army though Mago himself had died on the
voyage of gangrene from a thigh-wound. During the winter
negotiations got under way at Rome, and peace was concluded,
but by that time the damage was done.

During the winter a food-convoy from Sicily under Cn.
Octavius was caught in a storm. The escorting warships fought
their way through heavy seas and reached safety on Cape
Farina, but the supply-vessels were driven ashore in the neighbourhood of Carthage, some on the western side of Cape Bon
(Promonturium Hermaeum), but most of them on the off-shore
island of Aegimurus, about thirty miles from Carthage. The
people of Carthage were now desperately short of food, for
supplies from the interior had been cut off and Scipio was in
control of the sea. After a stormy meeting of the Senate, it was
decided not to let slip this opportunity of re-stocking their
larders, and Hasdrubal was sent with fifty warships to collect
the supply vessels and bring them into Carthage. Scipio at once
sent a deputation to protest, but now that Hannibal was back in
Africa the Barcids had the upper hand, and the protest was
rejected. Then the Barcid party decided to make a renewal of
the war inevitable by carrying out a treacherous attack on the
Roman envoys on their homeward voyage. The three emissaries,
Fabius, Baebius and Sergius, embarked on their quinquereme
and were given an escort of three Carthaginian triremes. When
they reached the mouth of the River Bagradas the escort left
them, but they sailed on unsuspecting. As they rounded the last

headland three Carthaginian triremes that had been lying in wait just beyond Utica swept down to intercept them. The enemy tried at first to sink the Roman ship by ramming, but were outmanoeuvred by the skill of the helmsman. Then they came alongside and tried to board, but the Roman marines lined the decks and drove them back. Then the Carthaginians drew off and swept the Roman deck with volleys of missiles. Soon most of the marines were dead or wounded and the ship was at the enemy's mercy. But the helmsman saw that Roman foraging-parties, out from the camp along the shore, had noticed their danger and were running at full speed down to the beach. So he ran the ship aground as close to the rescuers as he could get, and the envoys escaped.

Such a cold-blooded and blatant violation of the truce could only be expiated by war. Scipio at once launched a series of attacks on those towns that still remained in Carthaginian jurisdiction. He demonstrated the Roman attitude that no mercy can be shown to treaty-breakers by refusing to admit any of the towns to surrender but taking them all by assault and enslaving the inhabitants. However, when the Carthaginian emissaries arrived back from Rome, he gave orders that they should be treated with every courtesy and sent on to Carthage in safety.

These mopping-up operations occupied much of the summer. Meanwhile Scipio kept sending messages to Masinissa, who with the equivalent of a Roman legion was conquering and consolidating his hold on Numidia, to raise the largest possible force and rejoin him as soon as possible. At the same time the Carthaginian government sent orders to Hannibal to march north and oppose Scipio, to which Hannibal, who was still in the neighbourhood of Hadrumetum raising and training his army for the final struggle, despatched the cold reply that he would fight when he was ready.

It was in the autumn of 202 that the decisive battle took place. Hannibal moved up from Hadrumetum to Zama, a town five days march south-west of Carthage. This is probably to be identified with the later Roman colony of Zama Regia, now called Jama, not far from Seba Biar. Hannibal had about thirty thousand men. He was weak in cavalry, but had recently been reinforced by the Numidian prince Tychaeus, a rival of Masinissa, with two thousand horsemen, and probably by some of the

lesser chieftains. His deficiency in cavalry he hoped to make up
by a very powerful force of elephants, eighty in number. This
was, perhaps, a tactical error, as Roman troops, when well
trained and skilfully led, had always shown themselves capable
of dealing with elephants. However, they had been little used in
this war, and Hannibal may have thought that Scipio's men
would not have had the necessary experience to enable them to
stand up to an elephant-charge.

It is likely that Hannibal hoped to force a battle on Scipio
before Masinissa could arrive from Numidia, where the task of
subjugation seemed to have been rather prolonged, perhaps as a
result of resistance by Syphax's son Vermina. When Hannibal
reached Zama, he sent spies to Scipio's camp. They were
detected, and in the traditional manner employed by ancient
generals of a heroic type, they were shown round the Roman
camp, courteously entertained, and sent back unharmed. The
authenticity of this anecdote is often doubted, on the grounds
that it was told by Herodotus about Xerxes! But it is vouched
for by Polybius and is inherently probable. At this point
Hannibal sent and asked Scipio for a personal meeting at
which they could discuss terms. Hannibal had gained one vital
piece of information, that Masinissa was not in the Roman
camp, and he hoped that in his absence Scipio might prefer to
negotiate rather than be forced into a decisive battle. What he
did not know was that Masinissa was only two days' march
away. Scipio agreed to the confrontation, making it a condition
that he would choose the time and place. This gave him the
initiative, and, in effect, the choice of the battlefield, for he knew
the negotiations would come to nothing.

The next day Masinissa arrived. He had with him six thousand
foot and four thousand horse, a useful addition to Scipio's total
but nothing like the size of the forces that Syphax had been able
to put into the field. This indicates how precarious was Masinissa's hold over Numidia at this time. Thus reinforced, Scipio
moved camp, advancing to a place to which Polybius gives the
name 'Margaron' and Livy 'Naraggara', probably to be identified with the modern Sidi Youseff. He took up his position on
ground where, among other advantages, he could control a good
water supply. Hannibal, too, advanced from Zama, and encamped about three miles from Scipio, on a hill that provided a

strong defensive position but was a long way from water. It was only when he reached here that Hannibal realized that Masinissa and Scipio had joined forces.

The locality of the battlefield is hard to determine, because no site answering the topographical description, a plain lying between two hills, one with a good water supply, the other with none, can be found anywhere within fifteen miles of Naraggara. One can only suppose either that the name Naraggara denoted a fairly wide district rather than a precise town or village, or that Scipio passed through Naraggara and moved on to his final position. If either of these assumptions can be accepted, it would be possible to place the Roman camp on the hill of Koudiat el Behaima, the Carthaginians on Kat Bougrine, with the battle taking place on the plain of Draa el Meinan that lies in between. This is the most likely of all the various sites that have been suggested.

The conference between Scipio and Hannibal was dramatically important but diplomatically non-productive. Shorn of the rhetorical accretions, what Hannibal offered was a negotiated peace based on the surrender to Rome of all territories outside Africa which either side had claimed. He offered Scipio, in effect, all the glory of victory with most of the prizes. He dared Scipio to put fortune to the test 'to win or lose it all'. But Scipio had no option. As a Roman, he could not allow an enemy easier terms after the treacherous breach of a truce than they had been granted before. He could not concede a premium to the violation of Roman dignity and the outrage of Roman honour. The two generals parted and prepared for battle.

Next morning they moved their men into position. The two armies were of approximately equal strength, though the Romans were stronger in cavalry. Hannibal's front line was composed of mercenaries, Gauls, Balearics and Moors. His second line contained the local levies, Carthaginians and Libyans. His veterans from Italy were stationed about 100 yards to the rear. The Numidian cavalry held the left wing and the Carthaginian the right. In the very forefront were the elephants, to break up the enemy ranks in the first moments of the battle with a massive charge.

Scipio appreciated the danger and took steps to meet it. Instead of drawing up his three lines in staggered formation, with the *principes* covering the gaps between the separate units of the *hastati*, and the *triarii* covering the gaps between the units of the *principes*, he stationed the separate units in each line directly behind each other, to leave avenues between the formations running from front to rear. His light-armed skirmishers filled these avenues. Laelius with the Italian cavalry was on the left wing, and Masinissa's Numidians were on the right.

The battle opened with skirmishing between the opposing forces of Numidian cavalry. Then Hannibal ordered the elephants to charge. Some of them, insufficiently trained, were scared by the blare of trumpets and ran amok among the Numidian cavalry, enabling Masinissa to drive his opponents off the field. But the main body bore down upon the Roman line, only to come under a hail of missiles from the Roman light-armed, who drove them down the avenues until they passed harmlessly to the rear. Some of them, however, swung off to the flank and disorganized the Carthaginian cavalry that was facing Laelius, who took advantage of their confusion to put them, too, to flight.

Then the infantry came to grips. At first the skill and courage of the mercenaries gave them an advantage over the leading ranks of the *hastati*, but the rear ranks of the *hastati* moved forward in support and forced their opponents back onto their second line. Here there was some confusion, as the poorly-trained local levies would not support the mercenaries and had to be driven into battle at sword-point. But when they did move forward, their combined force pushed the *hastati* back. It was probably at this point of the battle that Scipio realized that he could not employ his tactics of using his *hastati* to hold the enemy line while enveloping them with his *principes* and *triarii*. Hannibal's scheme of holding back his best troops to form a strategic reserve would have exposed such a manoeuvre to a devastating counter-attack. Accordingly he changed his plan and put his *principes* into the battle in direct support of the *hastati*. The combined weight of the two Roman lines routed the enemy, and drove the survivors back onto Hannibal's veterans. Hannibal quickly redeployed them on his wings, while Scipio, too, reorganized his forces. He called back the *hastati* from the pursuit, halted them just beyond the scene of the recent struggle, where the ground had become slippery with blood and littered with heaps of dead, made his second and third lines form column and move through the battlefield in close order, and then deployed them on either flank of the *hastati*. Each side was now drawn up in one extended single line; they both charged, and the battle began afresh.

The two sides were well matched. They were about equal in numbers, since the Roman cavalry, in which Scipio had a decided advantage, were miles away in pursuit of the fleeing enemy. It is likely that the weaker Carthaginian cavalry had fled deliberately, on Hannibal's instructions, in order to keep the superior Roman horse from playing any part in the infantry battle. It was one of the few occasions when he had to give battle against an enemy superior in cavalry, and he did what he could to nullify the enemy's advantage. But at last Laelius and Masinissa returned and charged Hannibal's men in the rear. The Carthaginians broke and fled. Many were killed and many captured. The Romans had won the war.

The end soon came. Scipio returned to Utica, sent Laelius to Rome with the news of victory, and advanced on Carthage by land and sea. Hannibal had got away to his base at Hadrumetum, and from there hurried to Carthage to tell the government that there was no hope of any further resistance. As Scipio was approaching Carthage his fleet was met by a ship decked out with olive branches. On board were the ten leading men from Carthage, coming to sue for peace. Scipio ordered them to come to him at Tunis, and, after sailing into the Great Harbour at Carthage to impress and intimidate the enemy, he returned with all his forces to Utica.

While on his way to Tunis, a report came that the Numidian prince Vermina, Syphax's son, was approaching with a force of cavalry. He had been too late for the decisive battle and was now proposing to harass the Romans. Scipio detached his own cavalry, and they had little difficulty in intercepting and surrounding Vermina and annihilating his force. The only importance of the engagement is that it is dated as being the final clash of arms in the whole war. It took place on the first day of the Saturnalia, at the beginning of December. This helps fix the date of the battle of Zama at the end of October, a date that is to some extent confirmed by a report of an eclipse.

At Tunis Scipio received thirty emissaries from Carthage and dictated his terms. Carthage was to remain independent and retain its former territory in North Africa. The Carthaginians were to pay an additional indemnity for the outrages committed at the time when they broke the truce. The original war indemnity was doubled to ten thousand talents, to be paid in fifty years. Their fleet was to be further reduced to ten warships, and they were to hand over all captives, deserters and fugitive slaves. Masinissa's kingdom was to be restored to him in full: there were probably still some Carthaginian garrisons holding out in Numidia. The Roman army was to be supplied with provisions for three months, and with pay for such time until the peace terms were ratified. All the Carthaginian elephants were to be surrendered, and one hundred hostages were to be given. Finally, Carthage was forbidden to wage war on any people at all outside Africa, and on any people inside Africa without the consent of Rome. It was this clause that was to put Carthage at the mercy of Masinissa, and, in the end, lead to the Third Punic War.

These terms were ratified by both sides, though not without some opposition. At Carthage, a member of the Senate who tried to speak against them was peremptorily silenced by Hannibal, who pulled him off the rostrum. At Rome the consul, Cn. Lentulus, wanted the war to continue so that he could be voted Africa as his province and have the glory of dealing a *coup de grâce* to a now helpless enemy. But Scipio's supporters, the tribunes Acilius Glabrio and Minucius Thermus, had the decision referred to the Popular Assembly, and the People voted for peace. So, in the spring of the year 201 B.C., after seventeen years of uninterrupted fighting, the Second Punic War came to an end.

When one looks back on the course of this war, three things stand out. First, the early disasters that befell the Romans were the result of the poor quality of the Roman commanders and the inferior tactics employed. By the end of the war it had been shown that the Roman heavy infantry, when intelligently commanded and properly led, was a match for any type of troops on the Carthaginian side, and in most cases markedly superior. On the other hand, the poor quality of the Roman and Italian cavalry was making it clear that Rome would have to depend, for this arm at any rate, on foreign auxiliaries.

148

Next, this war is an interesting example of a conflict in which one side takes the initiative in the opening stages and establishes a dominant position in a main theatre of war, only to lose the initiative as a result of successes developed by the other side in subsidiary theatres. To students of military history a comparison with the 1939–1945 war in Europe may be enlightening.

Finally, in contrast to those of the First, the famous battles of the Second Punic War were fought on land, and it was on land that generals made or lost their reputation. Yet there have been few wars in history in which sea-power played such a pervasive and critical part. This is an aspect little appreciated by the ancient historians, who tend to treat naval operations as secondary to the campaigns by land, and in detached episodes which give little idea of naval strategy. Some general consideration of this topic seems called for in retrospect, such as may be given by a brief commentary on the map of the Western Mediterranean on pages 150-151.

At the outset of the war, the Roman fleet enjoyed a moral, material, and geographical superiority over that of Carthage. Their naval losses in the First Punic War seem to have blunted the offensive spirit of Punic admirals, and throughout the Second Punic War they showed little inclination to seek and destroy the enemy. True, they did not get much encouragement from their own government. At the start of the war the Roman fleet enjoyed a superiority of rather better than 2:1 (Rome, 220 naval vessels, Carthage 100, is a figure which seems reliable). The Carthaginians had the money and the means to redress this balance: so far as is known, they made no attempt to do so. Perhaps they were dazzled too long by Hannibal's successes in Italy: perhaps they were content with keeping control of the sea-routes to southern Spain, which they retained until the fall of Nova Carthago in 209 B.C. Whatever the reasons, their failure to wrest naval supremacy from Rome did more than anything to lose them the war.

A glance at the map will show the geographical factors working in favour of Rome. Her alliance with Massilia, and her possession of Corsica and Sardinia, gave control of the northern half of the western Mediterranean basin. Where Hannibal and Hasdrubal had to make long and dangerous overland journeys from Spain to northern Italy, Rome could move

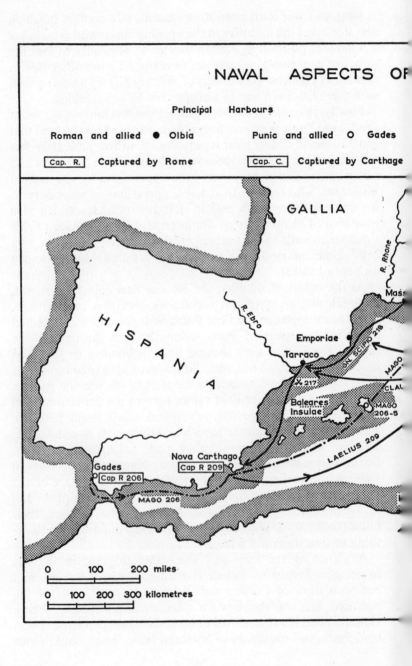

Principal Harbours

Roman and allied ● Olbia

Punic and allied ○ Gades

Cap. R. Captured by Rome

Cap. C. Captured by Carthage

GALLIA

R. Rhone

Mass

HISPANIA

R. Ebro

Emporiae ●

Tarraco

CN SCIPIO 218

MAGO

✕ 217

Baleares
Insulae

CLA

MAGO
206-5

Nova Carthago
Cap R 209

LAELIUS 209

Gades
Cap R 206

MAGO 206

0   100   200 miles

0   100   200   300 kilometres

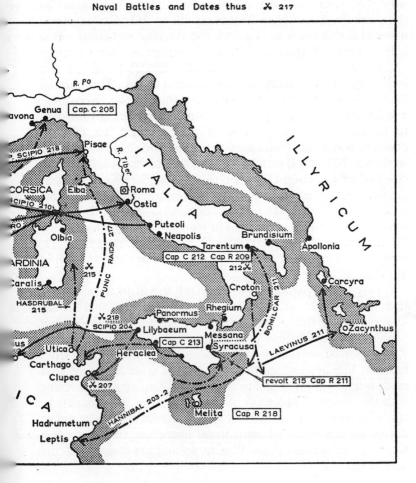

THE SECOND PUNIC WAR

Principal Fleet Movements

Roman LAELIUS 209 →   Punic ·—·—· MAGO 206 →

Naval Battles and Dates thus ⚔ 217

men and supplies by sea to Massilia, thence to Emporiae (Ampurias), and, later, to Tarraco, which became her main supply base in Spain. Her Italian bases at Pisae, Ostia, and Puteoli were never put out of action. It is true that Mago in 205 seized Genua and Savona, and so for a time controlled the Gulf of Genoa. This was the boldest Punic naval venture of the war, but it was belated, coming at a time when risks had to be taken because there was nothing else to do.

In southern Italy, Roman control of Tarentum and Brundisium gave command of the Ionian Sea and the approaches to the Adriatic. Even when Tarentum fell in 212, Carthage was never able effectively to penetrate the Adriatic and come to the help of Philip of Macedon. Thus the alliance between Carthage and Macedon could not develop its full potential. But the central factor was undoubtedly Rome's control of the harbours of Sicily, especially Messana, Syracuse, Panormus, Drepanum, and Lilybaeum. Lilybaeum was to Rome what Scapa Flow was to Britain in the First World War. It enabled her to keep constant watch on Punic movements towards Sardinia or the west coast of Italy; it provided a base for numerous raids on the coast of Africa, from Hippo on the west to Syrtes on the east; finally, it was the springboard from which Scipio launched his invasion of Africa. The naval command exercised by the governor of Sicily was cardinal in Roman strategy: the praetor T. Otacilius, who held it from 217 until his death in 211, deserves a place besides Fabius Maximus, Marcellus, and Scipio himself.

It may seem a paradox to assert that it was Roman sea-power that defeated Hannibal. Those who fought at Zama would scarcely agree. But it was respect for Roman sea-power that conditioned his strategy of invading Italy from Spain: it was Roman sea-power that prevented adequate reinforcements from reaching him in southern Italy: it was that same sea-power that made it impossible for him to concert an offensive against Rome with the power of Macedon. And if, at the last, he was able to effect his own withdrawal from Italy to Africa by sea, he did so during an armistice. Modern naval historians are right when they cite the Second Punic War to uphold the concept of 'the fleet in being'.

8

The Third Punic War

FIFTY-TWO YEARS after the peace treaty of 201 B.C., the third
war broke out between Rome and Carthage. This time the con-
testants were unevenly matched. Rome was by now the dominant power in the Mediterranean world. Carthage commanded
no more than the resources of a powerful city state. Once war
had begun, a Roman victory was inevitable, and in the end
Carthage was totally destroyed. Because the struggle of these
rivals has so many of the qualities of tragedy, it is tempting to
see this final war between them as though it were the last play
of a trilogy. Indeed, certain of its features support this view.
Rome found a pretext for a declaration of war in the breach by
Carthage of the terms of the peace treaty. As the fighting went
on, memories and attitudes properly belonging to the Second
Punic War revived. Scipio Africanus, with Laelius at his side,
had won the victories in Africa over Hannibal; a younger Scipio
and a younger Laelius completed the destruction of Carthage in
146 B.C. Yet in fact Rome and Carthage had lived in peace for
half a century, and there was nothing inevitable about the outbreak of war. Chance and the destiny of individuals played a
large part. If Scipio Africanus and Hannibal had lived longer,
and exercised continued power in their respective countries, if
Cato and Masinissa had died earlier, the war might never have
happened. Even so, it did not become likely until at least 157
B.C. and not before 152 was Cato able to make it the major
political objective for Rome.

When war did break out, the fighting was confined to the
territory of Carthage, and the belligerents were Rome, Carthage,
and Numidia. To understand the background from which

153

hostilities arose, one needs to know briefly what happened to each of them in the fifty years since the Second Punic War. Relations between them cannot be understood without reference to the Mediterranean world as a whole.

By 155 B.C. the salient factor was the supremacy of Rome. In Polybius' view, the Roman victory over Macedon in 168 had made this unchallengeable. 'For the future nothing remained but to accept the supremacy of the Romans, and to obey their command.' Yet this supremacy must be understood in its own terms. It was quite unlike the *imperium populi Romani* of the Late Republic, under which most of the Mediterranean lands were brought within the Roman provincial system. Still less did it resemble the *orbis Romanus* of the Principate, which united the entire Mediterranean world and much of western and central Europe under a closely organized and well administered political system. In the 2nd century B.C. Roman supremacy was an experimental and disjointed affair, which had come into being to deal with a series of emergencies. Cisalpine Gaul had been conquered, and Italy now extended to the foot of the Alps on the economic though not, as yet, on the political plane. The establishment of peasant farming in the Po Valley was some counter to the devastation of southern Italy in the Second Punic War. In the western Mediterranean, the only Roman provinces were the lands conquered from Carthage—Sicily, Corsica, Sardinia, and the two provinces set up in Spain. These provinces were badly organized and administered: there had been many rebellions: in Spain, in particular, the Roman conquest was far from complete. In that vast peninsula Rome was called upon to fight a series of harsh and grinding wars, the worst of which, the Lusitanian War, broke out in 154. In the East, Rome as yet administered no overseas territory, but she had shown up the Hellenistic kingdoms as paper tigers. She had shattered the power of Macedon, abolished the monarchy, and divided the kingdom into four independent republics. Antiochus the Great of Syria had been driven out of Asia Minor beyond the Taurus Mountains. Egypt, wealthy and weak, had come to look to Rome for protection. Over the 'liberated' city states of Greece, Rome exercised an increasingly tetchy patronage, favouring oligarchies and discouraging democracies. There were a number of powers of the second rank, which were allowed freedom and prosperity so long as they did what Rome wanted. The most important of these were Pergamum and Rhodes. Everywhere, the lesson had been learned that Rome could deploy her armies wherever she wanted.

The sources do not allow more than an outline history of Carthage at this period. It is however clear that she made a rapid economic recovery, so that by 191 she was in a position to offer to pay off the indemnity to Rome in full. It is usual to attribute this economic miracle to Hannibal and to the measures of reform which he instituted after gaining supreme power in 196, before his dramatic flight from Carthage in the next year at the prompting of Rome. The most important put a stop to the corruption by which the revenues of the state had seeped into the pockets of the magistrates. Others aimed at reforms in agriculture. But it should not be overlooked that other factors favoured recovery, besides the genius of Hannibal. During the Second Punic War, her lands in Africa had not been ravaged to anything like the extent of those of Italy. Since her armies were largely filled by mercenaries, losses in manpower had been proportionately less than those of Rome. She had untapped resources in the fertility of African agriculture, which had been previously underdeveloped because of the claims of her empire in Spain. Her mercantile marine was still a source of strength. It is true that she had lost her virtual monopoly of trade in the western Mediterranean. But contacts with Syria, Egypt, and Greece were still open, and it is known that Punic merchants also appeared in Italian markets. Her ships handled the carrying trade to Northern Africa as far as Morocco and beyond, and also to Gades in Spain. The rapid development of the Numidian kingdom under Masinissa must have brought economic gains to Carthage, though politically that monarch was a thorn in her side.

Masinissa was not only a friend of Rome, but also a favourite of Fortune. During his reign of fifty years, he turned Numidia from a loose aggregation of mainly nomadic tribes into a powerful kingdom with a well-developed agriculture. His loyalty to Rome was constant, and he sent men and provisions to her wars in Spain, Macedon and Greece. In return, he usually—but not invariably—received Roman support in his frequent territorial disputes with Carthage. Polybius and Strabo both praise his success in 'turning nomads into farmers'. Modern scholars are inclined to doubt whether he did more than exploit territories whose agriculture had already been developed by the Carthaginians. A similar doubt exists about the scope of his political ambitions. He has been credited with aspiring to an empire which stretched from Morocco to Egypt. Yet he must have been shrewd enough to know that such a development would never be allowed by Rome. Inscriptions prove that he did make diplomatic contacts in the eastern Mediterranean with kings of the same political standing as himself. And certainly he turned Numidia into the most powerful native state that had yet appeared in North Africa. His chief assets were the fighting qualities of the Numidians, and a remarkably flexible clause in the peace treaty of 201 B.C. which permitted him to make a series of territorial demands at the expense of Carthage.

The proviso that Masinissa was entitled to claim any lands within the territory of Carthage which had once belonged to his ancestors gave him virtually *carte blanche*. As one of his delegations to Rome pointed out, all that Carthage had legal claim in Africa was the ox-hide of land which had been granted to the original settlers in the Byrsa. In practice of course his claims had to be asserted with realism and without pushing Roman tolerance too far. His aggressions tended to recur at intervals of about ten years (195, 184, 172, 161, etc.), and usually at times when Rome was preoccupied elsewhere. The full extent of his encroachments on Carthaginian territory prior to 149 B.C. can be seen from the map on page 158. But there were also long periods of peace between Numidia and Carthage, and a pro-Numidian party grew up in that city. Their aim is said to have been the union of the two powers in a great kingdom which Masinissa should rule from Carthage. Matters came to a head shortly after 155 B.C., when the democratic party seized control in Carthage and embarked on a more militant policy. Annoyed by Masinissa's activities in the fertile district of Tusca (Thugga?) they appealed to Rome. The appeal brought Roman embassies but little satisfaction. But the embassy of 152 B.C., which included Cato and perhaps Scipio Nasica, was decisive. To examine disputed claims, this embassy had to travel around the country. It was alarmed by the prosperity and fertility displayed, and still more by what it saw in Carthage itself. In 151 B.C.

Carthage was due to pay the last instalment of the indemnity. What course would be followed by this powerful city, already so hostile to Rome? From this time onward Cato's mind became settled in the conviction that Carthage must be destroyed. There were as yet no reasons to justify war, but they would appear before long.

Throughout 151 the crisis mounted, with Numidia and Carthage sending embassies and counter-embassies to Rome. Late in 151 the Carthaginian government lost patience. The pro-Numidian party in the city was expelled: complaints from Masinissa were insultingly rejected: finally a Carthaginian army under Carthalo and Hasdrubal invaded his territory, in flagrant breach of the peace treaty of 201. Scipio Aemilianus, on a mission to seek elephants from Masinissa, was on hand to witness a great battle which followed. He much enjoyed it, and used to declare later that there had previously been only two such privileged spectators, when Zeus from Mount Ida and Poseidon from Samothrace had watched fighting in the Trojan War. Now fighting went in favour of Masinissa, who was later able to blockade the Punic army so that they could get neither food nor supplies. As a result almost the whole army was destroyed by hunger or disease.

Meanwhile, another and more important struggle had been decided in the minds of the Roman Senate. It is unfortunate that we know so little about personalities and factions in the Roman Senate at this time. Little more can be said than that Cato urged the destruction of Carthage, and that he was opposed by Scipio Nasica, who seems to have employed the argument that it was useful for Roman discipline and morale to have an enemy, and that Carthage should be left to play that rôle. Cato's view prevailed. Rome prepared for war.

There has been much discussion among modern scholars as to whether this decision was taken on good grounds. One thing is clear—there would never be a better opportunity for Roman intervention in Africa. Masinissa was in his late eighties and could not live much longer. The future of Numidia would have to be decided on his death. He had obligingly put out of action a large part of the Carthaginian army, and the city lay open to attack. A Roman invasion of Africa now would settle all problems there in the way most advantageous to Rome. So much may be granted, but why was it necessary to destroy Carthage? To understand this, we should need to know the terms in which Cato and his supporters presented the Carthaginian menace. Their arguments cannot have been confined to the ripe fig which Cato displayed in the Senate, with the remark that it had been gathered only three days previously in Africa.

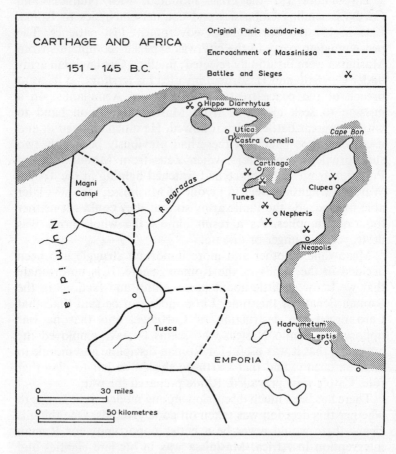

CARTHAGE AND AFRICA

151 - 145 B.C.

Original Punic boundaries ————

Encroachment of Massinissa ——————

Battles and Sieges ✗

Hippo Diarrhytus

Utica

Castra Cornelia

Cape Bon

Carthago

Clupea

Magni Campi

R. Bagradas

Tunes

Nepheris

Neapolis

Numidia

Tusca

Hadrumetum

Leptis

EMPORIA

0   30 miles

0   50 kilometres

This has been rather oddly interpreted as the excitement of Roman cupidity, and of vengeful envy at the fertility of North Africa. Roman cupidity was real enough, but scarcely to be set in motion by a fig. The moral of the story was that the fig was ripe; a ripe fig does not last long: the place where it was gathered must have been near. Ripeness, in fact, was all. When Virgil at the beginning of the Aeneid speaks of Carthage, he remarks that it is *Italiam contra*—opposite Italy. Opposite indeed, and only 90 miles from the coast of Sicily. It was a geo-political point that Cato was making. He supported it no doubt, from memories of the Second Punic War, and from considerations of recent political history. Something could have been made of the known fact that Punic agents had operated at many points among the enemies of Rome during the past half century; indeed a Punic general called Poenulus was even now in the armies of Viriathus in Spain. Again, Carthage had dangerous contacts in the eastern Mediterranean, notably with her kindred cities on the coast of Syria. Syria was weak, so was Egypt. Something like a domino effect may have been foreseen for this part of the Mediterranean world. In short, the grim prospect may have been held up of a powerful Numidian-Punic kingdom mustering a great southern coalition and leading it against Rome—*Italiam contra*.

All this is conjecture. But it is known that Scipio Nasica argued that, in any action she took, Rome must have regard to world opinion. Thanks to a passage of Polybius, we have a fair idea of what that opinion was. Polybius distinguishes the opinions of four groups of critics. The first regarded Rome's actions as a wise and far-sighted defence of her empire. The second remarked that Rome had entered a new and brutal phase of imperialism with the destruction of Macedon, and had given a yet more striking example of this by her treatment of Carthage. Others said that the Romans were in general a civilized people, but that their whole treatment of Carthage had been characterized by treachery and impiety. A fourth group—whose views are set out at length, which suggests that Polybius agreed with them—based their case on the fact that the Carthaginians had made a formal surrender (*deditio in fidem*) to Rome. (Elsewhere he had explained, for the benefit of a Greek audience, what such a *deditio* involved. It meant the surrender to Rome of the whole of their territory and the cities in it, all its inhabitants, all rivers, harbours, temples and towns, so that the Romans enter into possession of everything, and the party making the surrender remains in possession of nothing whatsoever.) This *deditio* was made by the embassy sent by Carthage to the Senate early in

149. War had already been declared by Rome: the army had left for Africa in charge of the consuls: Utica had anticipated Carthage by surrendering herself. A *deditio* was the only card the Punic ambassadors could play, and at first it seemed rewarding. The praetor (acting presumably in the absence of the consuls) announced that the Senate granted them freedom, their own laws, all their territory, and their public and private possessions. These apparently satisfactory terms would however, only be granted if Carthage sent 300 hostages to Lilybaeum, and obeyed the commands of the consuls. (The consuls, says Appian, had their secret instructions.) When the ambassadors returned to Carthage, a senator called Mago drew attention to the ominous fact that there had been no mention of the city of Carthage itself. But they had made their surrender, and now must obey any instructions, or else face war. In retrospect, the fourth school of Greek critics seized on this point. Rome received *deditio* from Carthage and full authority to act as she pleased: Carthage refused to obey instruction: Rome resorted to force. But she must stand acquitted of impiety, treachery, or injustice. Perhaps, on this legalistic plane, she must. Meanwhile, Carthage had condemned Carthalo and Hasdrubal to death. But Hasdrubal was still at the head of an army, and it does not look as though there was any move to enforce his condemnation.

The army which the consuls M. Manilius and L. Marcius Censorinus took to Africa consisted of 80,000 infantry and 4,000 cavalry. It was, indeed, larger than either of the two previous Roman expeditionary forces, those of Regulus in the First and Scipio Africanus in the Second Punic War. The campaign was popular: the prospects of heavy fighting appeared to be remote, pickings were certain to be good. Many of those young men who had dodged the unrewarding war in Spain were now ready to bear arms in their country's cause. It was an army with a long tail of camp-followers and shady dealers of every kind. If there was going to be peace, Carthage would have to buy it: war would open up the spoils of the wealthiest city in the world. The surrender of Utica offered a base and a bridgehead, and in April 149 the Roman forces were installed in Scipio's old positions at the Castra Cornelia. The consuls were ready for the next stage in what was as yet a war of diplomacy.

Appian is the best source for what followed. The Carthaginians had been promised a further instalment of what the Senate had in mind at Utica. Their embassy was received by the consuls in the open air, with the entire Roman army displayed in a tremendous show of military power. Censorinus—the better orator—spoke for Rome. What he had to say was simple and to the point. If the Carthaginians sincerely desired peace, what need had they of arms? 'Come now, hand over to us all your arms, public and private, both weapons and war-machines.' The Carthaginians agreed. Under the supervision of the Roman commissioners, an immense convoy of armaments was sent to Utica—complete armour for 200,000 men, spears and javelins too numerous to count, and 2,000 catapults; Carthage, to all appearances, was disarmed. (Scepticism, here, may not be out of place. Was there already some secret understanding between the Carthaginian Senate and Hasdrubal? In view of what happened later, was there not a substantial cache of arms in the city?) But Censorinus was confident enough to pass to the third, and final, disclosure. It was made to a Carthaginian delegation of unusual size, containing not only ambassadors, but senators, leading citizens, and priests; its purpose, says Appia, was to inspire respect or pity in the consuls. In this it failed.

For, at long last, the Carthaginians were made to realize why the Senate in Rome had omitted any reference to their city. 'Bear bravely,' said Censorinus, 'the final command of the Senate. Surrender Carthage to us, and retire anywhere you like within your own territory, so long as it is at least ten miles from the sea. We have decided to raze your city to the ground.' The Carthaginian reaction was frenzy, followed by a stunned silence. At last Banno spoke—of the loyalty of Carthage to the treaties made with Scipio Africanus, her prompt payment of the indemnity, her ready compliance with recent demands, her great history, and, finally, of the need for Rome to think of her own reputation, because of the mutability of human affairs. Censorinus' reply (in Appian's version) was strange but not, perhaps, wholly hypocritical. Sea-power corrupts. It had corrupted Athens: it was now corrupting Carthage. 'Whenever you look on the sea, you remember the great fleets you once had, the spoils you captured, the harbours into which you brought them, to fill your dockyards and arsenals.' Carthage must put away all thoughts of her imperial past, move inland, and enjoy the stable delights of peaceful agriculture. Like Rome—herself twelve miles from the sea. Whether Censorinus really delivered these Platonic moralizings on the evils that beset maritime cities we do not know. M. Picard, the great French authority on Carthage, thinks he did. But the gist of the speech sounds authentic. This is what *delenda est Carthago* meant—the city itself must be destroyed.

The ambassadors took back this fearful message to Carthage. The waiting citizens knew from their demeanour that calamity was impending, but they made way for them to reach the Senate. There, after one great outcry when the message was understood, they were heard in silence. But in the city there was fury and despair, leading to actions which Appian compared to those of the orgies of Bacchus. Pro-Roman Senators were torn to pieces. Italians in the city were assaulted and outraged, the temples were crowded, the gods abused for their failure to help. The same day the Senate of Carthage declared war on Rome. Its people emerged from their despair to a feverish attempt to make good the arms they had surrendered. This drive produced, each day, 100 shields, 300 swords, 1,000 missiles for catapults, 500 spears and javelins, and 'as many catapults as they could, for whose strings the women cut off their hair'. The consuls were asked for a thirty days' truce, but this obvious manoeuvre was refused. (If granted, the schedule of arms production just quoted would not have gone far to replace their losses. Something must have been kept back from the surrender, or else the declaration of war would have been a hopeless gesture.) Hasdrubal received an official pardon, and command of the army in the field.

The Romans would now have to take Carthage by force— a city protected by the strongest fortifications of the time. To reduce it by starvation—as had been done at Capua—meant gaining control of access to the city by land and sea, or of destroying the source of supply in Byzacena, the Carthaginian territory to the south and south-east. Here Hasdrubal and his army of 25,000 to 30,000 men were a factor. Their main base was the fortified city of Nepheris, some 18 miles (30 km) south of Carthage astride the lines of communication with the grain-lands. As for the fortifications of the city, a glance at the map (p. 163) will show the problems. The approach to Carthage from the landward side between the two lagoons was blocked by a great ditch, earthwork, and palisade. Discovered by French archaeologists, it ran across the neck of the isthmus immediately to the west of the city. Beginning at Sidi bou Said to the north-west, a line of fortifications ran parallel to the shore to the spit of land at Kherredine, then west to the earthwork, thence parallel to it to the north, and finally east to Sidi bou Said. Their circuit, according to Livy, was 21 miles: that of the Aurelian Wall at Rome is 12 miles (18·8 km). Although the wall is single on the seaward side, it became a triple system on the south and across the neck of the isthmus. The city was divided into two sections, Megara and Byrsa, each fortified like the wards of a castle. The Byrsa contained the Acropolis of Carthage and the Temple of Esmun; the great double harbour of Cothon, with its circular basin for warships and quadrangular harbour for commercial traffic, lay in its south-eastern quarter. Extensive quays flanked the Cothon on the seaward side to form an additional port, and there was a single entrance to the whole complex on its southern side.

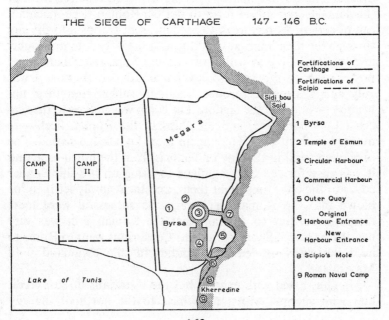

Finally, there was the question of Masinissa. He had hung back when the Roman force landed at Utica; a tardy offer of help met with the Roman reply: 'We shall let you know when we need you.' A grandson of his (another Hasdrubal) was one of the leaders of the democratic party in Carthage. What was clear about Masinissa was that, at this stage, he meant to play a waiting game.

The Romans achieved little in the campaign of 149. The consuls established themselves in two camps on the isthmus, in the belief that it would be easy to take Carthage by direct assault. Three concerted attacks were beaten off: obviously they would have to equip themselves with siege-engines to have any chance of success. Censorinus undertook this task, and crossed the southern lagoon in search of timber. Here one of his working-parties was roughly handled by the Punic cavalry commander, Himilco Phameas. But in the end he got his timber, and constructed two enormous battering-rams, one of which, says Appian, was operated and serviced by an assault force of six thousand men. With these units he attacked the fortifications at the south-western neck, and managed to make a large breach. The Carthaginians, working by night, repaired most of the damage, and sallied forth to put the Roman siege-machines out of action. At daybreak Censorinus sent troops into the city through the remaining gap, but the assault-party got into trouble and was only able to withdraw because Scipio Aemilianus had posted men on the walls to cover their retreat. By now it was July and Censorinus' troops began to suffer from their un-healthy position by the lagoon. The camp was moved to the sea-coast by Kherredine, and the ships of the Roman fleet were moored in front of it. Here again local knowledge scored. The prevailing wind in the Bay of Tunis is from the north-east, and it was easy for the Carthaginians to bring up fire-ships under cover to the city walls, light them, and then simply let them be blown into the Roman anchorage. So successful were these tactics, according to Appian, that the Roman fleet was very nearly destroyed. Shortly after this Censorinus went to Rome to hold the elections, leaving Manilius in sole command until May of 148.

Manilius acted with energy, but the historians do not credit him with success. Moving his base to the north of the city beyond Sidi bou Said, he abandoned the siege for the time being and concentrated on getting in supplies. Here again Himilco Phameas was a menace—except in actions where Scipio was present. Then, during the winter, Manilius conceived the plan of attacking Hasdrubal in his base at Nepheris. Scipio —a military tribune at the time—disapproved. But when Manilius got his army into a desperate position in a mountain gorge, it was Scipio who came to the rescue at the head of 300 cavalry. When four Roman cohorts were cut off and surrounded during the costly withdrawal it was Scipio who led an audacious and successful attempt to surround the besiegers. And finally, it was Scipio who persuaded Hasdrubal to bury the Roman military tribunes killed in this second action. There seemed little, indeed, that Scipio could not do: he even induced Cato to quote Greek. The Man of Destiny was on the stage. But there had been some adroit stage-management from Scipionic pro-paganda which found its way into the narrative of Polybius, and is echoed in Appian.

Scipio Aemilianus carried the burden of a family background almost intolerably illustrious. Son of Aemilius Paullus, con-queror of Macedonia, he had been adopted into the *gens Cornelia*. Inevitably, his achievements would be measured against those of Aemilius Paullus and Scipio Africanus, the two greatest generals Rome had yet produced. A famous passage of Polybius shows how much the Scipionic heritage, especially, weighed him down at a critical time of his life. Walking one day with Polybius, the eighteen-year-old Scipio asked: 'Do you have the same opinion of me which, I gather, the rest of my country-men have? They consider me unambitious and idle, wholly un-like the nature and habits of a Roman—because I do not choose to plead in the courts. My family, they say, needs a leader quite the opposite of myself. This is what especially distresses me.' Polybius offered reassurance and help 'to make you speak and act in a manner worthy of your ancestor'. Scipio took up the offer eagerly, and from that time onwards they had a relation of mentor and pupil which, in affection, was like that of father and son. It may well be that Polybius overestimated the effects of his tuition, as educators are prone to do. For Scipio responded to a compelling urge to improve himself. He sharpened his mind with his Greek tutors and Greek books: he hardened his body with a passion for hunting. In his military service, he deliberately sought the hardest assignment—reckless in pursuit at Pydna, in Spain, taking up successfully the challenge to personal combat with a Spanish chieftain, first on to the wall at a beleaguered city. The war against Carthage was for him a unique opportunity; he might rival the glory of his ancestors and also win preeminence in Roman politics. But first he had to gain command of the army, and, legally, he was too young to stand for the consulship. Propaganda, building on personal achievement, might brush the obstacles aside.

In the early months of 148, Scipio's family connections enabled him to perform a signal diplomatic service. We have seen the coolness between the Roman commanders and Masinissa, who had been told 'we shall send for you when we need you'. Now, in their lack of success, they needed him. A mission was sent to Cirta, and Scipio was on it, at Masinissa's request. For the old king 'best and most fortunate of the kings of our time', in Polybius' words, was near the end of his long life. There was the problem of arranging the kingdom after his death; his three (legitimate) sons were now middle-aged men, very different in their interests and talents. Scipio, who had inherited from Scipio Africanus a relationship of patronage to the King of Numidia, and was himself *persona grata*, was sent for to help in this task. But Masinissa died before Scipio could reach Cirta, having told his sons to abide by what Scipio decided. His solution was ingenious. Each of the three sons received the title of king and a share of the royal revenues, but they were to assume different functions. Micipsa, 'the oldest, and a lover of peace, was assigned the royal palace and the city of Cirta. Gulussa, next in age, and of warlike disposition, was placed in charge of foreign policy.' Mastanabal, an upright man and a student of law, was to administer justice. Gifts were also given to the ten surviving illegitimate sons (out of the forty-one fathered by Masinissa in his lifetime, the last at the age of 86!). Scipio went back to Carthage with Gulussa at his side, ready to go into action at once against Himilco Phameas. It was a solution of the Numidian problems much to the advantage of Rome. No longer would the country be under a single ruler. The prospect of a Punic-Numidian alliance—always a possibility so long as the Romans were doing badly—had receded. An advan-

tage that accrued was the coming over to the Roman side of
Himilco Phameas. The Numidians under Gulussa had cut down
his freedom of action: he perhaps saw the defeat of Carthage as
inevitable: he was certainly promised a rich reward for treachery.
The agent, once again, was Scipio.

When L. Calpurnius Piso arrived, with his legate Mancinus
to take charge of the fleet, there was a change of strategy. No
attempt was made to press the siege of Carthage, nor to destroy
Hasdrubal in the field. Instead, a number of cities still loyal to
Carthage were besieged—notably Clupea, Neapolis, and Hippo
Diarrhytus. The motive, it would seem, was booty, the only in-
centive that would still appeal to the thoroughly demoralized
Roman army. That this was so is suggested by the brutal sack of
Neapolis, although that city had given itself up. Even so, not
much was achieved. Carthage sent help to Hippo, and at the end
of the campaigning season of 148 the siege was abandoned.
In this unsatisfactory year for Rome, Carthage even won some
diplomatic successes. Trouble was effectively stirred up in
Numidia. The Mauri attacked the western frontiers of the
kingdom, the obvious move of causing dissension between the
three kings was exploited, and some Numidian cavalry joined
the Carthaginians. Further afield, Carthage was emboldened to
proffer aid and comfort to the Macedonian pretender Andriscus.

The situation was ripe for Scipionic propaganda. When
Scipio left Rome to stand for election as aedile, opinion was
loudly raised that he was the only man who could win the war.
It was supported by one of the most effective means of vote-
catching—soldiers' letters from the front. Scipio was accompanied to Rome by Himilco Phameas, whose surrender was
almost the only military success of the year. Each was to receive
an appropriate reward. Scipio was nominated for the consulship,
a motion proposed by a tribune providing a way round the law.
He was elected and, by a direct vote of the people, awarded
command in Africa. There he arrived in the spring of 147 B.C.,
bringing with him reinforcements from Rome and the allies.
His *legatus* was his close friend, Laelius.

His first task was to mount a rescue operation for a force of
men whom Mancinus had managed to get into the Megara
section of Carthage. On this operation the sources are at
variance. Appian reports a reckless venture, with disaster

averted at the last moment by the arrival of Scipio's ships. Livy, and other Latin sources, suggest that Mancinus did achieve a measure of success, which has been distorted by the pro-Scipionic account of Polybius. What can hardly be denied is that Scipio's major problem was to restore discipline in the Roman army. Appian reports a speech at a *contio*, in which the new commander ordered all except fighting soldiers out of the camp. Others must dispose of their goods by a given date: the general and the quaestors would supervise the sale. For the troops, there would be rewards—but only after victory. By some such measures as these he made the Roman army once again a fighting force.

The Carthaginians meanwhile had made what dispositions they could to confront the more vigorous assault in store. Hasdrubal was recalled to Carthage to take command of the city: a certain Bytheas took over the cavalry, in place of Phameas (deserted): the army at Nepheris was, according to Appian, placed under Diogenes, presumably a Greek mercenary general, like Xanthippus in the First Punic War. Hasdrubal with 6,000 men fortified a camp on the isthmus just west of the triple line of fortifications, in the hope of at least delaying Scipio's investment of the city on the landward side.

Scipio's first move with his rejuvenated army was an attack at two points on the western fortifications of Megara. He succeeded in getting 4,000 men inside the city, but found himself in an area unsuited to fighting, consisting as it did of numerous orchards, vineyards and olive-groves, intersected by many irrigation channels. Accordingly he withdrew. The topography of Carthage must by now have been familiar to the Romans, and a 'planned withdrawal' always raises suspicion of a defeat. (We must, however, remember the difficulties of the Flavian troops when they broke into a similar quarter of Rome in A.D. 69.)

At this point Hasdrubal withdrew into the Byrsa quarter and, in full view of the Romans, deliberately inflicted atrocities on the Roman prisoners in his hands. It was a calculated move to inspire his own men to resist to the end, but it misfired, as such moves are apt to do. Scipio saw that Megara did not offer an easy way in: the Byrsa itself and the harbour district of Cothon, both strongly defended, would have to be taken by storm. But first the city must be closely invested, to allow hunger to sap the enemy strength and will. So the rest of the summer of 147 was devoted to the great pieces of military engineering described in the historical sources, whose traces have been recently explored by French archaeologists.

The system of walls and ditches built on the isthmus was the first of these, and on their construction the entire army was engaged for twenty days and nights of unbroken labour, much of it under attack from the city. As described by Polybius, two parallel trenches were built across the entire length of the isthmus from lagoon to lagoon (a distance of 25 *stades* or about 4 km). Then two others were built at right-angles to them, and the entire quadrilateral of ditches was filled with sharp stakes, the ditches above them palisaded; and a twelve-foot wall with observation towers constructed on the eastern wall facing Carthage. The central tower had a wooden tower of four storeys superimposed. Appian is at pains to point out the multi-purpose nature of this system. It completely blocked the movement of supplies into Carthage, whether from the isthmus or the lagoons. It provided Scipio's army with a fortified camp and relative security against enemy sallies. Finally, it gave a view into the city, though as we shall see, not one that brought under range activity in the dockyard area.

Next Scipio turned his attention to the seaward approaches through which supplies were still reaching Carthage, while the Roman ships found it impossible to maintain an effective blockade. His plan was to block the common outlet from the two harbours of Cothon by building a great mole from Kherredine across to the southernmost tip of the outer harbour, a distance of some 700 metres (see map 11). This mole—portions of which still rise out of the water, and more can be seen from the air—is estimated by M. Jean Baradez to have involved the shifting of between 12,000 to 18,000 cubic metres of large boulders (the calculation depends on Appian's figures that, when completed, it was 24 feet across at the top and 96 feet at the base). The Carthaginians were not much alarmed at first, since it seemed a slow and perhaps impossible project. When they realized the deadly threat it presented they improvised a remarkable counter-plan of their own—the building of a new channel giving direct access from the circular naval harbour to the sea. Women and children helped with the digging; at the same time, within the circular harbour, there was feverish activity in the construction of a new fleet from old materials. The circular harbour was screened from view, and although the Romans could hear a loud noise by day and night, they had no idea of what was going on. Eventually, the new Punic fleet sailed down the channel and appeared off Kherredine. But the high spirits and daring shown in these plans did not meet a due reward. The Romans, concentrating all their efforts on finishing the mole, had left their own ships unmanned and unattended. An immediate attack might have wiped them out: instead, all the Punic fleet did was to make an empty parade of strength. It did not attack until the third day, by which time the opportunity had passed and the Roman fleet was ready. An indecisive but eventful naval battle followed. Towards evening the Carthaginians broke off the action, but their withdrawal was so badly co-ordinated that the mouth of the channel became blocked by their own small craft. The larger ships took refuge under the north wall of the commercial quay, bows facing to sea, where they could be covered by artillery fire from the city wall and from a strong point on the quay itself. They were sitting ducks for attack from the sea, but as the attacking Roman ships turned to draw off they were broadside on and exposed to heavy fire. Here they got a lesson in seamanship from the allied squadron of five ships from Side in Pamphylia, which had been sent 'out of friendship for Scipio'. Each of these ships dropped a sea-anchor and ran out long lines from it, so that they could warp back after running in to attack. The Romans followed their example, and were able to inflict heavy damage on the stationary ships of the enemy. Only after nightfall were the surviving Punic ships got back to harbour.

Next day Scipio attacked the commercial quay, and battered down part of the strong-point with siege-engines and rams. During the night Carthaginian divers waded or swam across with torches and burned the Roman machines. This desperate and unexpected attack caused such panic in the Roman camp that Scipio had to send a cavalry squadron to round up deserters. In the next phase of the fighting the Carthaginians repaired and strengthened their strong-point, but Scipio brought up more siege-engines, drove them out with incendiary missiles, and gained control of the whole quay. Finally he built his own fortifications on it, which included a long wall parallel with that of the city itself, from which he could sweep a large area inside with missiles.

These crowded events were the crucial phase of the siege of Carthage, in the sense that when it was over at the end of the summer of 147 there was no further chance of military success for the besieged. But the siege could yet be prolonged, for some supplies were even now reaching the city. Scipio planned to devote the winter to cutting off these supplies at source. The strategy was one of sustained pressure at the maximum number of points. Detached columns operated against a number of towns still faithful to Carthage. The main objects of attack were the Punic field army under Diogenes and the fortress of Nepheris. Two Roman forces converged on these, one under Laelius by land, the other, across the Lake of Tunis, led by Scipio himself. At the same time, Scipio kept shuttling to and fro between Nepheris and Carthage, to see that the blockade of the city was maintained. He personally supervised the final assault on the camp of Diogenes, most of whose troops tried to escape at an early stage. They were cut down in the open in huge numbers by Gulussa with the Numidian cavalry and elephants. Nepheris fell after a siege of twenty-two days in the depths of winter—a hardship for the besiegers. After this all the towns of Africa surrendered to Scipio, and only Carthage was left.

During this winter—it is not quite certain when—Hasdrubal made at least one attempt to sue for terms, using Gulussa as his intermediary. There was a faint hope that Scipio might grant acceptable terms, for fear that the new consuls for 146 might be sent out to supersede him. A fragment of Polybius describes the impression Hasdrubal made during these negotiations. When Scipio refused to spare the city, but offered survival to Hasdrubal himself, his family, and ten selected friends, Hasdrubal rejected them, saying that the finest funeral for men of spirit was to die in the flames of their native city. Fine words, says Polybius, but the man did not come up to them. Pot-bellied, red in the face, he showed the effects of feasting and carousing with his friends, while the people of Carthage starved. As for Scipio's command, it was extended for another year, to enable him to deal the *coup-de-grâce* to Carthage. Early in the spring of 146 B.C. he moved in methodically for the kill.

His first action was taken on the plane of religion—the recital of the terrible formula of *evocatio*, whose intent was to lure the protecting gods out of an enemy city about to fall. The archaic formula—a little touched up, perhaps—is preserved in a passage of Macrobius, writing about 400 A.D. The gist of it is in these words. 'O mighty god, who has taken under protection this city and this people, I pray, beseech, and request of you this indulgence, that you desert the city of Carthage and its people, abandon the places, temples, sacred sites, and their city, and go forth out of them. On that people cast fear, terror, and forgetfulness: abandoned by them, come to Rome to me and my people. . . . And if you accomplish these things, I promise that temples and games shall be established to honour you. . . .' Then followed the parallel formula of *devotio*, reserved to dictators and generals, and devoting the city and army of Carthage to the powers of the underworld. Such formulae had been used against the city of Veii by Camillus in 396 B.C.: when Titus besieged Jerusalem in A.D. 70, the gods were heard making a voluntary exit.

Military action started from the commercial quay. Hasdrubal himself fired the wooden buildings of the quadrangular harbour, and Laelius, in the confusion, forced his way into the circular harbour of Cothon. According to Plutarch, the two first men into Carthage were Fannius, the future historian, and the young Tiberius Gracchus. There followed a furious general assault on the wall between Cothon and Byrsa: by the evening Scipio had broken through as far as the Forum. The next day he brought in 4,000 fresh troops, but it was a day of plunder rather than fighting. For after the troops captured the Temple of Apollo with its gold-covered *cella*, they lost all discipline and proceeded to hack it to pieces with their swords.

When the assault was resumed, they were faced with the grimmest part of the task. Ahead lay the fortress of Byrsa, crowned by the Temple of Esmun. Three steep streets approached it from the Forum, each lined by tall houses of six or more storeys—like the old houses of Edinburgh. Every house was a fortress in its own right, to be stormed in the face of desperate resistance at every level. Heavy fighting was incessant, in the streets and on the flat roofs. As the Romans captured each block, they threw planks across the alleyways on to the next. Bodies fell from roofs and windows, often to be impaled on swords or pikes below. This, the fiercest street-fighting recorded in antiquity, lasted for six days. Wave after wave of Roman assault troops were thrown in, and withdrawn as they became exhausted, or unnerved by its horrors. Scipio (if Appian is to be believed) remained on his feet, without sleep and only stopping to snatch food, throughout the fighting which brought the attackers to the foot of the fortress itself. The last phase had brought a new climax of horror, for Scipio gave orders to burn down the houses and clear the rubble to provide ample space for the final assault. In these fires perished the old, the sick, and the wounded who had taken refuge in the secret parts of the houses. Others, living or dying, were shovelled into holes to make the roads passable. 'A man was used,' says Appian, 'for filling a ditch.' It was not, he explains, done deliberately, but in the heat of the moment (the ancients had a certain naivety lacking in our own times). On the seventh day, when the Romans expected many more days of fighting ahead, suppliants appeared from the citadel. They asked that those who were ready to surrender at that point should have their lives spared—no more. Scipio agreed. Then 50,000 men and women, survivors of the siege of Carthage, emerged through a postern gate. They were placed under guard, to be sold into slavery. There were left only Hasdrubal, his wife and two children, and 900 Roman deserters, who held out for some time in the precincts of the Temple of Esmun. Hasdrubal's nerve was the first to crack, and he came out to cast himself at Scipio's feet as a suppliant. The others set fire to the Temple: as they did so, Hasdrubal's wife cursed her husband as a coward and a traitor, then killed her two children and threw herself into the flames. So ended the siege of Carthage.

There remained the physical destruction of the city. Time was granted for private soldiers to search the city for loot, and for the best of the treasures to be gathered together to be sent to Rome or—in the case of sacred objects plundered from Sicily by the Carthaginians—to be reclaimed by their owners. Then the remains of Carthage were fired. It takes time to burn down a large city, and the fires of Carthage lasted for ten days. When they guttered out Punic Carthage had been destroyed as a physical and political entity. Its territories were to become the Roman province of Africa, whose capital and cultural centre would eventually be the Roman city of Carthage, colonized by Julius Caesar and Augustus. But that is another story.

It seems that it was during the final razing of Carthage that Scipio Aemilianus was moved to tears, and to his words on the inconsistency of Fortune and the mortality of all human affairs. The story is not in doubt: it originates from Polybius, a principal to the exchange: longer variants are preserved in Diodorus Siculus and in Appian. Scipio was no stranger to such themes. He had witnessed the surrender of King Perseus of Macedon to his father Aemilius Paullus after the battle of Pydna in 167 B.C.; he had been one of the young men to whom Paullus addressed a homily saying that they should refrain from exulting at the enemy's defeat, bearing ever in mind the mutability of Fortune. Only a few months earlier, in the winter of 147–6 B.C., such arguments had been put before him by Hasdrubal in his last desperate plea for mercy for Carthage. That plea had gone unheeded. Rome's greatest enemy was destroyed, and Scipio, as its destroyer, had surpassed his great ancestor Africanus. He was on a pinnacle of success; and so at his most vulnerable. His own father, Aemilius Paullus, was an example of this: shortly before his triumph in Rome, death had robbed him of two of his sons. So now, as he saw the flames rising over the ruins of Carthage, Scipio shed tears, and when Polybius asked him (so it appears): 'Is not this a splendid sight?' he grasped his hand and said: 'A splendid sight indeed, Polybius, and yet I am in fear—I know not why—that some day the same order will be given to destroy my own country.' (So the fragment from Polybius—the two later accounts add a quotation from Homer: 'The day shall come when sacred Troy shall perish, and Priam and the people of Priam of the ashen spear.') It is the sign of a great man, remarks Polybius, 'at the moment of greatest triumph, to think of his own circumstances and the possible reversal of Fortune. . . .' We may recall, perhaps, the words of Lee after the victory of Fredericksburg: 'It is well that this is so terrible. We should grow too fond of it.'

In spite of Polybius' gloss, modern scholars have spent much time in discussion of the meaning of Scipio's words, and indeed of his sincerity in uttering them. Into such speculations we shall not enter. For Scipio's words strike a plangent note that seems the proper end for an account of the wars between Rome and Carthage.

174

NOTES

1

The First Punic War

THE ACCOUNT OF THE First Punic War given in this chapter is based on Polybius I, 7–64. This is without doubt the most reliable version; it was written less than a hundred years after the end of the war, and was based on earlier works by Fabius Pictor and Philinus of Agrigentum, both men born during the war and writing from the standpoint of the Roman and Carthaginian sides respectively. Polybius therefore had the advantage of using two nearly contemporary accounts, and being able to compare their statements when they differed and test their veracity by other evidence or, in the last resort, by the criterion of inherent probability. Further information that can be used to supplement Polybius is found in the Epitomes of Livy XVI–XIX. Livy's account was probably derived ultimately from Fabius Pictor. An elder contemporary of Livy, Diodorus Siculus, dealt with the war in Books XXIII–XXIV of his *Library of History*, probably using Philinus as his source. Recent attempts have been made to demonstate that Diodorus, based on Philinus, is a better authority than Polybius (for example, V. La Bua, *Filino-Polybio, Sileno-Diodoro*, Palermo 1966, reviewed E. Badian, *Rivista di Filologia*, 1968) but the fact is that Polybius also used Philinus, but with far more discrimination than Diodorus, who followed his sources uncritically. In any case Books XXIII and XXIV of Diodorus only exist in abbreviated and carelessly compiled excerpts made in the Byzantine era. Other accounts are given by various later authors. Appian (2nd cen. A.D.) makes brief mention of it in *Sicilica* I–II and *Punica* I. It is described by Dio Cassius (c. A.D. 200) in Books XI–XII, which survive mainly in the Epitomes of Zonaras (12th cen.) 8, 8–17; by Florus (2nd cen. A.D.) in his Epitome I, 18; by Eutropius (4th cen. A.D.) in his *Breviarius* II, xviii–xviii; and by Orosius (5th cen. A.D.) in his *Historiae contra Paganos* IV, 8–11. All these later historians give details that do not occur in Polybius, but these details are generally confused, conflicting, and unreliable.

Of modern works relevant to the First Punic War and the

background to the conflict, the most important are: F. W. Walbank, *A Commentary on Polybius*, Vol. I (1957); A. J. Toynbee, *Hannibal's Legacy*, Vol. I (1965); G. Picard, *Carthage*; J. H. Thiel, *History of Roman Sea Power*; W. W. Tarn, 'Hellenistic Military and Naval Developments. Fleets of the 1st Punic War.' *Journal of Hellenic Studies*, 1907, pp. 48–60; A. Sherwin-White, *Army lists* 1960; B. H. Warmington, *Carthage* (2nd. edn., 1960).

2

The Origins of the Second Punic War

THE MOST RELIABLE ACCOUNT of the preliminaries to the
Hannibalic War occur in Polybius II, 1, 13, 36; III, 8–33.
Polybius gives a very shrewd discussion on the causes of the war
and differentiates between the real causes and the first actions.
In his description of the negotiations that followed the capture
of Saguntum he was unable to penetrate the overlying propaganda, but his version of the charges and countercharges is by
far the best that we have; it seems that the basis of the Roman
claim was that Saguntum was protected by a clause in the Peace
Treaty of 241, under which both sides agreed not to attack each
other's allies. The account in Livy (XXI, 2–19) is derived from a
very unreliable source. Of the later historians, Zonaras (8, 22)
gives details of a debate in the Senate after the announcement
of the capture of Saguntum, with L. Cornelius Lentulus Caud-
inus (consul 237) urging an immediate declaration of war, and
Q. Fabius Maximus suggesting a more conciliatory approach.

Of modern works the most relevant are: F. W. Walbank,
A Commentary on Polybius, Vol. I; H. H. Scullard, *Rome's Declaration of War on Carthage in 218 B.C.*, Rheinisches Museum,
1952, p. 209 ff.; E. Badian, *Foreign Clientelae*, pp. 49–52, 292–
293; T. A. Dorey, 'The Treaty with Saguntum', *Humanitas*,
1959, pp. 1–10; A. E. Astin, *Saguntum and the Origins of the
Second Punic War*, Latomus, 1967, pp. 577–596 (this work is
particularly valuable).

3

Hannibal's March

IT HAS BEEN ASSUMED in the narrative that Hannibal crossed
the Rhône in the neighbourhood of Orange; that the two rivers
enclosing 'The Island' were the Rhône and the Isère; and that
Hannibal marched up the Isère, turned off up the Arc, crossed
the Alps by the Col du Clapier, and came down the Dora
Riparia into the land of the Taurini whose capital was the
modern city of Turin. All these assumptions have been disputed,
but they fit in best with the evidence that is available.

The position of 'The Island' is indicated by two factors.
First, the description of it in Polybius III, 49. 7, that it is similar
in size and shape to the delta of the Nile, though with its third
side formed by precipitous mountains instead of by the sea, fits
the area between the Rhône and the Isère better than it does any
other region. Secondly, the junction of the Rhône and the Isère
is about one hundred miles from the sea, which accords with the
statement in Polybius that Hannibal crossed the Rhône at a
point four days' march from the sea and reached 'The Island'
after a further march of four days (III, 43.1; 49.5), especially
when it is remembered that during the four days after crossing
the Rhône Hannibal was moving as quickly as possible in order
to get away from Scipio and would probably have covered an
average of fifteen miles a day instead of the normal ten.

There are three possible routes that Hannibal could have
followed when crossing the Alps. He could have gone up the
Durance and over some pass like the Mont Genèvre, Col de
l'Argentière, or Traversette; along the Rhône and across the
Great St Bernard; or up the Isère and either straight on to the
Little St Bernard or turning off up the Arc at the bottom of the
valley of the Maurienne on to the Mont Cenis or the Col du
Clapier. Of these routes, the one up the Durance is based on an
attempt to reconcile Livy XXI, 31.9–12 with the rest of Livy's
narrative and with Polybius. This section in Livy is clearly an
addition to the basic narrative borrowed by Livy from some
other source, possibly the account of the subsequent crossing of
Hasdrubal, and should be excluded from all consideration of the

route taken by Hannibal. The route along the Rhône involves an unnecessarily long detour, and would bring the total distance of the march to a figure considerably higher than the nine thousand stades—approximately nine hundred miles—given by Polybius (III, 39.11). The ancient tradition that Hannibal crossed by the Great St Bernard is derived from the belief that the Poenine Alps were so called because the Carthaginian army had passed that way; in fact the name comes from *penn*, the Celtic word for a mountain-peak.

This leaves the route up the Isère, and it is this route that has most supporters. The main question at issue is whether Hannibal continued up the Isère, over the Little St Bernard, and down the Dora Baltea, or turned off up its tributary the Arc and went across the Mont Cenis pass or the Col du Clapier and then down the Dora Riparia. The answer to this question depends largely on whether the first tribe that he encountered were the Taurini or the Insubres, whose territory lay to the east of the Taurini, around Milan. The Dora Riparia would take him down among the Taurini, the Dora Baltea would lead him towards the Insubres. Now Livy states explicitly (XXI, 38.5–6) that all his sources agreed that the first tribe encountered by Hannibal were the Taurini, and expresses surprise that in spite of this most writers believed that he crossed by the Poenine Alps (Great St Bernard) or, according to Coelius Antipater, by the *Iuga Cremonis* (Little St Bernard); both these passes, Livy says, would have brought him out among the Salassi and the Libui, and it is not likely that they were open at that date. This is an occasion where Livy's personal knowledge of the Cisalpine Gaul —he was a native of Padua—would give his statement greater authority. Polybius is, at first sight, ambiguous on this point. In III, 56.3, he says that Hannibal, after completing the march from Nova Carthago in five months and the crossing of the Alps in fifteen days, boldly came down to the plains around the River Po and the nation of the Insubres. This indicates a wide area rather than a specific locality. Polybius mentions Hannibal's starting-point, Nova Carthago, the great barrier that he had to cross, the Alps, and the important river in North Italy that was to be the final destination of his year's march, the River Po, and the powerful tribe that lived along its banks. The Insubres are named in contrast to the other great tribes such as the Liguri, the Veneti, and the Boii, to denote the general area in Cisalpine Gaul that Hannibal was to enter. There is no contrast implied between the Insubres and any of the smaller tribes, such as the Taurini. In any case, if Hannibal came over the Great or Little St Bernard and down the Dora Baltea, he would have encountered first the Salassi and then the Libui before coming to the Insubres. It follows that, whichever pass Hannibal took, the Insubres cannot have been the first tribe that he met, and the mention by Polybius of that people cannot be taken as evidence that Hannibal came down the Dora Baltea rather than the Dora Riparia.

However, in III, 60, Polybius is more specific about Hannibal's movements. As soon as he came down from the Alps he pitched camp right at the foot of the mountains and gave his men time to recover from their exhaustion. Then, finding that the Taurini, who lived at the foot of the mountains, were at war with the Insubres and distrusted the Carthaginians, he first offered them his friendship, and then, when his offer was rejected, attacked and captured their chief town. The language used by Polybius indicates that the Taurini lived in the same locality as where Hannibal first rested his army after his descent from the Alps, and it has been shown that this passage is not really contradicted by the reference to the Insubres in III, 56.3. It can be concluded, then, that Polybius, too, supports the view that Hannibal came down among the Taurini. This would mean that he entered Italy by way of the Dora Riparia and not by the Dora Baltea.

As a result, the Little St Bernard can be excluded from consideration. In any case, it conspicuously lacked one of the most important features ascribed to Hannibal's pass by both Livy and Polybius—a splendid view of North Italy from the head of the pass. Such a view is obtained from both the passes leading up out of the River Arc, the Mont Cenis and the Col du Clapier. It is through one of these that Hannibal must have gone. Of the two, Mont Cenis is generally favoured, but there are three points against it. It is very doubtful whether this pass was open at that date; it is comparatively low—only 6,831 feet, and it is unlikely that any considerable amount of the last year's snow would have remained unmelted at that level; and the descent on the Italian side is not steep enough to have caused Hannibal all the difficulties that he encountered. On the other hand, the Col du Clapier is 8,173 feet high, an altitude sufficient for last year's snow to be still lying on the ground in sheltered places; it has a space at the summit three miles long and half a mile wide, large enough for Hannibal's army to encamp for two days, with a spur giving a fine view of Italy; and the descent on the Italian side is narrow, steep, and difficult, so that a landslide or an awkwardly placed snowdrift would cause very great trouble.

The evidence set out above indicates the strong probability that Hannibal crossed the Alps by the Col du Clapier. The route indicated certainly fits in with the facts related by Polybius, and the choice of this pass is supported by a recent examination of the ground by A. H. McDonald of Clare College, Cambridge. It is unfortunate that one of our most important guide-posts is one on which little reliance can be placed. The name of the river whose confluence with the Rhône formed 'The Island' is given both by Polybius (III, 49.6) and Livy (XXI, 31.4) but unfortunately they give different names. Polybius has 'Skaras' or 'Skoras', while Livy, whose manuscripts disagree on the reading, has 'Sarar' or 'Arar', though the preceding word ends in 'i', so that the original reading could have been 'Isara'. In view of this uncertainty it is not safe to try and identify the name of the river on philological grounds.

In many ways the most interesting question is not the identification of Hannibal's pass, but the reason for his unexpected difficulties and heavy losses. The Alps had often been crossed before, they were crossed by Hasdrubal ten years later with little difficulty, Hannibal had made enquiries about the route, and he had guides from Cisalpine Gaul. Yet he followed a route on which he was attacked, ambushed, and brought to a pass high enough to have last year's snow and with a very steep descent on the Italian side. It is difficult not to feel that the pass that Hannibal chose originally was not the one by which he finally crossed. It is possible that he was aiming for the Little St Bernard, and was led up the Arc to the Col du Clapier as a result of a misunderstanding or by the treachery of his guides. It has also been suggested that he originally intended to cross by one of the Durance passes, but the unexpected encounter with the Roman advance party made him strike inland to the Isère. This made it necessary for him to pursue a different route to the one he had planned, and to rely on whatever guides he was able to obtain in the course of his march. This explanation may well be the correct one.

The account of Hannibal's march is given by Polybius in Book III, 33–60 and by Livy in Book XXI 23–38. Of the countless works on the subject, the most interesting are: F. W. Walbank, *A Commentary on Polybius*, Vol. I; Sir Gavin de Beer, *Alps and Elephants*; see also the works listed under 'Hannibal's crossing of the Alps' in the notes to Chapter IV.

4

The War in Italy

ANCIENT SOURCES

Polybius Book III contains a narrative of the Hannibalic War to the end of 216 B.C. Important fragments of later books are, VII, (treaty with Macedon); VIII, 3–7 (siege of Syracuse); 23–24 (Tarentum); IX, 1–10 (siege of Capua, Hannibal's march on Rome): X, 2 (capture of Nova Carthago); 32 (death of Marcellus); 34–40 (war in Spain); XI, 1–3, 6 (battle of the Metaurus); 20–24 (Ilipa); XIV, 1–10 (war in Africa); XV, 1–16 (battle of Zama).

Livy's Third Decade (Books XXI–XXX), with its continuous narrative of the Second Punic War, must be considered the major source, despite its many problems. Appian, *Hannibalica*, *Libyca* 6–67, largely derive from Polybius. Plutarch's *Lives* contain biographies of Fabius Maximus and Claudius Marcellus. For a full list of ancient sources see *Cambridge Ancient History*, Vol. VIII p. 723.

MODERN WORKS

The Second Punic War is fully treated in *Cambridge Ancient History*, VIII, ch. II–IV (1930), and E. Pais, *Storia di Roma durante le guerre puniche* (2 vols) 1927. For a succinct and modern account see H. H. Scullard, *A History of the Roman World 753–146 B.C.*, pp. 177–227 and Appendix 8 (2nd edn, 1969). F. W. Walbank, *A Commentary on Polybius*, Vol. I (1957); Vol. II (1967), is fundamental, and gives very full bibliographies on important topics. For Livy see P. G. Walsh, *Livy, His Historical Aims and Methods*, 1961. On the preliminaries see G. V. Sumner, 'Roman Policy in Spain before the Hannibalic War', *Harvard Studies in Classical Philology*, (1968). The war is treated from the Carthaginian side by B. H. Warmington, *Carthage*, 1960, and G. C. and C. Picard, *The Life and Death of Punic War*, 1930.

Recent biographies are Sir Gavin de Beer, *Hannibal*, 1969, and H. H. Scullard, *Scipio Africanus, Soldier and Politician*, 1970. *See also* H. H. Scullard, *Scipio Africanus in the Second Punic War*, 1930.

Many aspects of the war and its aftermath are discussed by Arnold J. Toynbee, *Hannibal's Legacy* (2 vols: 1965). For maps and battle-plans see Kromayer-Veith, *Schlachten Atlas*, 1–2 (1922).

There is an enormous scholarly literature devoted to special problems of the war. The following is no more than a short selection:

HANNIBAL'S CROSSING OF THE ALPS A. H. McDonald: 'Hannibal's Passage of the Alps, *Alpine Journal*, LXI, 1956, pp. 93–101. (McDonald's arguments are answered, though not convincingly, by de Beer on pp. 215–217 of that volume.) F. W. Walbank, 'Some Reflections on Hannibal's Pass', *Journal of Roman Studies*, XLVI, 1956, pp. 37–45; T. A. Dorey, 'Hannibal's Route across the Alps,' *Romanitas*, III, 1961, pp. 325–330; W. W. Hyde, *Roman Alpine Routes*, pp. 197–210; W. T. Arnold, *The Second Punic War*, pp. 351–373; J. E. T. Brown, 'Hannibal's Route across the Alps,' *Greece and Rome*, New Series, X, 1963, pp. 38–46.

TREBIA G. de Sanctis, *Storia dei Romani*, iii, ii, 65–83, *Cambridge Ancient History*, viii, 709. J. Kromayer, *Antike Schlachtfelder*, iii, i, 478.

TRASIMENE G. Susini, *Richerche sulla Battaglia del Trasimeno*, Cortona, 1960. G. Susini, *Studi Annibalici*, pp. 132–6; T. A. Dorey, *Euphrosyne*, 1961, pp. 213–15; T. A. Dorey, *University of Birmingham Historical Journal*, 1959, pp. 1–2.

CANNAE T. A. Dorey (as above) 2–5; H. H. Scullard, *A History of Rome, 753–146 B.C.*, p. 438 (summary of views); A. D. Fitton Brown, 'After Cannae', *Historia*, 1955, pp. 365 f.

SYRACUSE E. K. Fabricius, 'Das antike Syrakus', *Klio, Beiheft 28*, 1932; J. G. Landels, *Journal of Hellenistic Studies*, 1966, 69–77 (for siege-engines).

TARENTUM E. St Denis, *Latomus*, 1954, pp. 25 f.

HANNIBAL'S MARCH ON ROME F. W. Walbank, *A Commentary on Polybius*, Vol. II, pp. 122 f.; E. T. Salmon, *Phoenix*, 1957, pp. 155 f.; R. Bloch and G. Foti, *Revue de philologie*, 1953, p. 75 (for Lucus Feroniae).

METAURUS G. Buroni, *Le diverse tesi sulla battaglia dei Metauro*, 1953; J. Kromayer, *Antike Schlachtfelder*, iii, i, pp. 426–494.
ZAMA F. W. Walbank, *A Commentary on Polybius*, II, pp. 446 f.; H. H. Scullard, *Scipio Africanus: Soldier and Politician*.

The War in Spain

THE ACCOUNT OF THE WAR in Spain given in this chapter is based mainly on Polybius and Livy, supplemented in one or two places by Appian's *Hispanica*. Polybius (III, 76; 95–99; IX, 11; X, 2–20; 34–40; XI, 20–33) deals with the events of 218–217; the excesses of the Carthaginian leaders after the destruction of the Scipios in 211; the arrival of Scipio Africanus and the capture of Nova Carthago; the battle of Baecula; the battle of Ilipa; the visit to Syphax, the mutiny of the Roman troops and the revolt of the Ilergetes. The rest of the account is derived from Livy (XXIII, 26–29; 48–49; XXIV, 41–42; 48–49; XXV, 32–39; XXVI, 17–20; XXVII, 19–20; XXVIII, 1–4; 15–23; 30–31; 35–37). At times Livy is able to correct Polybius. For instance, his figure of 50,000 for Hasdrubal's infantry at Ilipa is preferable to the 70,000 given by Polybius. But often Livy's narrative is over-dramatized and exaggerated; his account of the successes of Marcius in 211 and the operations of Nero in the following year are drawn from a bad source (either Claudius Quadrigarius or Valerius Antias) and must be regarded as highly suspect, as also is probably the case with Livy's story of the personal meeting between Scipio and Masinissa. The time-table for the probable movements of them both make it very difficult to see how this meeting could have been fitted in. But what makes Livy's account very unreliable is his habit (one typical of Roman historians) of converting a place-name of which he had never heard into one that was familiar both to himself and his readers, and, if necessary adjusting other relevant names to fit in with the topographical picture that he is adopting. This was a particularly dangerous habit in dealing with campaigns in a place like Spain. Here Appian is at times useful, in preserving (amidst a wealth of erroneous detail) the original Greek form of the name that would have been found in Polybius.

Of modern accounts of the Spanish campaigns, the two most important written in English are: B. H. Liddell Hart, *A Greater than Napoleon: Scipio Africanus*, 1926; H. H. Scullard, *Scipio*

Africanus in the Second Punic War, 1930. The latter book contains a most valuable and scholarly examination of all the geographical, chronological, and strategical problems. See also H. H. Scullard, *Scipio Africanus: Soldier and Politician*, 1970.

6

Sardinia, Greece, Sicily, and the War at Sea

THE MOST IMPORTANT SOURCES for the war in Sicily are: Polybius VIII, 5–9, 37; Livy XXI, 49–51, XXII, 37, XXIV, 4–7, 21–39, XXV, 23–31, XXVI, 40; Plutarch, *Marcellus*; Appian, *Sicilica*, III–V; Dio (Zonaras), 9, 4–5, 9–7; Diodorus Siculus. For Sardinia: Livy XXIII, 24, 40–41, XXVI, 6. For the alliance between Hannibal and Philip: Polybius VII, 9; Livy XXIII, 33–34, 38–39, XXIV, 40. For the subsequent development of the war in Greece, see F. W. Walbank, *Philip V. of Macedon*, and the sources quoted there.

7

The War in Africa

THE MOST RELIABLE ancient authority for the campaigns in Africa is Polybius, Books XIV and XV, 1–19. This has to be supplemented by Livy XXIX and XXX, which is derived from a mixture of sources, though with Polybius predominating. Appian, *Punica* II–IX describes these campaigns in a manner more suited to romantic fiction than sober history, but at times he preserves information that is not found in the better authors, while in some sections where Polybius does not survive, he seems to be following a source that is better than Livy.

Of modern works the most important are: F. W. Walbank, *A Commentary on Polybius*; H. H. Scullard, *Scipio Africanus in the Second Punic War;* H. H. Scullard, *Scipio Africanus: Soldier and Politician*; B. H. Liddell Hart, *A Greater than Napoleon: Scipio Africanus*; T. A. Dorey and C. W. F. Lydall, *Livy XXIX*.

The various problems of chronology and topography are fully discussed by Scullard.

8

The Third Punic War

ANCIENT SOURCES

Polybius was an eye-witness of the main events of the war, but his account survives only in fragments, notably XXXVII, 1, 3: XXXVIII, 1–3; XXXIX, 3–5. It is however fairly well represented by what is now the chief source viz, Appian *Libyca*, 67–136. See also Livy XXXII, 2; XXXIII, 45, 6–49; XXXIV, 49, 62; XXXVII, 5; XLI, 22: XLII, 23; XLIII, 3, 5, 6, 11; and also in the *Epitome* of XLVIII, L, LI. There is also Diodorus Siculus XXXII; XXXIV, 33; and Plutarch, *Life of Cato the Censor*, 26, 27.

MODERN SOURCES

For general accounts see *Cambridge Ancient History*, 1953 VIII, Chapter XV (B. L. Hallward and M. P. Charlesworth); L. Pareti, *Storia di Roma*, 1953, iii, Chapter II; G. C. Picard and Colette Picard, *The Life and Death of Carthage*, 7, (Eng. trans. 1968). On the outbreak of the war E. Badian, *Foreign Clientelae*, 125, 1958; F. E. Adcock, 'Delenda est Carthago', *Cambridge Historical Journal*, 1946, viii, 117 f.; F. W. Walbank: 'Political Morality and the Friends of Scipio', *Journal of Roman Studies*, 1965, 55, 1 f.

On Masinissa see P. G. Walsh, 'Masinissa', *Journal of Roman Studies*, 1965, 55, 149 f. On Scipio Aemilianus see A. E. Astin, *Scipio Aemilianus*, 1967, Chapters V–VII. On the harbours of Carthage see J. Baradez, 'Nouvelles Recherches sur les ports antiques de Carthage', *Karthago* 9, 1958, 45 f.

Index

In order to keep the index down to a reasonable size, it has been limited to personal and place names.

Roman personal names are normally given under the name of the *gens*, e.g. P. Cornelius Scipio under Cornelius. Cross-references are given where it seemed advisable.

Abbreviations: C., Carthage, Carthaginian(s). H., Hannibal. R., Rome, Roman(s).

Modern place-names are printed in italics.

Cornelius, P.—Scipio (Africanus), son of P.: rescues father at Ticinus, 104; rallies troops after Cannae, 67, 104; in 213 B.C. elected *curule aedile*, 104–5; elected to Spanish command; his character, 79, 104–5; arrives in Spain, 105–6; captures Nova Carthago, 106–8; defeats Hasdrubal at Baecula, 109–10; captures Masinissa's nephew, 110; moves down Baetis; decisive victory at Ilipa, 112–15; secures alliance of Masinissa, 116; visits Africa, treaty with Syphax, 116; his troops on the Sucro mutiny, 116; punishes various Spanish towns, 117; elected consul 205 B.C., 87; debate with Fabius in Senate, 87–8; given province of Sicily, 88, 90–1; captures Locri, 92; holds it against H., 92; atrocities of governor, Scipio blamed but acquitted, 92–3; sails for Africa, 134; defeats C. force, besieges Utica, forced to raise siege, penned in camp, 135; spies on enemy camps, attacks with complete success, 136–7; takes Anda, 138; occupies Tunis, 139; naval defeat at Utica, 139–40; peace negotiations, 141; marches to Zama, joined by Masinissa, meets H., 144–5; battle of Zama, 145–7; peace negotiated, 147–8

Cornelius, P.—Scipio Aemilianus (adopted by the son of Africanus): witness of battle between C. and Masinissa, 157; as military tribune prominent in fighting round C.,

Cornelius, P.—*contd.*
164–5; his heritage, 165–6; mission to Numidia, 166; at Rome, elected consul 147 and given African command, 167; restores army discipline, 168; unsuccessful attack on fortifications of C., city closely invested, 166–9; attacks C. posts, 171; final storm and destruction; meditations on C.'s downfall, 172–4

Cornelius, P.—Scipio Nasica: envoy to C., 156; opposes destruction of C., 167

Cornus, Sardinia, 120

Corsica, 2

Cremona, colony on Po, 46

Crispinus, see Quinctius

Croton, Bruttium, 92

Cumae, 71, 73

Damnippus, 127–8

Dio Cassius, R. historian, 2nd cent. A.D., 12

Diodorus Siculus, historian, 1st cent. B.C., 4

Diogenes, 168, 171

Dionysius, of Syracuse, 16

Dora Riparia (see map, 40) 44

Drepanum, N.W. Sicily, 16, 19, 24

Duillius, C., consul 260: first R. naval victory, relieves Segesta, etc., 9

Ebro, River, N.E. Spain, 32–3, 95–7, 103

Ecnomus, Sicily, 10–11

Edeco, prince of Edetani, 109

Edetani, 109

Emporiae, Spain, 95, 105

Epicydes, brother of Hippocrates, q.v., 125, 127–32

INDEX

Hamilcar Barca—*contd.*
of 2nd Punic War, 29; his policy, 30; commander in 'Truceless' war, 30; his influence at C., 30; hostility to C., 31; sent to Spain and extends C. power, 31; receives R. embassy, 32; his death, 31

Hamilcar, C. agent left in Liguria after 2nd Punic War, 90

Hampsicora, leader of Sardinian revolt, 119–20

Hannibal, C. commander in 1st Punic War, 7

Hannibal, son of Hamilcar, 17

Hannibal 'the Rhodian', 17, 23

Hannibal, son of Hamilcar Barca: his policy supported at C., 31; his attack on Saguntum, 32; succeeds Hasdrubal as C-in-C, 36; subdues tribes S. of Ebro, 33; and Saguntum, 33; R. ultimatum hastens his decision for war, 34; captures Saguntum, 34; R. embassy at C. demands his surrender, declares war, 35; aim at war, 36; childhood oath, 36; bitterness, 37; war aims, 37; preparations, moves from Nova Carthago, 38; crosses Rhône, 39–40; crosses Alps, 42–4; moves towards Po, 44–5; victories in Po valley, 48–50; crosses Apennines, 51–2; victory at L. Trasimene, 52–4; marches through Umbria and Picenum to Apulia, 56; attempts to lure Fabius into battle, 57; moves into Samnium and Campania, great devastation, 57; returns to Apulia, 58–9; winters at Gerunium, 60–2; moves on Cannae, 62; forces manoeuv-

Hannibal—*contd.*
res and conduct of battle, 63–7; refuses to march on R., 67–8; C. decide to send two fresh armies, only small forces arrive, 70–1; treaty with Philip V of Macedon, 71; Capua and other places go over, 68, 70–3; attempts to relieve Capua, 75; defeats R. near Herdonea, 76; fails to surprise Brundisium, 77; makes dash towards R., 77–8; retires to Bruttium, 78; in action at Grumentum and Venusia, 83; turns to Metapontum, 85; his plans to meet Hasdrubal, 84; halts at Larinum, 86; retires to Bruttium, 86; fails to retake Locri from Scipio, 92; alleged brutality in Bruttium, 93; recalled to Africa, 93, 139; lands at Leptis, 142; raises and trains army, marches to Zama, 143; interview with Scipio, 144–5; battle of Zama, 145–7; silences opposition to peace terms 148; his reforms at C., 155; R. envoys arrive; he flees into exile, 155

Hanno 'the elder', 7, 10–11, 24–5

Hanno, son of Bomilcar, 39–40, 73–5

Hanno, N. Spain, 39; captured at Cissa, 95

Hanno 'the Great': his anti-Barcid policy favours Rome, 29–31; unsuccessful commander in 'Truceless' war, 30

Hanno: brings reinforcements to Spain, 111

Hanno, defeated by Marcius, 117

Hanno, C. commander at Agrigentum: escapes to C., 132

198

Sempronius, Ti.—*contd.*
  disaster at Trebia, 49–50; his
  claims and recklessness, 50
Sena, River (*Cesano*), N.E. Italy,
  84
Sena Gallica, 51, 88
Senones, Gallic tribe, 51
Sergius, L., 143
Servilius, Cn.—Geminus, consul
  217: to defend N. Italy, 50–1;
  sends cavalry to join Flamin-
  ius, 54; brings legions to join
  Fabius, 56; watches H. at
  Gerunium, 62; asks Senate for
  instructions, 62; rendezvous
  with new consuls, 63; in joint
  command legions at Cannae,
  65; killed in battle, 66
Servilius, Cn.—Caepio, consul
  205, 88
Sicily, events in: First Punic
  War, 1–11, 14–25; Second
  Punic War, 90–1, 121–33
Siga, Africa, 116
Sila, Bruttium, 93
Silanus, see Junius
Sipontum, Apulia, 62
Sophoniba, daughter of Hasdru-
  bal Gisgo: married to Syphax,
  135; captured by Masinissa,
  139
Spain, events in, 31–4, 42, 95–
  118
Spoletium, Picenum, 55
Strabo, geographer, 1st cent.
  B.C./1st A.D., 155
Sucro, River, 116
Sulpicius, P.—Galba, consul 211
  B.C., 77–8
Syphax, king of Masaesylii in W.
  Numidia: Scipio's agreement
  with, 99; attacked by Masin-
  issa, 100; ally of C., brought
  over by Laelius and Scipio,

Syphax—*contd.*
  116; allied to C. and marries
  Sophoniba, 134–5; raises siege
  of Utica, 135; Scipio fails to
  bring him over, sends spies to
  his camp as negotiators, fires
  and attacks camp, 136–7;
  raises fresh forces, joins Hasdrubal, defeated on Great
  Plains, 138; Laelius and Masinissa invade Numidia, defeat
  and capture him, 139
Syracuse, chief Greek city in
  Sicily, ruled by Hiero, q.v.:
  after Hiero's death, C. envoys
  detach from R. alliance, 122–
  3; R. assault fails and siege
  formed, engineering devices,
  124–5; Marcellus captures
  most of town, 128–9; Achradina betrayed by Moericus,
  131; city plundered, 132
Syrtes, Lesser, gulf S. of C., 14,
  142

Tarentum, S. Italy, 73–4, 80, 83
Tarraco (*Tarragona*), 96, 105,
  109, 111, 118
Tartesii, name for Turdetani,
  q.v.
Taurini, Gallic tribe, 44
Tavoliere, Plain of, in Apulia,
  56, 60, 62
Teanum, Campania, 56, 58, 68
Telamon, Etruria, 46
Terentius, C.—Varro, consul 216
  B.C., 61; favours battle, 62;
  the battle of Cannae, 64–7;
  escapes, 69; appointed to Pice-
  num, 69
Thermae, N.W. Sicily, 15
Thurii, on border of Lucania and
  Bruttium, 80